WE ARE SUNDAY LEAGUE

WE ARE SUNDAY LEAGUE

A bitter-sweet, real life story from football's grass roots

EWAN FLYNN

First published by Pitch Publishing, 2017

Pitch Publishing
A2 Yeoman Gate
Yeoman Way
Worthing
Sussex
BN13 3QZ
www.pitchpublishing.co.uk
info@pitchpublishing.co.uk

A CIP catalogue record is available for this book
from the British Library.

ISBN 978-1-78531-321-9

Typesetting and origination by Pitch Publishing
Printed and bound in Great Britain by TJ International

Contents

Epigraph

'Glory days'

– Bruce Springsteen

Dedication

To my family. To the Wizards who are part of
my family. To Buzz Bissinger and Boobie Miles
for the inspiration. Thank you all.

Acknowledgements

I HAD long wanted to write a book about my experiences of playing Sunday League football as I felt it was a rich topic full of great stories that anyone who has ever put on a pair of boots and run out of a scruffy changing room onto a muddy pitch could relate to. However, as a first time author with a blank piece of paper in front of me, the prospect of bringing the idea to fruition was a daunting one. I attended a one-day course at *The Guardian*, led by Andrew Miller, called 'The Beginner's Guide to Starting a Book'. In those few hours Andrew, who probably won't remember me among the ten or so other people in the class, made it seem possible for someone like me to write a book – and that injection of confidence and possibility is something I am very grateful for. His advice not to worry about having a clear structure at the start, and to just begin writing where I felt comfortable at any point of the story I wanted to tell, was invaluable. I came to trust his insight that if I found what I was writing about interesting, or funny or sad, then other people would too. It may seem simple but the best advice often is.

One of Andrew's other suggestions was to get up every day and do what he called 'morning pages' to create the discipline and routine needed to start, persevere and one glorious day even finish writing a book. This is what I did every morning at 5am before heading off to do my day job and I'd like to thank

Melissa for not getting the hump when the alarm went off and for bringing me a cup of tea and two bits of toast like clockwork when it was time to stop writing, remembering to press save, and go to work. Mel isn't exactly what you'd call a football fan but she was a constant source of support and encouragement throughout.

My sister Rosanne gave me some shrewd advice at the outset that I should make the whole book about the Wizards and our players rather than a more general account or history of Sunday League football. She also let me attend her screenwriting group which hadn't really included someone writing prose before, but from where I got further good advice and encouragement from Anna McCleery, Camilla Bubna-Kasteliz and Johnny Lewsley.

I think writing this book has brought me closer to my parents as an adult, which is something I am very grateful for. I realise now so many of the things I'd take the piss out of Laurie, my dad, about or found embarrassing about him when I was a boy, are now the things I most admire. His commitment to social justice and treating other people decently, sometimes to the detriment of his own health and happiness, are inspirational. I also need to acknowledge that he drove me to and from the hospital for countless follow-up appointments and blood tests after the drama with my knee, which must have cost him a fortune in NHS parking charges. To my mum, Judith, I owe a debt which I can never repay, for the countless hours she put into editing this book to ensure it was in the best possible shape before I sent it out into the wide world. The days I spent with her up in Halesworth, Suffolk, working on it are some of the happiest I have had, and I couldn't have had better help and advice than that she gave me.

Donald McRae, in addition to giving such a lovely endorsement for the cover, helped me get the book to Pitch Publishing. He has been hugely generous in terms of both his time and encouragement and is someone I feel very lucky to be able to call a friend.

ACKNOWLEDGEMENTS

To all those people who agreed to be interviewed and took me seriously when I said I wanted to write about them, thank you for being so open and generous with me, and for being willing to share not just your happy memories but some painful ones too. I hope you feel I have done your stories justice and can see how much I respect you and value your friendship.

It's been a real team effort. Thank you all.

Introduction

IN the suburbs of north London, there are 15 or so men in their thirties – lads, well boys really – bound together by a great shared experience. Not going to war, thank Christ. Or the fact they all went to school together since the age of 11. But the experience of playing years and years (eight full seasons to be precise) of Sunday League football for their team, our team, the Wizards FC.

These boys are a family of sorts; dysfunctional at times, petty and jealous on occasion, but forever connected. And like a family, the years are now ticking by and we don't see each other as much. But, whenever we do, after the customary, 'How is the missus and kids?' the conversation always heads in the same direction, the Wizards. The Wizards played in the Edmonton and District Sunday Football League (EDSFL) from September 2002 to May 2010, with a brief hiatus to the more upmarket, but less fun, Mercury and Waltham League for a season in 2003.

A fella called Charles Dickens, who doesn't seem to have been much of a Sunday footballer, could have been writing the unauthorised history of the Wizards when he opens *A Tale of Two Cities* with, 'It was the best of times. It was the worst of times.'

That's how it was playing Sunday League in north London. We'd go from buzzing with euphoria when we won, to being frightened to death by 11 skinheads on the other side (some just out of prison, some soon to be on their way there, who, whilst questioning the virtue of your mother, girlfriend or family pet, broke you in half with an X-rated tackle).

It was on Sunday mornings that I learned the following crucial life lessons: having 11 men to start the game is better than having nine; never believe your centre-forward when he says, 'Don't worry mate, you can trust me to remember the clocks are changing on Saturday night'; and finally, if the opposition have a short fat fella in goal, he's probably not their normal keeper, so shoot on sight.

The chasm Sunday League football has left behind is not one that is easily filled. Which is why we all still love telling and hearing the stories. Some of them for the millionth time when we get together and have had a few drinks.

Real life is far harder than it was in those halcyon days. When all I really worried about was if I could get to 200 competitive appearances and win a league title. When Monday to Saturday was a blend of fear and excitement, with all roads leading to 11am on Sunday.

Reading this you might think, probably with some justification, this guy is a plonker. It's only Sunday League football. And rationally, yes that's all it was. Schoolboy dreams of being spotted for football stardom were long since gone. It was now simply about playing a game in the park with your mates against a team of strangers, just like you'd done every weekend for as long as you could remember. But it meant the world to me and the other boys who were the core of the team. It still does now. Winning the Division 1 title is the greatest achievement of my life. If it weren't for the fact that potential employers wouldn't understand, it would be at the very top of my CV. Only my fully completed collection of Panini World Cup™ sticker albums, 1986 through to 2014, gets anywhere near.

Now there are plenty of men who are more obsessed with football than I am. Some plan their whole lives around it. I am a Spurs season ticket holder, but I am not one of those superfans/

weirdos who hasn't missed a match, home or away, for 20 years, including both reserve team games and pre-season tours of Asia, wearing the fact that they missed their own daughter's wedding because she didn't refer to the fixture list when setting the date as some sort of badge of honour (you know who you are).

I know that there are other things in life than football. At 18, when being a football fundamentalist seemed a pretty attractive way of life, even I knew that there had to be limits. When a fellow Spur I met at university in Southampton told me he'd spent pretty much all his student loan to travel to Chişinău in Moldova to see Spurs play out a 0-0 draw with FC Zimbru, having won the first leg 3-0, I knew he wasn't quite right.

When it came to the Wizards, however, the same kind of obsession overtook me. I point-blank refused to drink or be out late on Saturday before a game for eight years during my twenties. Some of which time, it may shock you to hear, I didn't have a girlfriend. Even when I did finally meet a girl who would put up with this regime (thanks Melissa), we could never go away for the weekend anywhere between September and May.

Any trips to see her parents in Canada for Christmas had to be tactically planned, so they coincided with the Christmas holidays in the only part of the world that really mattered, the Edmonton and District Sunday Football League. One time we were booking Sunday flights from Heathrow to Vancouver. I remember making up some old bollocks about night flights being safer, owing to the estimated strength of crosswinds, in order to cover up the truth. The only reason I wanted to take the late flight was so that I could play in a cup game that morning, and still have time to go home, get showered and on the tube, even making a pit stop at Chase Farm A&E if needed.

Mercifully for my long-term domestic bliss, the game was called off that morning due to inclement weather, not crosswinds. (As an aside, I love the word inclement; you only ever hear it in relation to football fixtures being cancelled or as a warning at the precise moment you go arse over tit on rain-soaked surfaces by the escalator at Holborn tube.) I made the flight and arrived in Vancouver annoyed that if the game was not rescheduled, I would be down on my number of appearances compared to last year. It was only when Mel's lovely mum, Albina, said to me, 'I heard you were going to play football before going to the airport. What's wrong with you?' I realised my cover story had been blown and perhaps my priorities were a bit skewed. Next time just pay the extra couple of hundred quid and fly out Monday morning instead.

Chapter One

In the mixer

MY EARLIEST football memory relates to one of the most famous games ever played. It was the evening of Sunday 22 June 1986, England were playing Argentina in the quarter-finals of the World Cup in Mexico. As a four-year-old, the 'Hand of God' and 'Goal of the Century', both scored by Maradona within the space of five minutes early in the second half, passed me by as I slept under the gentle glow of my Thomas the Tank Engine night light. With nine minutes to go, substitute John Barnes crossed for Gary Lineker to score and bring England back into the game at 2-1.

I don't know if it was the shouts of celebration from my mum that woke me up or those immediately after of alarm, as straight from kick-off Argentina went down the other end and hit the inside of Peter Shilton's post. Either way, just as Barnes picked up the ball again on the left wing with three minutes left in the game, I sleepily made my way into the room in time to see him beat his man and send over another cross. Lineker threw himself at the ball, a scream went up from Barry Davies and Jimmy Hill in Mexico, my mum in north London and probably the entire nation. For a split second, they thought Lineker had scored the equaliser. However, my mum's wild shout turned from joy to anguish, making me burst into frightened tears. It was Lineker rather than the ball that had ended up in the back of the net. This was an early lesson for me of the strange and dangerous power football could have over people.

A year later came my next infant football trauma, the 1987 FA Cup Final at Wembley, Spurs v Coventry, with Spurs the firm favourite to win. By now I'd started school in Edmonton and I knew for a fact that Tottenham are the greatest team the world has ever seen. Lo and behold, Clive Allen put Spurs one goal up inside the first two minutes! And then he scored again! And then again from a different angle!

As a five-year-old I hadn't quite gotten my head around instant replays. I couldn't believe my mum when she tried to explain away what I'd seen with my own eyes, albeit in slow motion. Spurs went on to lose 3-2. The sharp correlation between supporting Tottenham and disappointment was to be a key feature of my experience of football.

It was in the 1988/89 season that my football consciousness really took off. Although I was born in Edmonton, we'd moved to a bigger house in more upmarket Palmers Green. Now, we had a long back garden that served as my own personal training ground and later, both FA Cup and World Cup Final pitches. It was a place notorious for decisions favouring the home team, where the 'ref' always gave me a penalty to win the game in the last minute from age six to 29.

But my sister Rosanne and I still both went to Latymer All Saints Infant and Primary School in Edmonton. My mum and dad thought changing schools was a bad idea. Edmonton is a very working class area, where people new to London from other parts of the UK or the wider world in the early 1980s tended to arrive. Then, if they'd made a bit of money, they'd get out as quickly as possible. Edmonton borders on Tottenham. If you went to Latymer All Saints you had the choice; support Tottenham and play football at playtime or play kiss chase with the girls. Naturally, I opted for the former and the direction of my life was decided.

Anytime there was a day at school where we were allowed to wear non-uniform, I would faithfully turn up in full Spurs replica kit, complete with matching Spurs shin pads. As would pretty much all the other boys in the class, other than the weird ones who didn't like football. I went to my first game at White Hart Lane in the 1988/89 season, a 1-1 draw against Charlton Athletic with Gary Mabbutt scoring the goal for Spurs. I continued to wear full kit and shin pads whenever I went, in the hope that an injury would lead to a call across the tannoy for any seven-year-old boy already in the kit, to make himself known to the stewards so that he could be brought on as sub.

It was during this season that my sister came home from school one day early in December and coolly announced that she and some of her classmates had been selected to sing Christmas carols on the pitch at White Hart Lane during a league game. All the good Christian lessons we had been given in assembly about not being jealous of your neighbour's ox went completely out the window. I was fuming. She didn't even like Spurs and was now going to get onto the pitch. She had even said that she supported Arsenal just to wind me up when I pushed her on the subject. When the day came, off she went to the Lane leaving her younger brother sat sulking at home, in full kit of course. Being so overcome with jealousy, I came to believe afterwards that Terry Venables dressed up as Santa and gave them all presents. Given that the singing took place at half-time this does seem unlikely, although thinking about some of the managers Spurs have had subsequently, anything's possible.

I was at home one sunny day in spring 1989 with my big Spurs mate, Terry Mordecai, thrashing out a deal to swap his Spurs pencil case and stationery for one of my Centurion action figures (Ray, the green one with the 'tache). Terry was always a shrewd operator and didn't take a lot of convincing as he was definitely getting the better deal, but I wanted the pencil case so badly. That day, 15 April 1989, as it unfolded, turned out to be one of the very worst in the history of English football and English policing. Terry and I listened in shock as news of people dying at a football match came through on the radio from Hillsborough.

On Monday at school our teacher, Mr Hindell, Spurs mug on his desk as usual, tried to explain to a class of seven- and eight-year-olds what had happened. He chalked a picture of the terrace behind a goal on the board and explained that too many fans had been allowed into the same part of the stadium and that this had led to a crush. Hillsborough has always been burned into my memory, as I am sure it was for every football fan old enough to remember those awful events. It probably speaks volumes as to why the families of the 96 victims of the disaster have had to fight so long and hard for justice, that my primary school teacher did a more accurate job of explaining what had happened 48 hours after the horrendous events than elements of the press and authorities did for over 20 years. *The Sun*'s disgraceful coverage of the disaster, blaming Liverpool fans, meant that when the Premier League launched, there was to be no talking my dad into getting Sky to allow me to watch the games. His disdain for anything owned by Rupert Murdoch ran deep. He told me how 6,000 people lost their jobs when News International moved operations for *The Sun*, *News of the World*, *The Times* and the *Sunday Times* to Wapping, and how union resistance was crushed.[1] While I have grown to respect this principled stance, annoyingly typical of my dad, it didn't hold much weight in the school playground, where the division between the haves and have-nots in terms of who had been able to watch *Ford Super Sunday* was all too clear.[2]

---

1   The defeat of the strike at Wapping hit my dad's family hard. My dad's dad, Vincent Flynn, had been a lifelong trade unionist, and was general secretary of the print union SOGAT (Society of Graphical and Allied Trades) before retiring in 1974.

2   After years of my own kind of campaigning I reached a compromise with my dad whereby we got the Sky Sports channels through Cable London.

IN THE MIXER

The only sort of football coaching I received at Latymer
All Saints Primary School was when a man came in just before
the start of World Cup 90 to do a demonstration of skills in the
playground. He had a sack full of red, white and green Coca-
Cola mini balls, emblazoned with 'Ciao', the Italia 90 (and
unquestionably best ever) World Cup mascot.

It wasn't until a family holiday at Center Parcs, that I finally
got some proper coaching. Our family holidays were always a
bit strained; my mum and dad didn't seem to have much fun
together. Dad was a journalist, specialising in industrial disasters
and asbestosis, that kind of thing. He can be quite a serious
character and his idea of holiday reading would be a book about
the Holocaust or the suffering of those working in the blood
diamond trade in Angola. Perhaps my dad thought that bringing
along his elderly Scottish parents, and us all staying together in
the cabin fever conditions of a self-catering lodge, was just the
tonic for a flagging marriage. Unsurprisingly, this did not result
in a romantic reawakening for mum and dad. It did however, give
me one of the few vivid memories I have of my granddad before
he died. The years rolled back as he momentarily forgot that he
needed his crutches to move around and tried to get on the end of
a loose pass from me that fell in his direction. Thankfully, my dad
got hold of him just in time before he lost his balance completely,
saving a trip to the Center Parcs medical centre. Beyond this
memory, I was delighted to have granny and granddad there
that holiday as they had bought me the full Hummel Spurs kit
for my birthday with Holsten across the middle – although they
then lectured me on the evils of advertising beer on children's
clothing.

This was a more innocent time, when those killjoys in
government hadn't yet outlawed alcohol firms displaying their
names across the front of children's football shirts. It certainly
didn't have any impact on me; I'm confident my requests to my
dad to henceforth only buy Holsten were purely coincidental. I
think this was one of the last children's Spurs kits to bear Holsten's

name. I remember getting the 1990/91 season goalkeeper's shirt as worn by my hero Erik Thorstvedt as a present soon after, and being horrified that there was no sponsor on it, so much so that I immediately cut the letters H O L S T E N out of a piece of paper to affix them to the shirt with Copydex glue. Not only was my shirt sponsor-less, it now had glue stains down the front. From then on I insisted on having men's sized Spurs shirts to avoid the embarrassment of not having a sponsor. It meant I could lord it over all the other boys whose shirts didn't have the all-important Holsten, even though my shirts looked like I had stolen them from the men's lost property.

Having learned that it was best to join some sort of club or activity on holiday rather than be around mum and dad all the time, I signed up for football coaching with Dennis Longhorn. Dennis was the first professional footballer I ever met. I was in awe to hear that he had only just retired from a career that had taken in spells at Mansfield Town, Aldershot and Colchester United among several other teams that, like these, I had never heard of. Accrington Stanley? Who are they? Exactly! At the end of the two days of football training all the boys had a penalty competition, which I won. The prize I received from Dennis was a copy of *Shoot!* magazine, which he pointed out had a poster of the whole Liverpool squad with their (printed) autographs on it. I wasn't fooled; I knew it was a rubbish prize. Dennis then said it was traditional for the winning boy to have a penalty shoot-out with his dad. My dad had come by to pick me up in some ill-fitting 80s tennis shorts and brown leather boat shoes and reluctantly agreed to take part.

Dad wasn't at his athletic peak at this time; once he went to university his boyhood interest in football had been pushed aside in order to make plans for a socialist world revolution, and long, slow marches from the LSE to Hyde Park or Trafalgar Square were never going to be optimum for keeping fit. Nevertheless, when Dennis said the loser of this competition between father and son would have to do 20 press-ups, I saw something change in him. I remember him saying to himself loudly enough for me and several of the other young boys to hear, 'I'm not doing any fucking press-ups.' He then proceeded to smash five of the hardest penalties he could muster past his helpless, shocked eight-year-old son. Poor old Dennis Longhorn didn't know where to look, and the competitive dad sketch on the *Fast Show* will resonate with me for the rest of my life. I should say I took my revenge on dad a few years later playing tennis on our last-ever family holiday. In the sweltering Portuguese sun, I hit the sweetest forehand into his bollocks from the back of the court before fleeing the scene shouting over my shoulder, 'That's for Center Parcs.'

With my sister moving up to secondary school, my mum and dad decided it would be better for me to move to a school nearer to our house for my final two years in primary. They claim that they had for some weeks gently told me this was on the horizon. In fact, we all went together to meet the head teacher and look round the other school. I have no memory of this at all. Maybe I thought it was some kind of wind-up; maybe I was in denial. Anyway, one day when rifling through their wardrobe looking for my birthday presents during the summer holidays I found a red Hazelwood school jumper. It seemed clear it was destined for me to wear. All the crying in the world and threats to run away held no sway, and at the start of the new school year off to Hazelwood Junior School I went. In hindsight, it was absolutely the best thing for me; having school and new friends walking distance away was great, and I was able to be at the park by 9.30am every weekend to play 2-on-2 games of football, which seemed to last the whole day long.

It was at Hazelwood recreation ground that I first encountered Sunday League football. Seeing teams in full matching kit playing with referees and sometimes even linesmen just down the road was more exciting to me than going through the back of a wardrobe to discover Narnia. I remember one time being down the rec kicking about with some pals just as the nets were being put up for a Sunday League game that morning. Usually at this time, we were politely asked to 'Fucking get out of the goals', but this particular week the goalkeeper asked us to warm him up by taking a few shots at him. It is safe to say that he must have seen us playing before as he felt sufficiently confident in his own ability, or our lack thereof, to offer us a tenner if we could score past him. Suffice to say after ten or so scuffed shots, none of which required him to make a save, it was time for us to 'fuck off'. Upon reflection, of all the things a small boy might be offered cash for by a stranger in a public park, I think we got away lightly.

Although I had broken into the school team at centre-back, it was around this time that my love of Erik Thorstvedt, and a new story about a young goalkeeper in *Roy of the Rovers* who I thought looked like me, inspired me to start playing in goal. I tried to do everything like Erik the Viking, right down to wearing a knee strapping when playing despite having no knee injury, only to pretend I did when people asked what the bandage was for.

The early 90s was not a vintage period for English football. Graham Taylor was presiding over the national team as it stumbled through qualification for the European Championships, and direct 'up and at 'em' football was very much in vogue. 'Put it in the mixer' – a phrase repeated up and down every Sunday League pitch in the country – also seemed to be the go-to tactic for half of the Barclays First Division. Even as a nine-year-old, especially now playing in goal, I realised that it was perhaps asking a lot of primary school children to play on full-size pitches with full-size goals. Basically, the surest way to score a goal was to give the other team a goal kick. Their goalkeeper, barely able to kick the ball out of the penalty area, would then present the ball straight to your striker who knew even if he shot wide the goal kick that followed would immediately present him with another chance to score.

The fortunes of our school team peaked and then troughed with the arrival and departure of a boy called Abdi part way through the year. Abdi was from Somalia. He was a lovely, quiet boy who was infinitely better than any of us at football. He was also well on the way to six foot tall, and as is so often the way in boys' football when there is one boy who has developed much faster than the rest, he would basically win our matches single-handedly.

The tactics were always the same: 'Get the ball to Abdi!' All was well and we were unbeatable until Abdi moved to another school in the district. When it was our turn to play his new school, Abdi demonstrated just how much of a one-man team Hazelwood had been. With him on the other side, it was a non-contest. We consoled ourselves that although we maybe weren't a very strong side anymore, at least we had a pitch. Our Lady of Lourdes Primary School played *their* school games on a pioneering new all-weather surface – a concrete playground. Playing them we came away with the win plus matching battle scars, cut knees and elbows. That school literally used jumpers for goalposts.

The Metropolitan Police would organise an annual five-a-side tournament for schools on the immaculate pitches of the Tesco Country Club at Goff's Oak, which incidentally were used for training by the Swiss national team during Euro '96. Playing there was obviously a Very Big Deal. However, thanks to the meddling of Esther Rantzen, I nearly never got to share my gift of pretty average goalkeeping with the wider world.

Esther Rantzen's programme, *That's Life,* was compulsory viewing on a Sunday evening in our super-safety-conscious house. Most of the time it had funny items, like people being stopped in the street and asked silly questions, or being set up in some ridiculous scenario. But then it had some serious items too. The Sunday night before the tournament, with timing that seemed to be aimed deliberately to cause me the maximum embarrassment, Rantzen ran a feature on the dangers of five-a-side goalposts and how up and down the country there had been a spate of serious and even fatal injuries to young goalkeepers caused by the collapse of the goal on top of them. With hindsight,

I should be grateful that my mum was so concerned with my wellbeing that she took it upon herself not just to drive me to the sports ground, but also to linger. This was a public safety matter and she wanted answers. She set about inspecting all the goals to see how they were fixed to the ground, and was not satisfied. There are few worse things in a ten-year-old's life than having to tell your team-mates that you might not be allowed to play because your mum says it's not safe. But that's what I had to endure that night. Eventually, she spoke to the police officer in charge and gave him an earful about what she had seen on Esther's ever-helpful show, and how there should at least be sandbags on the back of the goals weighing them down. At this point, I started to cry and prepared to make the walk of shame back to the car in front of carloads of other boys whose mums had correctly understood that child safety should not get in the way of five-a-side school football. Thankfully the police officer, no doubt drawing on years of professional experience in handling overly vocal people, while at the same time mourning the loss of manliness in the youth of today, said, 'Well it's up to you madam!' Mercifully my mum saw the light, and I was able to play on.

Goalkeeping did turn out to be a hazardous occupation for me all the same. Around the time of 'goalpost gate', I started going to midweek football lessons in a local secondary school gym. Back then, the only credentials you needed to run football lessons seemed to be owning a few footballs and the ability to hire an indoor space for an hour each week. Having ticked these two boxes, our coach was a man in his early twenties who clearly modelled himself on Roberto Baggio. Right down to 'the divine ponytail', glitzy earring and Juventus leisurewear. Two weeks in, he was putting on a training drill, the title of which might have been, 'How to impress the younger mums sitting on benches round the edge of the gym to watch the session'. As I was the only goalkeeper in the group, he made me stand in front of a high jump crash mat propped up on its side to represent a goal, and then demonstrated just how hard he could shoot. What exactly this was meant to teach any of us was unclear. However, the ball arrowed directly into my face and left me dazed on the floor with a bloody nose. Baggio's apology, he hadn't expected me to try to save it – didn't cut the mustard with my mum. That was the end of the course for me.

The year after I left junior school a friend of mine, let's call him 'David', in the year below me was made captain of the school team. A new teacher had taken on responsibility for coaching them. David recalls that football training that year consisted of very little football, but was more about lots of stretching or walking on hands and knees across the floor of the dinner hall, that doubled up as a sports hall. Towards the end of the school year, before he was to join me at secondary school, David and one of the other boys got word that the teacher wanted to see them at lunchtime on important football team business. The two of them duly reported to the teacher's classroom, where he explained that as they were soon to be leaving the school and had been such good footballers, they could really help next year's boys by appearing in a training video. David recalls feeling immensely proud, thinking he would be forever immortalised in the folklore of the school football team. He was only too keen to participate.

There was a video camera in the classroom and the boys were asked to change into their football kit before being asked to do some role-play. Firstly one boy had to do some stretches touching his toes, while the other boy acted as the teacher and told him where he was going wrong. Then they were given a wooden metre stick and told to tap each other on the backside when the stretches weren't done properly. Finally, David remembers being asked to do a 'sit-up thing on top of each other'. Attempting to rationalise this, he describes it as an assisted stretch even though, now in his early thirties, he understands what was going on. At the time, however, the teacher said the video was to be a special surprise for the school and the boys were not to tell anyone. At that age, there is little more important than the school football team. So at the end of the session, when the camera was turned off, he didn't say a word to anyone about what had happened, but took great pride in having been selected for this honour. It confirmed what every schoolboy wanted to hear, that he was one of the best footballers in the school. Now, future generations would know it too.

Surprisingly, however, it appears that the teacher had not made the definitive football training video after all, as the following year he made the same request to another boy. This boy must have gone home and told his parents about it. David, at this point in his first year at secondary school, recounts that he was contacted by the police to inquire if he had been asked to do anything unusual in relation to the junior school football team. When I suggest to him that probably the video was viewed by more men than just the teacher who filmed it, there is a brief flicker of discomfort in his eyes. But reflecting back over 20 years since it happened, he says he doesn't feel like he went through a harrowing experience, and doesn't feel as if he was abused or groomed by a paedophile. He also remembers that in his first Sunday League team, the coach on occasion required him to wear a black bin bag and do laps of the pitch because he needed to lose weight. I have heard that professional footballers in the late 1980s and early 90s employed this as a way of excreting the alcohol from their system if they had had a skinful the night before and were trying to go undetected by the manager, but the fact that someone would ask a child with a bit of puppy fat on them to do the same is perhaps indicative of how unregulated youth football was, and how easy it was for well-meaning volunteers, let alone sexual predators, to do massive harm to young boys who would turn up week in, week out, to play the game they loved.

Happily, David channelled these experiences, which never diminished his passion for football, into setting up his own business delivering brilliant weekly football coaching to hundreds of youth footballers across north London and

Hertfordshire. He takes great pride in ensuring that the children in his company's care have a safe environment to develop, and most importantly enjoy their football. He still feels there are companies and coaches out there who cut corners and don't perform the necessary Disclosure and Barring Service checks or have properly robust safeguarding policies. Having been with him on the sidelines when coaching his team in matches against other clubs, it is immediately apparent to me how upsetting he finds it when the conduct of the coach of the opposition team does not meet the standards he sets for anyone in his employ. He says he doesn't ever think about the teacher anymore or feel hatred towards him, but 'now I know if I ever did see him, he would deserve a good kicking'.

At secondary school I was still playing in goal. I'd left the Cubs, which for a while was a great source of organised football and knot tying. This was the time I joined my first proper Sunday League team, Winchmore Hill FC, made up of several of the boys I had played against in the Cubs, and who I now went to school with. Four of us would travel together to training every Thursday, and matches on a Sunday, often driven by Dominic Slatter's dad, Malcolm. He was a rather stern police officer, who would tell us with increasing dismay not to slam the doors of his Vauxhall Cavalier and reprimand me for my goalkeeping gloves. After a couple of weeks of wearing, they smelt like a dead animal and completely overpowered the air freshener each time I entered his pristine vehicle. Looking back, I have to credit Malcolm as he would always be willing to do the driving, even though his son was a perennial substitute and would only be given the last few minutes of a game if the scoreline meant the result was already a formality. Toni Cannas, the dad of Daniele, one of my other mates on the team, was another regular source of lifts to and from games and training. Toni was a small man with a warm, friendly face, dark hair and big moustache which, given our age and his strong Italian accent, made comparisons to Super Mario of Nintendo fame inevitable. I will always be thankful to Toni in those formative Sunday League years, where I came off the pitch having made at best one bad mistake in the game, but oftentimes many more, for having a kind word to say to me. Which would encourage me to do it all again the following week.

Winchmore Hill was a big club that ran multiple men's football teams and cricket in the summer. The youth football team wore purple and white shirts and short 1980s-style football shorts – unfortunately the longer style ushered in by Spurs and Umbro in the 1991 FA Cup Final took longer to trickle down to amateur football. We were managed by a policeman called Jimmy. Unlike most youth football managers, Jimmy did not have a son in the team. You can usually tell the teams where the manager's son is in the side as he'll be the captain, taking free kicks and penalties and always completing the full 90 minutes despite being the worst player on the pitch. Jimmy was a nice enough guy, although I do remember him laughing when one of the players I didn't know mispronounced my name as 'Urine'. Mercifully, it was only a few years before *Trainspotting* came out and Ewan McGregor made the name familiar to everyone south of the border. I joined part way through the season after the clocks had changed. Training was conducted on a muddy bit of field with one big goal close to the clubhouse. There was a floodlight (singular), which emitted about as much light as would a hand torch gaffer-taped to a pole; you could just about see the person next to you or the ball speeding out of the shadows a split second before it hit you in the face.

Training mostly involved forming a queue, the player at the front of which would pass the ball to Jimmy or one of the dads who served as his assistants, who would then lay it off for the player to have a shot at goal. That was the theory, but this rather depended on firstly the player making an accurate pass to the adult, and then, equally unlikely, the adult returning the ball with any sort of quality to the onrushing player. Should these unlikely stars align, more often than not the player would proceed to either shank his shot wide or miss the ball altogether.

He would then return to the back of the queue and wait for the other 15 boys to do the same before getting another go, by which time he had completely forgotten the sophisticated 'coaching point' he had been given, namely, 'Try kicking the ball next time.' As the goalkeeper in these exercises, I wasn't getting very much practice. While I would like to put it down to that, truth be told, I just wasn't very good in goal.

The team itself was not bad though, with a couple of really talented players. The first was Simon, a pacey forward who was twice the size of everyone else and rattled in the goals every week. He was soon cherry-picked by Tesco, the dominant force in youth football in our area. The second was a boy called Edward. I never actually saw him play, but his prodigious talent at age 11 was constantly spoken about by the dads. Sadly, though, Edward had contracted gangrene, which at school I had learned about as something afflicting soldiers in WWI rather than youth Sunday League footballers in the 1990s.

My debut for Winchmore Hill came in a cup-tie against Bedfont Eagles that necessitated a long drive across London to their home ground right by Heathrow's Terminal 4. As the various cars pulled into the car park and we made our way over to the changing rooms, we all noticed daubed in massive letters across the front of the building, 'Hounslow I had your mum'. This was particularly unfortunate for one boy in our ranks, poor Ben Hounslow. At age 11, there was no greater insult than someone besmirching, or as we all put it, cussing your mum. But Ben received very little sympathy from the rest of us – quite the opposite in fact. We were blissfully ignorant that Hounslow was the name of a town nearby to Heathrow and the insult more than likely related to a team of that name. The game from that point is now a blur. The only real memory I have is of finding it hard to concentrate with the roar of the jets as they barely cleared the crossbar of the goal I was keeping.

But the environment at our home pitch had challenges of its own. A few minutes into the second half of my first league game a shot went wide, and flew into the trees a few feet behind the goal. I went back into the trees to retrieve the ball, already panicking about the inept goal kick I would shortly be taking. The ball, however, had gone through the trees and out the other side into the stream behind them. After what seemed at least 15 minutes, I finally managed to get the ball and return to the game with sopping wet boots in what would become a regular routine whenever we defended that end. So much so, that I would often dive and try and save the ball even if it was going wide, just to save myself the river walk to fetch it back.

Once I felt established in the team, I noticed that no one seemed to be wearing a captain's armband, even though a blond lad called Mark was clearly captain in that he would do the coin toss before the game. In the garden at home, I would often wear around my upper arm the tennis headband that had come with matching wristbands. I wondered if I just turned up to the game on Sunday doing the same, would I be allowed to be captain from then on? The fact that my captain's armband was white and fluffy and said 'Wilson' in rainbow-coloured letters was a slight cause for concern but it was surely worth a try. I pressed ahead with my plan, until the manager asked me what I was doing and I embarrassedly took it off. Funnily enough, though, the very next week Mark turned up with a proper captain's armband of his own.

Once Simon had left, and with the injured Edward no closer to returning, we went from being a team that won more than we lost, to a side that got beaten regularly and often heavily. As the fact that I could only dive one way, never a strength in a goalkeeper, became more and more exposed, my confidence took a similar one-way nosedive. I would get home obliterated in mud, miserable from having had to pick the ball out of the back of the net over and over. One of the watching mums, called Anne, became my tormentor in chief. Clearly, she believed her son was on course to play professionally but for the limitations of the players around him. Perhaps she was right.

One week at training, after a particularly dismal display by the team, Jimmy lined up all the boys along the goal line. He and the other dad who helped oversee training, plus the boys who had been absent that Sunday, smashed balls into the goal with strict instructions that moving out of the way was not an option. I have ruminated many times since on exactly what this was supposed to teach us, and how it would improve the team. I am still unsure today. The main thing I took from it was that losing Sunday League football wasn't fun, and maybe that was the aim of the lesson. But I think we had already figured that out for ourselves.

Eventually, I came to training to be greeted by the sight of another goalkeeper already there and in the sticks being warmed up. I knew the writing was on the wall for me as the Number 1. Initially we would take turns to play in the matches, like Ray Clemence and Peter Shilton had done for England all those years before. If Clem and Shilts could be imagined as slightly chubby schoolboys, decked out in multi-coloured Umbro replica goalkeeping kits that were big enough to fit two people, with fluorescent Sondico gloves.

We used to receive the team sheet for the coming Sunday's game in the post on a Friday, once Jimmy had overseen training and knew who was available. Thankfully, he stopped this practice of informing us of the team in writing before it got to the point when I was dropped altogether.

In one last attempt to improve my goalkeeping skills, I nagged my mum to pay for me to go to Bob Wilson's three-day residential goalkeeping school, which used to run adverts in *Match* magazine that I also received by post every week. Wearing the full turquoise Spurs keeper kit to Arsenal legend Bob Wilson's school at least made me stand out, and although I did learn to wait to see where the shot was going before diving, it was clear to me when I shook special guest David Seaman's hand at the end-of-course ceremony, that goalkeeping wasn't for me. It was a turning point. I realised I had to get back to playing centre-back, where my height and love of heading the ball really far would make me a much better and happier footballer for the rest of my school years.

Chapter Two

Grass roots, Green Lanes

THE Wizards began life in the summer of 2002 as the much less whimsically named Winchmore Arms. Yes, we were essentially a pub team at first. The Winchmore Arms was a pretty unremarkable pub on a small roundabout somewhere between Southgate and Winchmore Hill in north London; regular patrons wore Reebok Classics long after their heyday and there was always a queue to put your pound down to be next on the pool table.

Jon Davis, a lifelong friend of mine, was the founder of the team. I had shared many of Spurs' worst defeats of the mid to late 90s with Jon, either in the stands at White Hart Lane or listening to Capital Gold's live commentary on a school night. Games like (Championship or whatever the second tier of English football was calling itself in 1996) Bolton, 6, (Premier League) Spurs, 1. This sort of result left you with two options: asking your mum to write you a sick note so you could avoid school and more importantly, the Arsenal fans in the common room the next day; or the braver option of defiantly going to school but hiding in the toilets during breaktime. Jon and I would also stay up every fourth Sunday in each month to watch World Wrestling Federation pay-per-views on Sky until 4am, which he chose to do rather than spending time with Nicole, his extremely beautiful girlfriend at that time.

Jon's dad, Gary, had been behind the success of the Planet Hollywood restaurant in London, and Jon had learnt a lot of enterprise and negotiation skills from him. This undoubtedly helped Jon always to have the most stunning girlfriends, that and perhaps also his ability to dazzle them with the finest dinner an American film-themed restaurant had to offer.

Following my return to London after three years at university in Southampton, Jon floated the idea of getting together a team of our old schoolmates. He used his business acumen to convince the landlord of the Winchmore Arms to put up some money for a kit and the fees for joining the Edmonton and District Sunday Football League. My memory is that there was a kind of gentlemen's agreement that a quota of the pub regulars would be picked for the team, but since they weren't very good, this soon fell by the wayside. One of the pub players a few of us remembered a bit from school (he was two years ahead of us) made the fatal mistake of telling people that in his late teens he'd been signed by Crystal Palace under Terry Venables. Such claims were more difficult to debunk in the late 1990s, when the internet was still a rare and mysterious commodity even in the fairly affluent homes of N10 and N13. Four years on, however, as we started playing Sunday League, the poor chap was reminded of his supposed pedigree every time he misplaced a pass at Pyms Park.

We played our first game as the Winchmore Arms in Edmonton Division 5 after a long pre-season of fitness work, by which I mean five minutes smashing shots at the keeper before the match kicked off. Jon had made me captain of the side, which meant I got to proudly wear a proper captain's armband and finally exorcised that particular childhood ghost. The result was a 5-0 win against Enfield Crusaders. I scored the first goal in the club's history. It was a bullet header that got more powerful and from further out each time I subsequently described it.

After the game, the team headed back to the Winchmore Arms in euphoric mood and were served a complimentary plate of potatoes and mystery meat sausages. Jon had evidently negotiated a sausage-based bonus deal with the landlord if we won. It's fair to say this became a bone of contention as the season progressed. For one thing, the nucleus of the team was taking the games very seriously, which meant a huge sausage bill for the landlord. For another thing, in order to keep winning we'd frozen out the actual pub players. Maybe it was the rumblings of discontent among the regulars, or maybe the more committed players weren't buying enough post-match drinks. Anyway, after a few weeks the landlord did his sums and reached his decision. He cut off the sausage supply.

In a very short time the relationship with The Arms deteriorated to the point where the landlord asked Jon to give back the kit. We stopped going to the pub at all after this, so never found out if the bar staff were now decked out in blue nylon with a number on the back. We honourably kept the Winchmore Arms team name for the rest of the campaign – the league wouldn't let us change it mid-season when we asked.

As an aside, I should record that a few of us did make a covert visit to The Arms a few years later, in order to watch Spurs play West Ham on TV live from Upton Park. The game became known as 'lasagne-gate'. A win would have seen Spurs qualify for the Champions League for the first time. But instead, with several players allegedly suffering the ill effects of a dodgy lasagne, they lost to West Ham, which meant they were edged out of fourth place in the league by Arsenal.

Having had our kit confiscated, we knew that playing in bare skins, although acceptable down the park when you're a kid and need to distinguish the teams, wasn't an option. We turned out for the rest of that glorious first season in a borrowed all-white Prostar number which looked great, making us the Division 5 Real Madrid and smelt like a spring meadow for exactly one week. Unlike Madrid, we were playing on pitches that resembled First World War battlefields. A rectangle of thick mud which just happens to have some corner flags, goalposts and white lines on it, in amongst the elaborate trench and tunnel systems. The kit quickly deteriorated from brilliant white to pound-shop grey; as young men, none of us had yet learned that cramming the whole team's muddy kit straight in the machine on boil wash wasn't how our mums would have done it.

Our main rivals on the field in this year were a team called Pantel FC, who had opted to play in the Edmonton League rather than the Greek League for which they were also eligible. The area of north London where we grew up has a large Greek Cypriot community, so at school I was an honorary Cypriot and inevitably learnt lots of Greek swear words and ways to insult someone's mother. Our high street, Green Lanes, not that cleverly dubbed 'Greek Lanes', had the highest concentration of hairdressers in the western world separated by amazing fruit and vegetable shops that seemed to be open 24 hours a day, presumably supplying a quick hit of broccoli and red peppers to those who didn't want their night to end after the pubs had closed. Even more intriguing, however, were the other establishments on the high street that as far as I know were unique to north London at that time. Shop fronts shrouded in mystery, or more precisely a tobacco-stained net curtain preventing anyone from seeing inside. The signs above the premises always looked the same: the name of an exotic-sounding football team together with an image of a 1970s-style hexagonal football or delightfully drawn, blocky figure, attempting an overhead kick.

In all my years living in the area, I never once saw anyone go in or out of these places or got a glimpse of what was happening behind the curtain. This all changed, though, one glorious day after school when one of the Cypriot lads from my class who I hung out with said that he could get us inside. Hanging back behind him, a group of us nervously entered through the front door. What we found was something better than any 13-year-old boy could hope for, a pool table, a colour TV high up on a stand in the corner showing non-stop football from across Europe, and posters of legendary Cypriot players of yesteryear with improbably short shorts and haircuts identical to those displayed on the windows of the Greek hairdressers next door. The only woman anywhere to be seen was Samantha Fox, also wearing short shorts but as was often her way whenever I saw her, no shirt!

Sadly, after a couple of games of pool, our access to the forbidden kingdom was revoked as abruptly as it had been granted when a couple of regulars arrived and wanted to use the table. They had a word or two in Greek with a fella behind the bar, presumably about why a bunch of spotty teenagers had gotten into their sanctuary, especially as one of them was an 'Englezo'. We made for the exit excited at the rich rewards adult life would have in store for us, and looking forward to the day we were old enough, or Greek Cypriot enough in my case, to be formally invited to become members of N.Salamis FC Supporters' Club.[3]

It was with these memories from my youth that we turned up to play Pantel FC on 20 October 2002 for the first time that season. I fully expected to be playing against some middle-aged, overweight fellas operating out of a supporters' club on Green Lanes. However, when they came out of the dressing room they were actually boys like us but in a much more pristine white kit, doing an impressive set of drills at the commands of a coach in full Pantel FC tracksuit, matching tops and bottoms!

They say in professional football games are often won or lost in the tunnel before a ball is kicked. That is where the

---

3   When a totally unfancied Greek national team won Euro 2004, it was no surprise that Green Lanes became the happiest place on Earth for a good 48 hours.

psychological warfare takes place. In Sunday League, where there is no tunnel to come out of, you'd be amazed by how much stock one team puts in the opposition's kit and warm-up routines. In my experience having more than one ball to warm up with, or a set of cones to jog around, is worth at least a two-goal head start.

Most remarkably, Pantel was the only team in the league, maybe any Sunday League, which had a fan base. There were about a hundred people present to see the highly anticipated first leg of our 5th Division cup tie, which was played before we had faced them in the league itself. The table showed we were the two strongest teams in the division, and even though there were no points at stake this was going to be an important barometer for the eventual destination of the title and subsequent promotion.

As the game got going I remember being nervous, anxious that the presence of a crowd would affect my first touch. I needn't have worried, it was exactly the same as always. Crap. We went behind in the first half, a goal greeted with a shout from the side of the pitch that would put the atmosphere at many present day Premier League fixtures to shame. It was then that I became aware that one of the people in the Pantel ranks on the sideline was filming the game with a video camera on a tripod. How seriously are they taking their football? I wondered. Does the coach then make them sit down and review the game during training? Is he wearing a bluetooth headset and is his assistant up a tree to get a bird's eye view of the action?

The presence of a camera had gotten our backs up, so when we equalised a few of us got a bit silly and I ran towards it to celebrate, screaming 'Get in!' See Maradona's amphetamine-charged goal celebration, incidentally against Greece in World Cup '94, for an idea of our pathetic antics.[4] I knew as soon as I had done it that I had been a dick, as it was actually a middle-aged woman doing the filming and my celebration was pretty classless, even if I did feel provoked. It was also stupid given that

---

4   Maradona failed a drug test and was sent home.

they had a hundred fans on the sideline and there was not going to be a police escort from the pitch to the car park like in the pros. As captain, I got an especially severe and public telling off from the referee, and then got dog's abuse from the crowd every time I touched the ball for the remainder of the match. We lost 3-1.

It was an interesting experience in humility for me early in our club's journey. From then on I did my best to stay calm and keep the rest of the boys level-headed because there's not much worse than giving it loads on a football pitch and then losing – there is literally nothing you can say. We lost the second leg 2-1 a week later with a depleted side, and Pantel went on to win the cup. Our minds, however, were very much focused on what really mattered to us, the league title.

Our first league meeting against Pantel came on 16 March 2003, by which time we were fully recovered from the fall-out with the pub and winning fairly comfortably most weeks, as were they. We dispatched them 3-0 away from home, but due to slipping up early on in the season, we knew we would probably have to take maximum points from our last five games to secure the title. One of these games was against a team called Corinthians. I tell the following story, still slightly worried that I may have to hand back my Division 5 winners' medal. Just to be clear, Edmonton Sunday League officials, you can't have it as I have drilled a hole in it and wear it as a medallion. The game was locked at 1-1 and Corinthians appeared to have improved considerably from when we played them earlier in the season, but any moral outrage we might have had about them potentially playing ringers has to be tempered by our own misdemeanour.

Regularly during our season in the bottom tier of the Edmonton Sunday Football pyramid, we would have no referee. Sometimes this would be known ahead of time when none was allocated to our game on the weekly fixture list. Other times, however, it would be because the home team had failed to call the ref to confirm the game during the week, or the ref had just decided to do something else with his Sunday morning. The

realisation as both teams warmed up and kick-off approached
that no referee was in attendance tended to cause universal panic.
It meant one of the club secretaries or substitutes would have to
be forced, kicking and screaming, to take the role of ref in order
for the game to go ahead.[5]

On this occasion, however, it worked to our advantage. One
of our regular players, Alex Clayton, the unofficial world record
holder for the number of foul throws in a season, was currently
out injured. This meant he was available to referee the game.
Alex has a strong moral compass, but when it comes to Sunday
League it's the type that has been tampered with, to make it
never point north no matter where you're standing. In addition to
this, despite not enjoying or very often attending school, he is one
of the brightest and most savvy people I know. I credit him with
this even though on the evening we got our GCSE results, where
we broke the mould and did something unheard of for teenagers
in the UK, that is, went to the local park and got smashed on
cider and lemon Hooch, I witnessed him rolling about on the
floor under a picnic table telling a bewildered girl called Lindsey
that she was his She-Ra, which presumably made him He-Man.

With the game all square and Alex knowing that we needed
a win, he proceeded to officiate the longest 90 minutes of
association football ever played to enable us enough time to
score a winning goal. What was particularly magnificent about
his refereeing performance was that at one stage, Alex had
honestly answered one of the Corinthian players who had asked

---

5   As we progressed to the higher echelons of the Edmonton League the
occurrence of there not being a referee for the game became much less
regular. Although there was one time in Division 2 where one of our players
Daniel Abrahams came over to watch the game unable to play due to illness.
In addition to possessing a highly cultured left foot, Dan is a primary school
teacher and made the mistake that particular morning of confessing he
had a whistle affixed to his key ring, a necessary tool of his work. A few
minutes later he was press-ganged into refereeing the game despite having
a temperature well into the hundreds and a green tint to his complexion. At
the end of the game players on both teams acknowledged he was the best
referee they had ever had in Sunday football.

how much time was left in the game, only a good five minutes later to tell the same guy who asked again that now more time was left to play than the last time he'd asked. Alex said this with such authority that none of their players batted an eyelid. Little did they know that they were essentially playing a game of next-goal-wins (only if *they* conceded) and so it happened as deep, deep, deep, into added time we forced a goal. Again Alex played a blinder, barely allowing the opposition to take centre before blowing up for full time. I think at this point one of their players did actually question how time that had been moving so slowly suddenly seemed to have evaporated now that they needed some to try and equalise. But with all the front of his hero Del Boy winning over punters on Hooky Street, Alex just pointed to his watch and said time was up, and we trooped off three points closer to the title.

When it comes to suspect refereeing, this is not the most extreme story I've come across in the Edmonton and District Sunday League. My friend Tony Speller, one of the few adult males I know who never played for the Wizards, which I know is one of the biggest regrets of his life, once played a Brigg Cup tie for the Academicals, when they didn't have a ref for the match.

I should explain that the Brigg Cup is a competition with workings so arcane it makes doing your tax return seem like a doddle. Essentially the Brigg Cup is there to act as a filler to ensure that teams that have gone out of the other cup competitions early, and would otherwise only have league games to play, have enough matches to fill up the fixture list. This meant you could win all your group games in the Brigg Cup but because you had advanced a few rounds in another competition you then could not qualify, whereas the team you might have beaten 8-0 in one of these Brigg Cup games *would* progress. The way to succeed therefore was to lose. I guess if the Brigg Cup had an official song it would be 'Every Loser Wins', by Nick Berry of *EastEnders* and *Heartbeat* fame, which spent three weeks at the top of the singles chart in 1986.

Tony told me that in this particular cup tie, following a discussion between the two club secretaries, it was somehow agreed to allow an opposition player to referee the game at the same time as playing in it; whistle in mouth while stepping up to take the free kick he had just awarded himself. I suppose it was a small mercy that the fella played outfield rather than in goal, where keeping up with play may have proved difficult. Tony thinks that his team won the game, which means they were immediately eliminated from the competition.

Following our ill-gotten three-point boost courtesy of Alex's creative timekeeping, we knew going into our penultimate league game versus Pantel that a win against them would wrap up the league title. So long as we won, our goal difference would make our final game of the season academic. The crucial clash with Pantel was set to kick off on a gloriously sunny morning at the end of April 2003, in front of another bumper crowd, none of whom were there to support us despite it being our home game. (I should record in fairness that with inscrutable Sunday League logic our 'away' game earlier in the season had been played on exactly the same pitch.)

Since our schism with the pub, Jon had become our regular goalkeeper. But as we warmed up for our most important match to date he was nowhere to be seen. As the minutes ticked down to kick-off, we tried hard to hide the fact that anything was wrong, but already I was playing out the awful scenario of my own enforced return between the sticks. At last, with seconds to spare, Jon came running up the field, clearly the worse for wear and in suit trousers and shirt from the night before. For the first spell of the game he was still wearing the trousers, until an appropriate-length break in play enabled him to slip into something more comfortable. Luckily the ball didn't get near his goal too often in the first half as Jon reported being able to see three balls for most of the time until he sobered up.

On the day, however, it was Michael Pearce who was our star performer. A shout came from the sideline after Mickey had scored a goal that Pantel weren't coming back from. 'Their number 10 is shitting all over you!' Mickey, who was never a shy character, in fact he was confident enough to wear a rat's tail deep into his secondary school career, actually put his foot on the ball following this remark and pointed over his back with both his thumbs to the number 10 on his shirt, with the most deliciously smug gesture on a football pitch since Andy Möller's hands-on-hips strut having scored the winning penalty against England in the semi-finals of Euro '96.

As we played out the final few minutes of the game, 4-1 up and with the title in the bag, I reflected genuinely how sad it was for these boys we had beaten that their girlfriends, family and friends were there to witness their misery. Some people might revel in getting one up on a rival in front of everyone they know, but on this occasion I didn't feel like that at all. Football can be a horrible game when you lose, and I can vouch for suffering some of the most desperate feelings after losing important games. Even if we were 'only' playing for the Edmonton 5th Division title, for those of us out on the park during that 90 minutes and the period of celebration or desolation afterwards, depending on what kit you were wearing, it mattered to us as much as any game of football ever played. Having reflected on what a wanker I had been in the cup game against Pantel earlier in the season, before joining in with our celebrations I went over to have a word with their captain. He'd been a good player whenever we played them, and a nice guy on the occasions when I'd seen him along Green Lanes, and he stopped for a chat out of the window of his car. (I should mention another thing about the Greek Cypriot lads where we grew up – they always had the flashiest cars.) Anyway, at the final whistle, I gave him a pat on the back and we shook hands and I offered some pretty hollow words of encouragement and commiseration, congratulating them on a good season. At this point he said to me that the main thing was that they had won a cup for 'their boy'. It turns out that far from being named after a Greek or Cypriot football team, Pantel FC had been founded in memory of one of their friends, Paul (Pantelakis) Michael, who had been tragically killed in horrific circumstances in July 2002, aged just 21.

Paul Michael was murdered by a fellow student by the name of Mustapha Maher, who suffered from paranoid schizophrenia. Maher had become obsessed with Paul Michael during their time studying A Levels at college, and then followed him by enrolling at the University of Buckinghamshire. According to press reports at the time, Paul, having initially been friendly, had tried to distance himself from Maher as his behaviour became more erratic and obsessive. Maher was unable to accept this; he made threats and stalked Paul Michael before ambushing him outside his home, stabbing him in the back.[6]

Paul Michael was exactly the same age as most of our players when he died. At a point in his life where all options and possibilities seemed open, suddenly they closed forever in the most brutal and shocking circumstances. I can't imagine how hard it must have been for the boys who came together to found Pantel FC, to take to the pitch that season of 2002/03 so soon after this tragedy had taken place. Lining up on a field to play football with your mates, knowing that someone who should be out there with you never would be again. It's something I don't think I would have been able to process at age 21, or now for that matter. Setting up a team to honour their friend and keep his memory alive was a great and touching response to the tragedy. I really hope that winning the cup in their first season, which obviously meant so much to their players at the time, helped them and their fans in some way.

In July 2003, we had our first ever end-of-season do at Planet Hollywood, Piccadilly Circus. Thanks to Jon and his dad, drinks and dinner were on the house. My brother-in-law, Johnny, tells a story of how a television executive he knows, who had worked on *Baywatch*, was one day accosted by David Hasselhoff. The Hoff had just heard that *Baywatch* was currently the most watched

6   These details are taken from the *Evening Standard*, 13 November 2003.

show in the world, and without any degree of irony, declared that as he was the show's star he must therefore be the world's best actor. In similar vein, having been voted players' player of the season at our Planet Hollywood celebration, I drunkenly reasoned to myself that this made me the best player in the whole of the 5th Division. Surely it was only a matter of time until I received an international call-up.

The drinks continued to flow into the early hours, until it was time to find an unlicensed taxi touting for business and offering the best fares in London to transport us home. I remember it was a silver people carrier with maybe six of us in it. About halfway through the 40-minute journey the self-proclaimed 'best player in the Edmonton 5th Division' realised he was going to be sick. The penalties for being sick in a taxi, expulsion and a slap depending on how many of you are in the car, are well established as the poor fellas who make their living this way have to deal with this routinely on trips from central London along Green Lanes on a Saturday night. As I considered my options, I noticed the bright pink shirt I had on had a pocket on the left-hand side, and reasoned that as I was sitting in the back row in the left hand corner I could discreetly transfer vomit from my mouth into said shirt pocket without the driver noticing. While I successfully managed to move the offending deposit from A to B, I neglected to consider that the retching noises and smell might give me away. Upon being questioned I assured the driver that all the sick 'was in my top pocket' and our journey home was completed with no further incident. It was only the next morning, when my mum opened the washing machine to find my shirt and the contents of my stomach/top pocket inside, that I realised I hadn't been half as cunning as I thought.

For a lot of Sunday League footballers the post-match and sometimes pre-match drinks are more important than the games. I was never into this and spent huge time and effort advocating moderation in drinking and drugs to all our players, particularly during the season. Nevertheless, following our expulsion from the Winchmore Arms the team found a new base in a pub called the Kings Head, which is situated on a three-sided green in Winchmore Hill. It's a funny set-up; there are three pubs all within a stone's throw of each other. If JFK's motorcade had ever come to Winchmore Hill, this would have been the perfect spot for the assassination, assuming you believe the multiple gunmen theory of that terrible event. The notion of a president visiting this part of London may seem ridiculous, but the Kings Head back then was full of aspiration; all expensive jeans, Italian shoes without socks and yacht club chic. This despite the nearest coast being a two-hour drive away. No one went to the Kings Head for football, it just wasn't that sort of place. Over time, I began to notice the regularity with which people went to the toilet in little groups of two or three; and when they came back they seemed to speak much more animatedly than they had done a few minutes before.

Even at 21 I have to confess I was quite naive to the whole world of drugs. I was always happy to have a bit of a straight-edged image. In fact my mum, Judith, had written several factual books for children about the dangers of drugs and smoking and this had put the fear of God into me at an early age. I never felt in any sort of physical danger from my mum, but somewhere inside I knew that if she had found me with cigarettes, she would have murdered me, thereby proving the point beyond reasonable doubt that smoking kills. This and the fact that in year two of secondary school they sat us down in Personal and Social Education and showed us a video of Gary Lineker doing some very staged training, and then explaining he would never have made it as a footballer had he messed about with tobacco and drugs. The secret of Gary's success, as we all know, was saturated fats and salt.

Chapter Three

The Wizards

A REGULAR topic of conversation at these nights out at the Kings Head was that the Edmonton League wasn't the right fit for us as a team. Some might say we had delusions of grandeur, but the number of times we had played games during that season without a referee had started to wear on lots of the boys. We were unaware at the time, but the Edmonton and District Sunday Football League had a particularly rich heritage that directly impacted on the number of referees it was able to call upon to officiate games. The EDSFL is believed to be the oldest Sunday League in England. It was formed at a meeting in the Horse and Groom Pub on Fore Street, Edmonton, in June 1925. The League started life as a rogue organisation created against the wishes of the Football Association, which was opposed to amateur football being played on the Sabbath, a stance it maintained until as late as 1960. Ken Martin has been involved in the Edmonton League since the late 1960s, initially as a club secretary then selflessly fulfilling a variety of roles on the management committee ever since. He explained to me that the FA banned referees from working in unaffiliated leagues. Despite this, the Edmonton League managed to survive on its own for 79 years, at one point boasting ten divisions and a hundred teams, before eventually succumbing to the pressure of needing access to more referees and affiliating to the Football Association in 2004.

Some of the elder statesmen in our team spoke of a paradise beyond the A10 and M25, a land of milk and honey, where referees were plentiful and teams shook hands before and after the game and politely encouraged each other during the full 90 minutes. And so it was, we made an application to join the Mercury and Waltham League for the start of the next season. News of this defection meant that at the Edmonton and District awards night, we were the only team not to receive the actual championship trophy shield for fear we would never return it. Ken, as financial secretary for Edmonton, gave us back our deposit for the next season and was good enough to say if we ever wanted to come back in the future we would be welcome.

Launching out into deepest darkest Hertfordshire to attend an interview with the Mercury and Waltham League, and getting thoroughly lost on the way, I began to wonder if we had made a mistake. Getting 11 players to the pitch in time for kick-off had been a challenge when we all lived locally and played at the same ground every week. Now we would be playing away games in places like Cheshunt and Hatfield, it would be necessary for players not only to remember their boots but also to read and follow a map, which I for one felt was not a personal strength.

Arriving late was clearly much more of an issue in the Mercury League. We were greeted by the executive committee, all of whom were wearing league-branded ties and blazers, and the chair of the meeting made a point of tapping his watch as we entered the room. This was in stark contrast to what we had been used to in Edmonton, where cans of Skol lager and chain-smoking were more the order of the day. We answered the questions as best we could, and showed the committee a spreadsheet demonstrating that if we collected subs from 14 players every week we would have enough money to make it to the end of the season. Unbeknownst to them, though, our real plan was to spend the little money we did have in the coffers on the most important thing a Sunday League team can have – a brand-new kit with shorts that actually matched the shirts. I remember the most friendly chap on the interview panel, who also served as the secretary of one of the Mercury League's more well-established teams, Wormley Rovers, asking me what measures we had for controlling our spectators during games. I confidently answered that we were an extremely well disciplined club and had never had any such problems in the previous season, omitting the fact that both our maximum and minimum attendances during the last campaign had been zero.

While it was clear that the board were somewhat hesitant, they did decide to offer us a place in their 3rd Division for the upcoming season. It was now time to decide on a new name for the club. We wanted to retain the Winchmore in a nod to our prestigious (12 month) history, but then also wanted something to set us apart from all the other Sunday League teams. 'Hotspur' was of course unpalatable to half our players, although looking back there was nothing to stop me writing it on the Mercury League form and then revealing the sting to the Arsenal boys just before the first game of the season. Instead, much like the young men of Tottenham who borrowed flashy Harry Hotspur's name from Shakespeare when founding their team, we decided to take inspiration from the greatest literary talent of our time, namely JK Rowling. And so was born the Winchmore Wizards FC.

We decided that it would be beneficial ahead of our first game of the season to have a couple of friendlies, and booked a pitch at a local school. The summer months were miserable without football to play. The prospect of a game of any sort was always highly anticipated, even if the pitches not yet being marked out at the parks meant the only option was to play on astroturf. Only those of us born before the new millennium will know the particular misery of astroturf; thankfully it has long since been replaced by third generation (3G), 4G or even 5G pitches.

But back then the height of all-weather technology involved laying out a pitch-sized green scouring pad, dumping a beach's worth of sand on top, and then asking people in football shirts and shorts to cannibalise their bodies by diving around on it. When you factored rain into the equation, an essential ingredient of British summertime, even those players who you could see had made a conscious decision not to make a sliding tackle during the game would find it impossible not to come away with the skin from their knees and elbows horribly shredded. Worse still was the bit of flesh, where the top of your thigh meets your arse, which was particularly vulnerable to a sliding tackle and then would stick to your bed sheet at night as it wept, becoming a particular hit with the ladies. I tried inventively to combat astroturf misery, whether it be covering every exposed part of skin in Vaseline, or cutting up pairs of sports socks to fashion makeshift knee and elbow pads under my kit, but nothing would work. Once knees and elbows were ripped, seven days was never enough time for them to heal before they were opened up again the next time you played. If you had scraped a cheese-grater across your legs you would have done less damage. I'll always remember another occasion when we were short of players for a friendly, when Mickey somehow convinced the father of his then girlfriend to come down and play in goal for us. Butch, as he was introduced to us, was a big, heavily-set man. The sight of him, well on the way to 60, diving around on the astroturf in the short-sleeve shirt he insisted on wearing was an inspiration.

In our first friendly game, ahead of our fresh start in the Mercury and Waltham League, now wearing new green-and-white hooped shirts, we took on Edmonton Rangers. This was a team that featured my next door neighbour, who I had never played against before. I was keen to demonstrate my footballing excellence but was having trouble with long balls which on the astroturf were bouncing higher than a house. Being pre-season, the basic tenets of Sunday League defending, not letting the ball bounce, or calling your name to avoid two players going for the same ball and in the process neither getting it, had been left behind on the various beaches the boys had been holidaying at. Determined to set a good example off the next goal kick, I told myself, 'Get your head on this at all costs!' As the ball approached, I called for it and jumped high, meeting it well and sending it back with aplomb from whence it came. So far, so good. But unfortunately, on the way back down I went over the shoulders of our left-back, Toby, who was trying to get out of the way, and landed bang on my left hand, which now appeared to be attached to my wrist at a different angle than it had been previously. There are always a sweet few seconds between a serious injury occurring and the local nerves sending the signal along their complex pathways to the brain. I have often thought if you could just control and extend those seconds before the pain kicks in, you could do almost anything. Sadly, I had wasted those precious few seconds thinking about what a deeply profound thought that was and was now in agony.

One of the boys, Darren, said he thought it was a dislocation and made towards my hand as if to push it back into place. Let's just say I politely declined, and so saying went off to A&E at Chase Farm.

Sunday in A&E is never the happiest scene. Seeing the ranks of the sporting injured, parachuted straight from the pitch in full kit plus blood stains and whatever bandages happened to be in the club medical bag, I had a couple of hours to reflect on the cost to the NHS of so many people putting so much effort into keeping fit. Most of all I was calculating, if my hand was broken, how many games I would have to miss. Broken it was. But being Sunday, it seemed there was no one available in the fracture clinic to do the plastering. Using a combination of my teeth and good hand to open the flip screen of my annoyingly small mobile phone, I steeled myself to do the only thing I could. I called my mum, broke the news and asked her to come and collect me. I think it's fair to say by this stage that my mum was despairing of the many and frequent injuries I had sustained playing football.[7] I remember her compassionate response on this occasion as I relayed the admittedly frustrating news of my broken hand. 'Oh for fuck's sake, Ewan!'

It was a long night at home with my hand held bent and bruised in a sling. I remembered that Pele had scored an overhead kick against Nazi Germany in the film *Escape to Victory* in similar circumstances and hoped I would be back doing likewise before too long.

On my return to the hospital, my hand had been plastered on the palm to keep it straight, with a softer dressing over the top. Unfortunately, after a week or so it became clear that the bones in my hand were starting to push up through the dressing. Returning to the hospital I was told that it would now need an operation to insert some temporary metalwork, otherwise my hand would become deformed. As a result I missed my cousin's wedding, which was on the same day.

This was to be the start of what would become a quite intimate relationship between me and the anaesthetists' team at Chase Farm and Barnet hospitals over the next decade. But neither the prospect of having a permanently crooked hand, nor the problem of being away from my new job for a couple of weeks, much to the chagrin of my employers who had taken me on to cover their busiest time of year, bothered me as much as my main concern. How long would I be out of the team and would I get my place back?

In the meantime, I was reduced to watching from the sideline as summer turned to autumn in 2003. I gained a wholly new perspective on Sunday League football, namely that a lot of it is not very good. When you are out there in the middle of a game, I realised, you have no real concept of the quality of the football. You can tell if your direct opponent has a nice touch or is better than you, but you don't really get an overview of the game itself.

---

7   One of the more random had occurred to me as a schoolboy as I headed the ball only to find another boy's teeth embedded in the back of my head. That one required stitches.

Being on the touchline, however, you do start to tot up how many misplaced passes there are, or players who try to Cruyff-turn themselves inside out in their own box rather than use their left foot. As a team, the Wizards were OK and we had some decent players. Still, we were finding results harder to come by than we had in Edmonton. To make matters worse, our administration was not very clever. During one match that wasn't going to plan, AJ, who was picking the team, decided to bring on a sub and change formation. Matthew Berou, fired up having watched a pretty inept performance from the bench, came sprinting on to the pitch, primed to make a difference. He was barking out the orders: 'We are changing to a back three, you go there, you there, you two are wing backs!' As the players rotated into these new positions the referee came over and asked Matthew for his name. He then pronounced that as Matthew had not been named as a sub before kick-off he couldn't come on and had to get off the pitch. I made a mental note that things had to be tightened up if we were to get anywhere.

About six weeks after the operation, it was deemed time to have the metalwork removed from my hand. The doctor unwrapped the dressing to reveal half an inch of wire poking up through the back of my hand just below my little finger. He then opened a tool kit with a collection of tools that looked like they had been passed down through several generations of his family, father to son, took out some pliers, grabbed hold of the protruding wire and pulled it out of me, just like that. Had it not been for the small girl quietly enduring much worse without even a whimper in the bay next to me, I would have broken down in tears it hurt so much. It was also immediately apparent that my hand would no longer run straight from my arm but instead was effectively a skateboard ramp down from my wrist to my fingers.

Predictably, a couple of months into the season the main proponent for the move to the Mercury and Waltham League decided he could no longer be involved. A few of the other boys were complaining about the journey time and our numbers started to thin out. I had got back playing by this stage wearing a strapping on my hand that I liked to think made me look like Eric Cantona, circa 19 September 1993, when he memorably scored a great free kick against Arsenal complete with broken wrist, but actually, given that I had found it in a specialist shop for old people with mobility problems and it was that beige colour that everything in those shops is, I probably did not. When I first got back into the side, I found my confidence was even more fragile than the surgically repaired bones in my hand. I was making mistakes in almost every game, and spent the midweek dreading the approach of Sunday. It is a horrible feeling when you don't feel like your team-mates trust you on the pitch, and worse still if you don't trust yourself. When my confidence completely flat-lined, I remember even thinking about going down with a phantom injury shortly after kick-off, just to escape the misery of playing so poorly and the disparaging looks, imagined or real, I felt were being aimed my way from the other boys. Thankfully, I never implemented this emergency exit strategy. I'd started playing for a midweek five-a-side team called the Bears with some Irish lads I knew. After scoring a couple of really good goals for them, I remembered that I actually enjoy playing the game of football. As if by magic my form on a Sunday came back and I begged it to never abandon me again. 'I'll do whatever you want, just don't leave me.'

Light relief during this difficult period was supplied by one of our best players, Mickey Pearce, when he ordered a new pair of Adidas boots as worn by his idol, Patrick Vieira, at that time. Mickey had taken advantage of the latest development in boot technology, the ability to customise your boots by having a significant or inspirational message embroidered on them, provided you could say it in no more than the maximum allowable eight characters. Mickey thought it would be flash to have his date of birth, '06/09/80', embossed on the tongue of his new boots. It seemed that it had not even crossed Mickey's mind as he lovingly unpacked them from his kit bag that rather than admiration, his purchase would be greeted with epic ridicule. As one opposition player put it within seconds of noticing, 'Is that your birthday on your boots? What in case you forget it?' Sadly the boots only got a few outings before Mickey had to hang them up for the best part of three years. He had been preparing to do 'The Knowledge' to become a cabbie, which involved going out on a moped on his own, day after day, and learning all the different roads and routes in London that he might be required to navigate. During this period he started to find that he was having serious back pain, which eventually required two operations on his spine. The surgical removal of Mickey's damaged disc deprived us of a player and personality we couldn't easily replace.

Another of our regulars went out injured about the same time. Towards the end of a cup game at Donkey Lane, our dependable left-back, Toby Alterman, got caught with a bad tackle and landed awkwardly with a terrible scream. Toby was not the sort of player to stay down, and so it was clear as he lay prone on the muddy wet ground that something serious had happened. His kneecap appeared to be pointing in completely the wrong direction. As we all crowded around Toby, not knowing what to do, the referee brought the game to a premature end and ran off the pitch without a word. Some of our boys sprinted to the changing room for their phones (Donkey Lane being one of the few grounds where the doors could be locked to keep valuables safe) to call for an ambulance. All this time Toby was screaming in the most horrible way.

The referee reappeared and was taken aback when questioned as to why he'd disappeared. But he too had gone off to call an ambulance. Even so, we had to wait in the rain nearly an hour for help to arrive. It seemed like a very long time with Toby in such pain. When the ambulance did finally drive onto the pitch one of our players remarked to the paramedic, 'Why has it taken so fucking long? This guy has been in agony.' But he replied irritably, 'It's not life-threatening, mate.' Maybe so, but it was a horrible dislocation, the worst looking injury I've ever seen on a football pitch, and it held Toby back from playing much competitive football ever again.

Chase Farm Hospital was only five minutes' drive from Donkey Lane and as Neil and I followed the ambulance in Neil's car, we debated whether we should have tried to get Toby straight into the back seat and take him ourselves. Probably not, but seeing a friend in so much pain for so long was horrendous. In future years I would always wince at the monthly Edmonton League meetings when the officials made a regular point of asking club secretaries to tell players not to park in front of the ambulance access gate at grounds.[8]

With so many players missing, we were now dependent on drafting in ringers every week. Robbo, who had taken over running the Wizards, was constantly sourcing players from his work or randoms he had met at the pub, just to get a team out. Also, as players left they took their kit with them, so halfway through the season we found we no longer had enough of the new kit to go round; we ended up wearing an old Wingate and Finchley kit Robbo had inherited from a Sunday team he had played for previously. The team was feeling less and less like our group of mates, and this, combined with the two-hour round trips to get to the games, made it a real prospect that we would not make it to the end of the season. Moreover, we had started to incur debts whether for not having matching corner flags, not wearing matching socks, or just the fines we were picking up for yellow cards, which players turning out as a one-off under someone else's name tend not to want to pay.

One week, one of our regular players, Ian Kiely, brought his mate Paddy Gallagher down to play. Paddy was a centre-forward and it was immediately clear in the warm-up that he could play.

---

8   As part of registering with a league each season the team was required to have insurance, which meant filling out forms listing the macabre level of compensation your pals could expect to receive should they lose an eye, limb, set of teeth, or even die while playing Sunday League football. In all our time I don't recall us ever making a claim.

He was a small, pale lad with an absolute rocket of a shot. The first time he got the ball in the game from an impossible angle far out on the right wing, he lashed a shot into the top corner. It was one of those moments where both teams stop and the world goes very quiet as something incomprehensible has just happened. To even think to shoot from there, let alone score, was something fundamentally different to what anyone else could do on the pitch. When I got home and put 'Paddy Gallagher' into Google, it soon became clear he wasn't your average ringer; my search returned a picture of him in that classic football-sticker pose, sat down in kit for the individual and team photos before the start of the season. Paddy had been playing professionally for Queen's Park in Scotland.

It was a matter of time before we would be undone. The Mercury and Waltham League, unlike Edmonton, had a photo ID system, and as we reached the business end of the season, teams started to require that these be checked prior to kick-off. Thanks to bad weather earlier in the year, we had to play Wormley Rovers on a Wednesday evening. It was hard enough to get players even to play on a Sunday by this point, and so to save the day Robbo had managed to tap up some boys who'd been a couple of years below us at school. This presented one of Sunday League's great creative dilemmas; whether to call ringers by the name of the player they are replacing, which means if you try and call for the ball from them you are unlikely to get it as they don't recognise the name, or whether to call them by their proper name and risk being rumbled by the referee. My experience was that in practice neither would happen. Instead, halfway through calling their real name you would remember you were supposed to be calling them something else and try to adapt mid-shout. As if it weren't obvious enough to a referee that something dodgy was happening, it got worse when a player playing under someone else's name got booked and couldn't remember the name he had been told before the game started. This required great on-pitch management by the rest of us, to get in the player's eyeline behind the referee's back and try and mime the name he was supposed to give. Some players who turned out for us just once wouldn't care about the consequences and would just give the first name that popped into their head, often straight from the news headlines. Referees sometimes raised a sceptical eyebrow as they wrote M. Jackson or T. Blair in their notebook.

We travelled as a convoy from Winchmore Hill Green to Wormley in Hertfordshire on a balmy evening. When we arrived it transpired that the referee would not let us wear the kit we had brought with us as it was not in the colours we had logged in the League handbook and was too close to the home team's kit. Consequently, we had to play in our own clothes, only adding to the sense that we were becoming the real-life Rag Arse Rovers.

Wormley were riding high at the top of the League and badly needed the points to cement their title challenge. Under the floodlights at Wormley's pretty fancy ground we played out a highly competitive draw, perhaps the first ever 0-0 in the history of Sunday League football. Eighteen days later, we were set to play them again in the corresponding league fixture, which was supposed to be our home game but was again to be played at their ground. It seemed that both Wormley and the chairman of the League had their suspicions aroused during the first game where they had not checked our photo ID cards prior to kick-off. Had they done so it would have been fairly easy for them to spot that we were fielding unregistered players. For one thing, at that time we didn't have any non-white players registered, but they must surely have noticed that not all the players in our team were white. In any event, ahead of the second fixture, where Wormley needed a result to seal the title, the referee decided to line us all up in the middle of the pitch and compare our faces to the mug shots we'd submitted at the start of the season.

Of the squad of 14 players we had that day, six were ineligible to play. Inexplicably however the referee mistook one of the unregistered players, Danny Grimsdell, for Mickey Pearce whose photo card he was holding. They both had short-cropped hair and were good-looking lads, but you wouldn't exactly say they looked alike. Even more amusingly, the referee made a big play of talking to Danny and saying, 'Oh yes, Mickey Pearce. I remember you from the first game, how could I forget you, son.' In a way he was right. Danny had been Mickey in that game too.

We therefore had a decision to make. The referee said we could start the game with the nine registered players we had (eight plus Danny) or we would have to forfeit the points. There was a long discussion among the boys where we even offered to forfeit and then play 11 versus 11 with no points on the line, but Wormley were not willing to do this. Maybe it was pride, maybe it was honour; they seemed keen to play against our nine men or not at all. With the benefit of hindsight, I realise that it was nip and tuck between them and Cheshunt at the top of the table, and they probably saw a game against nine men as a way of racking up their goal difference.

Well, we had all gotten up early and made the trip out of north London, and so we decided to go ahead and play the game with nine men. Matthew, our right-back, did the honours in goal, though it was clear to anyone from his appearance alone he was not a goalkeeper. In front of him we played a 4-3-1 formation and held our own in the opening exchanges. At some point in that first half Danny/Mickey, who shouldn't technically have been on the pitch, picked up the ball around the halfway line, burst through a couple of players with a driving run showing an exceptional touch on a bobbly pitch, and was through on goal, clinically dispatching the ball into the bottom left-hand corner. Naturally, the nine of us found this highly amusing but were now fully expecting the Wormley onslaught to descend on us good and proper. Nonetheless, we defended stoutly, minutes passed, time stretched, and next thing we'd reached half-time, one goal up. The mood of the boys was buoyant: all the cliché words of footballing wisdom were trotted out as we huddled together and had a drink. Keep it tight. Let's see how long we can keep it for. Maybe they'll start to get frustrated.

The second half kicked off and Wormley upped the pressure but they weren't really making inroads into our defence. We started to grow confident. Neil Connor even began to provide commentary in between heading or volleying the ball away from centre-half: 'Is that all you've got?' – header; 'We've only got nine men!' – hoof up the park. Wormley were indeed becoming increasingly frustrated, and midway through the second half, as Robbo describes, 'One of their players came up to me, looked me in the eyes, grabbed me by the nuts and squeezed them.' Robbo, never one to count to ten, chased after the perpetrator and kicked him in the leg. The player went down and as the ref came over Robbo declared loud enough for everyone on the pitch and sidelines to hear, 'I don't care! Send me off! He grabbed my bollocks, send me off!' The referee duly obliged and we were now down to eight men. Five minutes later, the *same* Wormley player rattled into a tackle on Matt Godwin after the ball had long since gone. Matt got to his feet and threw the ball in the face of the player who must have been thinking he could get every Wizard on the pitch to bite. Matt was also given his marching orders by the ref.

A full-size football pitch is a very big place when you only have seven men, which is in fact the minimum number you are allowed before a game is abandoned. With no subs and the sun beating down on us, the remaining six outfield players sank further and further towards our own box and tried on the odd occasions we had possession in what remained of the game to launch the ball as far away from goal, and as far off the pitch as possible. Remarkably, time was ticking on and we still had our one-goal lead precariously intact.

Andy Michaelides vividly recalls as we defended a corner late on in the game that he desperately screamed as we tried to mark up, 'I've got four men at the back post, I've got four!' but even then somehow we managed to scramble the ball away. Finally, after what seemed like two days had elapsed, the referee blew the whistle for full time. Those destined to become known, at least to us, as the Magnificent Seven had recorded the most unlikely of 1-0 victories. As we left the pitch, we were greeted by accusations of being cheats by both the Wormley players and those who had watched the game from the side. It was easy to understand their frustration as a single point from that game would have seen them crowned champions. Instead, having insisted on playing us, they missed out on goal difference.

2003/04 Mercury and Waltham League Division 3

		Pl	W	D	L	F	A	PTS
1.	Cheshunt	20	12	4	4	68	24	40
2.	Wormley Rovers	20	11	7	2	46	18	40
3.	Winchmore Wizards	20	12	1	7	56	41	37

For those of us that played that day it's a story we'll take to our graves. Andy says even now, more than ten years on, he often finds himself thinking about it at work and will occasionally tweet about it. 'Definitely something I'll tell the grandkids.' He was even recently able to advise a work colleague who had confided in him that he was apprehensive about a fixture the youth team he coached was facing because they only had nine players available. Andy introduced him to the merits of the 4-3-1 system.

We made the journey home exhausted and sunburnt and deliriously happy. Robbo remembers that he had decided to go topless for the drive back in his Peugeot 206 Quicksilver, which isn't at all out of character; nor was his decision to flag over the two attractive women who pulled up next to him at the traffic lights in a convertible on the A10, who he then chatted up and got to know even better over the coming week. Robbo describes it as the cherry on the cake of a beautiful day. Evidently the damage done to his bollocks by the Wormley player wasn't too severe.

Chapter Four

Attitude

BY the end of the 2003/04 season the club had run up debts that we could not afford to repay, so when it came to finding the fee to stay in the Mercury and Waltham League for the next season we politely declined. A plan was then formulated to return to Edmonton with our tails between our legs. All our lofty talk about wanting to play somewhere more organised was actually our undoing. As a club, we weren't organised enough. A lesson I think every person who has ever run a Sunday League team soon learns is that the promises people make about sharing the workload, even if well intentioned, are emptier than the posh seats at White Hart Lane five minutes before the full-time whistle when Spurs are taking a pasting at home.

The sooner you realise you will have to do everything for everyone, be it attend the meetings, wash the kit, bring tape because no one else will, the happier you will be. Thankfully the Edmonton League was good enough to take us back. Winchmore Wizards were officially banned from playing in any FA competitions, which now included the newly affiliated Edmonton and District Sunday League, until such time as all debts were paid off, and so the simple solution was to reboot with a streamlined name: Wizards.

Alex Clayton, who had stepped away from playing part way through the previous season having become disillusioned that fewer of the original players were involved, now took on responsibility for the administration and tried to return to the fold all the veterans of the Division 5 title win. One urgent area to address was the position of goalkeeper. We had not had a regular custodian, arguably the most important position in Sunday football, during most of the previous season. The answer presented itself to us in the shape of a Moroccan called Wadi. Wadi worked in the Cherry Tree Pub, Southgate, with one of our other players and let it be known that back in Morocco he was quite the goalkeeper. He also seemed to have a penchant for the ladies. Having joined the team he would regularly bring along a series of poor unsuspecting women to our games each week, leaving each one standing on the sideline alone in the driving rain for 90 minutes and more with no one to talk to. Worse was the embarrassment when one of the boys trying to be friendly would say, 'Hello…,' using the name of the girl he'd brought along the previous week. And so it went on.

Wadi wasn't the tallest of lads, and in the most tired of footballing stereotypes about foreign goalkeepers, he wasn't particularly comfortable with high balls. In my experience very few keepers are. On occasion, he could take your breath away with an impossible save. Nevertheless there was a uniquely fatal flaw in Wadi's game. He had a temper that could combust at the slightest feeling of injustice; he could go from the sublime to the ridiculous without so much as a comma to punctuate the two. If Wadi made a great, brave save at a forward's feet and felt that the player had left a boot in on him, he would put the ball on the floor while it was still in play and leave his goal unattended to remonstrate with the referee in his strong Moroccan accent, getting increasingly animated as the referee shooed him away. This would sometimes lead him to seek his own retribution by squaring up to or even swinging a kick at the player he perceived had done him the injustice in the first place. Another thing about Wadi was that he was an incredibly hard man and he looked it. He would wear all black to keep goal except for a gold chain that would swing out from his collar as he dived around. He had a chipped front tooth that suggested he wasn't afraid to take on the world single-handed if he felt someone had looked at him the wrong way.

All this presented a challenge for the more conflict-averse members of the team in the early weeks when we played with him, as he would be getting entangled with the opposition players and bench. While you naturally want to back up your team-mate, or better still prevent him getting involved in the first place, it does help if you know what might spark him off. With Wadi, you never knew. Consequently, whenever he caught the ball from a cross and took a bit of a bump, my default was straight away to get myself back on the goal line in case he did set down the ball and go walkabout; then at least I could try and block any shot the opposition might take while he was off looking for a fight.

Of course, sometimes Wadi was justified in feeling injustice.

We played a team called the Rose and Crown, who were far from progressive in their views and had a hugely overweight manager with a completely bald head, not even with stubble on top, the sort who takes a Bic razor to his scalp every morning. This gentleman always wore a full pale-blue Sergio Tacchini tracksuit, the official leisurewear of football hooliganism in the 1980s, of which I am certain he was fully aware. During a game against them where Wadi had gotten upset with the overtly aggressive nature of their play, which we were all feeling the brunt of, their manager turned on Wadi and shouted from the touchline, 'You fucking dirty Kosovan! Shut up you fucking Kosovan!' It was a truly shocking moment. My contempt was split between disgust at this horrible man who had no qualms about hurling racist abuse, and his complete ignorance of basic geography. Kosovo is part of eastern Europe and a long, long way from north Africa. The referee declined to hear what was said and it was left to us players to remonstrate with the Bic-head manager and keep Wadi away from him. In a way there would have been justice in Wadi tearing him to pieces, which I have no doubt he would have, but for us trying to win the game of football always came first. It was a sad reminder, though, that the Sunday League park was a place where those so inclined could say and do what in other areas of life they would not get away with.

Perhaps inevitably, it seems Wadi's temper did catch up with him in the end. Although he only played two seasons for the Wizards, a few of our players were still in touch with him a couple of years later. Then, suddenly, he fell off their radar. The story goes that Wadi was on a night out in London and got into an altercation with a man he apparently hit so hard that he was hospitalised; as far as we know Wadi was arrested and deported back to Morocco.

Our first game back in the Edmonton Division 4 was against a new club in the league called Attitude. They were run by a short, Italian Londoner called Carlo. For 18 years Carlo had played for one of the most well established clubs in the League, called the Bricklayers, but having turned 40 it seemed he was surplus to requirements, and so he set up his own team. There were a couple of players from the Bricklayers and then friends of friends, mostly a group of lads in their late teens and early twenties from Kingsmead School. Kingsmead was one of those schools that had a bit of a reputation for being tough; when we were playing school football, a trip to play them was certainly not one we'd relish. As Carlo explains, life away from the pitch wasn't the easiest for a lot of the Attitude players. 'Many of them weren't working. A few of them were working a few days here, a few days there. Half of them were from [the notoriously tough] Tottenham estates… God knows what they got up to.'

When I talked to Carlo recently, he told me the choice of name for his new Sunday team was an attempt to tap into this background. 'If you remember my team, we were full of attitude.' The name definitely made other teams in the league view them in a certain way, which he saw as a positive; as he says with a certain degree of understatement, the team would get into a lot of 'scuffs' over the next few seasons.

Carlo and his players were seemingly oblivious to the fact that Attitude was also the title of the UK's leading gay lifestyle magazine, a monthly publication featuring topless, tanned and waxed men lolling around in their pants on its front cover. This is probably not quite the image an amateur team in rough and tumble north London is going for, although to be honest our changing room before a game might have made a good front cover for said publication, Deep Heat muscle rub standing in for baby oil. Trips to the mirror, discussions about the best brand of hair gel, and what colour boots went best with yet another new kit we could ill afford seemed to have overtaken talk about events in Saturday's Premier League games. Since I know you're wondering, the kit this time was fetching orange shirts with black shorts and socks.

As always seemed to be the case, the first game of the season occurring on the first Sunday in September was played out in brilliant sunshine. A closely fought game saw Attitude turn us over 3-2. They had a very talented forward, who despite being tall had excellent pace and could finish from both inside and outside the box. Carlo told me his star striker had been a goalkeeper on the books of Colchester United, but now as a Sunday League player he was playing up front, and to great effect. I remember him giving me a real test that first game, and thinking if all the forwards in the league were as good as him it might be a tough season ahead.

He later appeared on a television programme where people, particularly young drivers who might be inclined to drive under the influence, were put on a driving simulator to show the negative effect alcohol had on their reactions and overall driving skills. Who'd have thought it?

The protocol in the Edmonton League was that the home team was supposed to provide a match card on the day, which both teams had to fill out with the names and signatures of those playing. As home team you had to show it to the referee before kick-off, ring in the final result to the League's dedicated results line, then post the match card off to the fixtures secretary to arrive no later than the middle of the week.

In theory, this was a straightforward system. It was, however, based on the misguided assumption that the full complement of players for both teams would have arrived at the playing field more than two minutes before kick-off. What tended to happen *in practice* was that the secretaries of both teams would resort to signing the card on their players' behalf, forging the signatures from the players' registration forms, and chucking in a change of biro part way through the list to throw the league officials off the scent.

As the weeks and years went by, and it became clear that the checking of the signatures on these cards was less than watertight, even these basic measures of deception fell into disuse. We would just scribble 'signatures' for our boys, who having turned up late, again, were getting changed by the side of the pitch. Amazingly, though, there were some teams who did fall foul of the match card checks. I think this can only mean they were playing ringers and unthinkingly wrote their real names rather than giving them the name of a registered player on the match card. It may have been this difference in attention to detail that led a player on one team we were playing against to dismiss us as 'fucking university boys'.

At the end of our first home meeting with Attitude, Carlo said to Alex that as he hadn't had a chance to get all his players to sign prior to kick-off, he would get the match card completed and send it to the League. We foolishly agreed, but unfortunately that match card never arrived. Neither did another match card a few weeks later, this time sent by Alex. As a result we were docked three points.

Now that the Edmonton League had affiliated to the London FA, it came under the jurisdiction of the Football Association. Consequently, if a team felt it had suffered an injustice, it had the right to appeal to the FA, on the proviso it could afford to foot the bill for the appeals process. We believed that the deduction of three points could cost us the league title, so an appeal was made based on the time-honoured, lost-in-the-post defence.

On the appointed day, Alex in his capacity as secretary/chairman, and I in my capacity as someone who can recite both sides of the Tom Cruise/Jack Nicholson face-off in *A Few Good Men*, duly arrived at the hearing in front of officials from the Edmonton League. We were pleased to see we'd won at least the opening salvo of the duel, as we had both worn suits, although to be honest, I somewhat undermined our sophisticated look by lamely leaving the manufacturer's tag on the left sleeve, and conspicuously folding my arms in order to show it off. While we put up a spirited defence, which basically involved me thinking up the longest words I could muster to express, 'If Alex says he put the match card in the post, then he put the match card in the post,' our case soon collapsed on cross-examination from the arbitrators sent from the London FA. Not only had the match card failed to arrive twice where it was supposed to, but as Colin, the chairman of the Edmonton League at that time, pointed out, the referee scorecard which we were supposed to send to a different address had also not materialised. To lose one bit of paperwork could be considered unfortunate, but for two to go missing suggested carelessness. Alex confessed that he had not sent the referee's card but still categorically maintains to this day that he did send that match card. Whether or not he put a stamp or wrote an address on the envelope perhaps will be his deathbed confession to me.

Colin and Ken from the League were very reasonable about the whole thing, even after Alex lost his temper with them as we made our way to the car park, especially given that our stubbornness to accept the three-point deduction had forced them to give up yet another evening of their lives to Edmonton Sunday League football administration. From that point on the Wizards had an excellent relationship with the League, and I had a newfound respect for all the work these gents put in behind the scenes to enable us to have an organised game of football on a Sunday morning. Alex, however, had had enough and soon after decided that running a Sunday League side at this point in his life wasn't for him.

Years later, he would reappear as the secretary, chairman and oligarch of Zenit St Whetstone in the Barnet Sunday League. It was a role that for a time came to dominate his whole life, starting with the need to pretend to be of the Jewish faith in order to play for a team called the Whetstone Eagles, who were regularly losing by double figures in the lower realms of the Jewish League. Eventually, through force of personality, he turned them into a powerhouse of a side that, with a change of name and location, competed in the top flight of the Barnet League. Against all odds, Zenit won a spectacular Middlesex County Cup Final in a dramatic penalty shoot-out against the equally brilliantly named Athletico Bill Plough.

Alex became a member of the board in the Barnet League and lobbied for rule changes, even pulling the odd stroke to ensure his better players could play when they were due a suspension. As he puts it, that appeal in Edmonton over the match card was the only time he came out on the losing end. In Barnet, he says, 'I had a ten out of ten appeal success rate… it wasn't worth arguing with me because of the shit I'd cause… and probably because I lost that one I never lost another one.' Alex would also talk his way into being co-opted on to the board of the Tottenham Hotspur supporters' trust, which afforded him a meeting in the executive inner sanctums of White Hart Lane with Tottenham chairman, Daniel Levy, a meeting of personalities I wager Mr Levy remembers to this day.

In order to keep the Wizards going it was left to me to assume the role of secretary for the remainder of the season, and what became a further six years. I never wanted to take responsibility for picking the team – who wants to pick one mate over another? But happily, for the remainder of that season we usually only had 11 players so the side picked itself. Nevertheless, I had to miss a couple of games towards the back end of the campaign because of an injury acquired off the pitch.

It was Sunday 13 March 2005. I'd been round at Jon's watching Spurs lose in the quarter-final of the FA Cup to an equally average Newcastle United. I returned home later to find the inner glass doors of our house bolted from the inside. There was no response from my mum either when I rang the doorbell repeatedly or when I called the landline phone.

I should explain that my dad, who was now separated from my mum, dividing his time between Edinburgh and Finchley, had been working on a book published under the title, *Untouchables*. Rather than being about the Arsenal Invincibles, who in going the previous season unbeaten had made my life a misery, it was instead about *dirty cops, bent justice and racism in Scotland Yard*. It was causing dad a lot of stress. A few days earlier, he had phoned to warn me that, owing to the nature of his research and the fact it had upset some less than savoury characters in both the Metropolitan Police and London's criminal fraternity, I should be vigilant. He had found a dead rat conspicuously decaying at his address, which he took as a shot across his bows rather than a random natural occurrence. Having played that Sunday morning, and sat through yet another limp Spurs exit from the FA Cup, I arrived home to find the inner doors to the house bolted for the first time I could remember in all my years. My mind began to race. I did the only thing a young man can do when his blood is pumping and he fears his mum is in mortal danger. I called my sister and asked her what to do.

Unbeknownst to me, my sister had independently received a different but equally helpful warning from my dad about keeping an eye on my mum because he said there was suicide in the family. Tragically, her brother had killed himself in a state of distress in a head-on car crash not long after I was born.[9] Given that we now had two seemingly serious reasons to be concerned for our mum's welfare, my sister's advice was to break into the house as quickly as possible. Above the inner glass doors was a fixed panel of glass that I could smash so as to reach through to the bolt. I should use my trainer to bash it, being careful not to break the antique etched glass of the door itself. She suggested I should take off my sock and use it as a glove to remove the bits of broken glass, then reach through to undo the bolt. Sadly, however, she assumed I would have the foresight to put my sock and my trainer back on before proceeding through the debris of the shattered glass, omitting to mention this crucial step in her instructions. Adrenaline pumping, still talking on the phone, I smashed the glass, undid the bolt, ran in, and charged up the stairs, ready to do I don't exactly know what to the captors I expected to find holding my dear mum hostage. Only to find her safe and soundly asleep in her bedroom. 'She's here! She's fine!' I shouted down the phone to my sister. This caused my mum to come to in a drowsy state of surprise. 'What's going on?'

It turned out that my mum had absent-mindedly bolted the inner door before going to bed unusually early because she had a crack of dawn start for work the following morning. Her bedroom was at the back of the house and she hadn't heard a thing until I burst in. By the time we'd each figured out what had happened, and my heart rate had returned to normal, I became aware of a pain in my heel. As I started to retrace my steps along the corridor and down the stairs, I noticed an unmistakable trail of blood. I couldn't deny what was now very clear. I had a fragment of glass lodged in the sole of my foot.

The shard had gone in too far for it to be retrieved with tweezers, so the next morning I limped along to the GP's surgery at the end of our road. Whereupon Dr Parkinson said it would be a job for the hospital, so off I went again to reacquaint myself

---

9   The coroner delivered an open verdict, but there was always uncertainty about what had happened.

with Chase Farm Accident and Emergency department. Here another doctor explained that, due to the angle the fragment of glass had gone in at, it would be necessary to have me lie flat on my stomach and be intubated, under what was becoming my annual general anaesthetic, in order to remove it. 'Well done,' the doctor said by way of consolation. 'If you had to get a bit of glass in your foot in ridiculous circumstances, it might as well be some antique leaded glass like this, because it shows up on the X-ray.'

The anaesthetist this time round, despite being a very friendly chap, had multiple piercings all over his face. I reflected, rather melodramatically, that if it did turn out to be curtains for me during surgery, his face wouldn't have been my first choice for the last I would ever see. My sister had arrived at the hospital while I was still under. Apparently my first comments on coming round from the operation were to her. I giggled weirdly and told her that she was the female me. Many years later at a Christmas dinner when she first told me what I'd said (I myself have no memory of it) it was clear that she had been deeply moved by it. Feeling pretty guilty, I confessed that the first thing I remember saying was addressed to the doctor: 'How soon can I play again?' 'Three to four weeks, son,' was the answer. In the event, I took pride in only missing two games while the cut in my foot healed. I didn't however come clean to the boys about the farcical way the injury had occurred in the first place.

Later in the season we were able to avenge our opening day defeat by beating Attitude 4-3 in the return fixture, but despite lots of notable, high-scoring victories, featuring some classic Sunday League scorelines of 8-3, 7-1, 10-1, 6-2 and 8-2 all in our favour, even the 5-0 win in our final match only saw us finish in fourth place. Although this was one place above Attitude by virtue of goal difference, we would have needed more than the three points deducted on account of the missing match card to be promoted. Another year in Division 4 beckoned.

Chapter Five

Silverware!

ICKEY Pearce had been away from the Wizards for
nearly two years with an injury that would likely
prevent him from playing again. Over the summer
of 2005, he decided that if he could not play Sunday League
football, the next best way to stay involved was to become the
team's manager. Mickey, who was always a bright and popular
character, realised very early on in this process the value of
having a number two to bounce ideas off. They could also
play good cop/bad cop. There would always be times when the
team wasn't playing very well, or tough decisions needed to be
made and communicated regarding the starting line-up. Andy
Michaelides, who had played in the Magnificent Seven game but
had then been struck down by a cruciate ligament injury, came
on board as assistant manager and that's how the Edmonton
and District Sunday League version of Brian Clough and Peter
Taylor was born. It speaks volumes for the spirit we had built up
within the core of the team over the previous three seasons, that
Mickey and Andy were willing to take on these roles knowing
full well that this ruled out from September to May the delights
of a lie-in on a Sunday morning: they had traded the sanctuary of

a cosy duvet for standing on the sidelines of a completely exposed playing field. Where if the rain didn't get you the wind certainly would, with only tepid solace available in the Firs Farm catering van's version of a cup of tea.

We had an excellent pre-season training at Trent Park, which is located between the final two stops on the eastbound Piccadilly Line and formerly housed the most picturesque campus of Middlesex University. Many of the team remember being dragged up there as sixth formers for a fair about the merits of higher education; however, the main thing I had remembered about the huge wooded grounds was that it was believed to be the place George Graham had brought his Arsenal team to do cross-country running ahead of the 1988/89 season, which unfortunately would see them win the championship for the first time since 1971. Mickey, being a huge Arsenal fan, (he actually missed his SATS exams to travel with his dad to Copenhagen in May 1994 to watch a distinctly average Arsenal side somehow beat a star-studded Parma in the Cup Winners' Cup Final) would take every opportunity to remind the Spurs contingent of the Wizards about this bit of local history as we jogged between the trees. Judging by the alleged drinking habits of some of that Arsenal squad, they were spiritually much closer to Sunday League football than to the Premier League of today. Nowadays, the sports science and nutrition departments, a feature of all the top clubs, have determined definitively that a skinful of alcohol is not the ideal preparation for a big game.

Feeling better prepared than ever before at the opening of the season, we began our league campaign with a hard-fought 3-2 victory over Downhills Park. They were one of the more amiable sides in the Edmonton League. The following week, however, we were turned over 3-0 by a team called Hop Poles, a side based out of a pub in one of the rougher parts of Enfield Town. Hop Poles were not a particularly talented bunch, but had a lot of players with shaved heads who weren't shy about telling us that not only could they beat us at football but if necessary they would beat the shit out of us after the game as well. I am ashamed to say that even at 24 and 25, we were the sort of characters that could still be intimidated by this kind of thing; we would sometimes lose to sides we should have beaten comfortably because we effectively bottled it, perhaps the most unforgivable of Sunday League sins. Coming off the pitch in this situation is very awkward. There is a silent, unspoken understanding between all of us that we know what has just happened and are embarrassed by it; none of us really wants to admit that we have just been bullied into losing a game of football largely via the haircuts of the other team and a few empty threats. Mickey and Andy, two big specimens themselves, were not about to let this go so easily. They had strong words with all of us after the game and made us vow that it would not happen again under their stewardship. This was a big turning point for the Wizards. It speaks well of Mickey's abilities as an orator that he was able to deliver some of his most impassioned team talks and get through to all our players, despite often wearing a t-shirt featuring Arsene Wenger lighting the fuse of a cannon that had a startled-looking, cartoon Spurs cockerel loaded in the barrel. Suffice to say he'd sourced this masterpiece from somewhere other than the official Arsenal shop.

Mickey and Andy faced one particular challenge in the early months of their reign. Difficult parents. However, unlike in youth football, the players they were dealing with were in their mid-twenties, as well as being lifelong friends. Parents in this case might be expected to realise that if their offspring were going to make it to the Premier League, it would have happened by now. One keen dad, called Phil, had taken to making the short walk from his house in Winchmore Hill to Firs Farm to watch his son, Robbo, who was an exceptional athlete and fine technical footballer. Robbo played on the left wing for the Wizards. Now Phil is a fascinating character, who even at retirement age has a full head of hair and the physique of a marathon runner; he could probably outrun most of our players despite being more than twice their age. Robbo recounts that Phil used to play on the wing for Enfield and Finchley, and it's not hard to hear the frustration in the story that he might once have been taken on by Chelsea. There's no denying Phil was extremely knowledgeable about football. His other great love was giving his opinion. So it was that his passion for the game and for his son led him to become increasingly vocal from the sideline with comments that were not always constructive.

While Phil would also get himself entangled in disputes with the opposition or referee, the majority of his remarks were aimed at players from our own team, perhaps because Robbo was not seeing enough of the ball or when the ball did get to him it wasn't coming quickly enough. Inevitably feedback in this form didn't go down at all well, and a feisty dialogue often ensued, ending in Phil being asked in less than refined language to keep his opinions to himself. Obviously, this was embarrassing and distracting for Robbo and, from my perspective as captain, I felt it was having a negative impact on his performance and hindering the team. Such was Phil's passion for watching his son play the game, that when Robbo asked him to take a step back or keep quiet, he continued to come and watch. As Robbo explains now, even if he had been asked not to come at all, he would have walked over anyway. It may have been unusual for a father to be so involved in his son's amateur football deep into his twenties, but to Robbo that shows how much his dad cared about him, even if his feelings sometimes surfaced in a non-productive way. When Robbo was at secondary school he'd shown great promise as a runner. He says he'll forever be thankful to Phil for taking him regularly to the athletics track at Donkey Lane in Enfield, watching in the pitch-black under an umbrella as the rain hammered down. 'I never had to ask him, he was always there.'

Events came to a head one Sunday morning when Mickey decided to substitute Robbo during the second half, a decision Robbo disagreed with. On this occasion his dad, mum and younger brother were all watching the game and so they pitched in with their opinions. Mickey and Andy defended their decision, words were exchanged and after the game ended it seemed the whole incident would blow over. However, Mickey went out that afternoon to watch Arsenal. When he got back, his mum Pat explained that while he was out the doorbell had rung, and it was Robbo's mum with the goal nets which Robbo had been storing at home each week. His mum dropped them on the doorstep and left.

It was clear we couldn't let this rumble on. So the following evening Mickey and I travelled to Robbo's family house to try and resolve things. For the team's sake, we needed to make sure Mickey and Andy would be able to make the selections and substitutions they saw fit without confrontation. We also needed Robbo to continue playing as an important member of the team. Casting his mind back, Robbo recalls that Phil had actually said to him that he was not to play for the Wizards again, which does seem an incredible thing to say to a 24-year-old playing for a Sunday League team of his school mates. Perhaps it underlines how seriously we all, including Phil, took our football. Robbo's memory is that he was regularly not starting games, which a look back through the immaculate team records kept by Matthew Borou shows was absolutely not the case. The only times Robbo didn't start were when he was injured. There were instances at the start of that season where he was substituted towards the end of games, and Robbo's feeling was that this was being done to wind up his dad. Mickey and Andy don't remember this being the case, but who knows, perhaps subconsciously they felt a need to exert their authority.

Even now, years later, the perception of being mistreated at this time in his Wizards career still permeates Robbo's thinking. It was definitely influencing his and Phil's behaviour at the time. When we went to Robbo's house, his mum was actually very friendly; we sat down in the kitchen and had a cup of tea and chat. Phil was mostly in the living room, watching *Monday Night*

Football, but was obviously listening to what was being said and would pop in and out to add his opinion. It was clear that he was driven by a genuine wish to do what he thought was the best for his son, rather than any malice towards Mickey. Even with this better understanding of where this was all coming from, Mickey and I reflected afterwards as we sat in his Renault Clio outside the house, that we had endured a couple of the most surreal hours of our lives up to that point. We'd never thought that running a Sunday League team would be training us in high-level diplomacy.

As we speak a decade on from these events, Robbo, always a bubbly and energetic character, becomes very serious. Almost as if processing this for the first time he explains, 'Maybe my dad didn't achieve what he wanted to when he was younger. I don't know if you know this but he was involved in a serious car crash in his late twenties and he lost his three best friends. They all died and my dad broke his neck, his legs, and his arms and was in a coma, in intensive care in Saudi Arabia. He was a body builder at that time. He gave up football to do body building and he was huge, they called him Legs, he used to train with people that competed for Mr Olympia. The only thing that kept him alive then was the size of his body, his muscle mass. But I do feel he never really achieved his potential because he was a very good 110 metre high-hurdler, a very good footballer and he was tough. Even now he is running, cycling, fit as a fiddle, fitter than me, not a pound of fat on him ever. I think he tried to instil that discipline into me and I thank him for that. But there were times I didn't need him there shouting at me, what to do, do this, do that; it was distracting, I'm not going to lie to you. But… not many other boys' dads were down there watching, so I can't knock him. But it was distracting for the team and that's what I regret most.'

Things did improve with Phil from that point, even though Robbo recalls his dad initially telling him that he was 'fucking crazy' to go back to the team. Credit to Phil in future years, he would come down to our pre-season training and put us through our paces, pushing us to work harder, run faster and be the best we could. Sometimes, he would even pop out unannounced from among the trees at Trent Park where we trained. One night, Mickey gave Phil the green light to take over training, even though it turned out Andy had already planned the session. Andy admits he felt undermined and threw his toys out of the pram a bit, to the extent he even briefly considered walking away from the Wizards. But it was clear to us all that Andy enjoyed it too much to ever go through with his threat. Maybe Mickey had shown his adroitness for man management, shrewdly judging that any harm done in putting Andy's nose out of joint on this occasion would be easier to resolve than another conflict with Phil. As the years went on the emergence of Anthony, Phil's younger son, as an exceptional player, who also had games on a Sunday morning, meant he had another outlet for his passion, which made things easier for us at least! Still, the record will show that no one attended more Wizards games as a spectator than Phil. In fact he regularly made up 100% of our crowd.

It is worth noting that for the rest of the Wizards' existence Mickey would be responsible for stowing and bringing the nets. Robbo ironically became Mister Football Equipment, purchasing brand-new match balls out of his own pocket seemingly on a weekly basis, and providing a medical bag so extensively stocked with equipment that it sometimes seemed a shame not to use it.

To a large extent, I think this shows how young we still were, even in our mid-twenties. There were all sorts of tensions with father figures lurking around and needing to be worked out. This was exacerbated by the ridiculous London property market, where soaring rents and house prices meant many of us couldn't afford to move out of the family home, even if we'd wanted to. But it was mostly due to us being mothers' boys who had grown too comfortable to fly the nest. My mum would despair as boots were washed in the kitchen sink with the washing-up brush, mud splattering over the counter tops; then the washing machine would be running in relays every Sunday afternoon, 16 full kits being washed and hung out to dry, either on the washing line or on the radiators. With my dad not in the house anymore it was left to my mum's new boyfriend, a tall, bald man called Andrew, with adult sons of his own, to try and assert himself and take me to task. While I certainly didn't make it easy for him or welcome him with open arms into the family, which was less than helpful on my part, I did have some legitimate misgivings about the way he came and went and messed my mum around, which could send her spiralling into bouts of depression. One damp Sunday afternoon in autumn, when he and she returned from a walk, they found the radiators all around the house had been decked as usual in orange and black nylon. Andrew decided to make his stand. He pointed out angrily that my mum had specifically asked me not to do that. After a pretty embarrassing coming together (more playground than prize fight) where no blows were thrown, he went away satisfied that he had made his mark. However, for me the needs of the Wizards were paramount; players couldn't be trusted to remember to wash their own kit and bring it with them, and a short-lived rota system had resulted in the whole team once memorably starting a game in ripe, muddy kit seasoned in the back of Trigger's car for a week. If having a full clean kit meant me taking the whole lot home to wash, so be it. The kits were back on the radiators the next Sunday and every Sunday thereafter, until spring came and they could be hung on the line outside.

On the pitch Mickey and Andy were enjoying a much less stressful time. The team was beginning to flourish and started a long unbeaten run. I, on the other hand, continued my personal game of football injury bingo. It was in an after-work kick-about with some players from a midweek 11-a-side league team I'd started playing for, the spectacularly named Godzilla Express II FC. I took a shot and followed through into the sole of the defender's boot, thereby breaking the fourth metatarsal and two toes of my right foot. The foot was plastered up, leaving me to attend matches with a plastic bag taped around it to keep out the damp as I stood propped up on crutches on the touchline for nine Wizards games between October and December.

The final game of the period when I was laid off was on 11 December 2005. It was a cup tie against Enfield Crusaders at Donkey Lane. Mickey and Andy were both away that week and so I got to try my hand at picking the side, a task made easier by the fact that we had the bare 11 players available. Even though we ran out comfortable 4-0 winners, the game was not without its challenges, being played as it was under a thick layer of smoke, which made it not only hard to see across the pitch but also to breathe. In the early hours of that Sunday morning, fire had broken out at the Buncefield fuel depot in Hertfordshire a few miles up the road. This facility processed around 2.37 million metric tonnes of oil products a year, mainly petrol, diesel and aviation fuel. According to the BBC, what followed was the UK's biggest peacetime fire as further explosions engulfed 20 large storage tanks, and by the early afternoon black smoke from the blaze was hanging over a large area of south-east England. The incident was declared a major emergency and saw at its peak 25 fire engines, 20 support vehicles and 180 fire fighters in action before the fire was finally extinguished five days later.

Soon after I was fit enough to play again, coming up to Christmas, we hit the top of the league, and from that point onwards I was in a state of anxiety, spending hours each week working out the permutations and forecasting what our nearest challengers could do. This continued until the point we were mathematically uncatchable. In this state of eternal vigilance I noticed that Hop Poles, our main challengers, were scheduled to play Edmonton Rangers in the league for a third time that season. But the Edmonton League, like most leagues, was run on the basis that each team plays every other team twice, once at home and once away. I busily pointed this out to the fixtures secretary. Being a volunteer, running the league out of the goodness of your heart and possibly not being the most confident user of a computer was no excuse to my mind for an error of the utmost seriousness; I couldn't understand why no offer was made to fall on a sword, but no one else shared my outrage. Nevertheless, Hop Poles versus Edmonton Rangers part three was rightly cancelled.

Our good form had seen us progress to two cup finals. The first was another clash with Hop Poles, this time in the lofty surroundings of the Henry Barrass Surround Stadium at Jubilee Park. This was the pitch reserved for cup finals and was distinct in that it had a rope around the perimeter and a few concrete rows from where people could watch the game. For many of us it was our first cup final ever. The nerves were very much apparent as we met in the Stag and Hounds pub car park to make the drive in convoy to Jubilee Park. Convoy is stretching it a bit; the distance between the two was so short that by the time the last car had left the car park, the first had already arrived at the ground, which possibly diluted this show of strength. But Mickey had decided to leave nothing to chance on this showpiece occasion, a lesson he learned as a youth footballer. Back then he was in a team that reached a prestigious cup final. The manager roped the parents into paying for the boys to stay in a hotel for the night, to make them feel like professionals before the big game. Unfortunately, however, being young teenage boys, they loaded up on fizzy drinks and sweets, barely slept, and lost the game. This was despite all 11 players wearing the little strips across their noses that allegedly helped you breathe and play better, then the height of football fashion, as worn by Robbie Fowler. He, unlike them, may have got some benefit from the product by being paid to wear it.

For cup finals the Edmonton and District League used to produce match programmes, which were circulated in the dressing room before the game. The League required teams to submit their probable starting line-up plus substitutes so that the list could be published in the programme. Mickey and Andy had a full complement of players to choose from; it was amazing how slight knocks or family commitments that ruled out players so often from routine league fixtures were seldom an issue on cup final days. The League also required you to provide a brief history of the club and provided space in the programme to give a nod to your sponsors. Since we had broken free from the shackles of the Winchmore Arms and evolved into the Wizards, we had not secured a new sponsor. I thought I'd be creative and give the boys a bit of a laugh before the game.

We entered the changing rooms, which had certainly seen better days; small windows caked with dirt and an ancient treatment table that someone in Chiswick could probably sell for a fortune as antique furniture. I sat back waiting patiently for my comedy genius to pay off when the boys opened the programme and found our sponsor listed as Hogwarts School of Witchcraft and Wizardry. But in the event the joke got lost since most of them were only interested in looking to see whether they had made the starting 11 or were on the bench. The Harry Potter-based humour seemed a lot less funny as the banging and guttural shouts grew louder and louder through the wall that separated us from the Hop Poles. We remembered how they'd bullied us the last time we played them.

I cannot ever in my life recall being more nervous at the prospect of playing 90 minutes of football than I was that day. I wasn't the only one of our players feeling that way. The cup final changing rooms were unique in comparison to the ones we used most weeks in that they had their own 'en suite' toilet. This was a challenge for me particularly as part of my pre-game ritual was that I had to make a secret offering of the sit-down variety to the football gods before going into battle. The set-up at Jubilee Park required me to walk through the dressing room very publicly holding a toilet roll. I had learnt over the years always to bring my own, since the odds on there being some provided were as long as on an eight-team accumulator bet, and the risk far outweighed the reward. Of course, the door would neither fully shut nor lock and nor would the toilet flush, which became an increasing issue as the minutes ticked by and a number of nervous Wizards made the pilgrimage to the porcelain altar.

Our nerves were heightened when we were finally called from the dressing rooms to go out onto the pitch. Some Hop Poles players had red marks on their foreheads, presumably from nutting the changing room wall. We were then required to shake hands with the League's guest of honour, a silver-haired gentleman who had come specially to present the Harry Ash Cup. It was a nice touch by the Edmonton League and brought a real sense of history to the occasion. The ensuing 90 minutes had no such class about them. Hop Poles were clearly wound up to the point where any prospect of them playing actual football was remote and several of our players decided to meet fire with fire. A fight broke out very early on in the proceedings and punches were exchanged. Unfortunately for Robbo, sporting a brand-new pair of bright red Puma boots for the occasion, he was identified as the perpetrator. He duly received his marching orders from the referee, a Mr Stevenson, who coincidentally was his cousin. As Robbo reflects, 'What kind of cousin sends you off in a cup final, and actually he'd got it wrong it wasn't me, he got the wrong person. I don't speak to him now. I never forgave him for that.' To the best any of those who played or were in attendance that day can remember it was young Graham Sawkins, our fantastically gifted forward, who had actually aimed the blows and while we were all sympathetic to Robbo as the victim of mistaken identity, we were happy that Graham stayed on the pitch as he scored two superb goals. We ran out 3-2 winners, but not before several further players saw red from the referee, who at one point even threatened to abandon the game.

Both teams were admonished at the next monthly League meeting for their behaviour. Although when I subsequently wrote a letter to the League's board apologising for our role in what had transpired, but explaining that we were provoked, and thanking them for all they did, word came back that the League sympathised with us and understood what sort of team Hop Poles were. Nonetheless, they said, any repeat of these events in our upcoming second cup final of the season against Attitude would see the referee instructed to abandon the game immediately. All of this didn't detract from our memory of what had been a great victory and the celebrations that followed.

The truth of the old adage, about cup finals only being enjoyable if you win them, was made starkly clear to us a few weeks later when we returned to Jubilee Park for our encounter with Attitude. Mickey and Andy decided to play all the players who hadn't played in the earlier cup final, which was a noble intention but which backfired as to a man we played terribly that day. In fact, we were lucky to get away with only a 4-0 scoreline against us – bad enough on any Sunday but coming against Attitude all the more galling. I have managed to block out memories of just how poorly I played that day. All I can remember now is feeling pleased with myself at 4-0 down for making use of the official linesman, the presence of whom also added to the sense of occasion at cup finals, by stepping up as last man and catching Attitude's forward offside. From the resulting free kick from just inside our half, which was to be played long into their box, I thought I would be clever and force Carlo (playing as well as managing on this occasion), who was about half my height, to man mark me. I stood in front of him as he tried to mark one of our other players, and then moved wherever he moved – a rubbish tactic given that he just moved away from the middle of the goal thus rendering our tallest target at set pieces, namely me, completely useless. This all proved to be academic anyway as the free kick was scuffed and never reached anyone, at which point the referee mercifully blew the full-time whistle.

But our consistency throughout the season meant we had already won the league 12 points ahead of Attitude, who were in second place and promoted with us. We could take solace in having secured a double and in the prospect of playing at a higher level the next season.

Chapter Six

He should have been a contender

WHILE any management team who win a double in their first season deserve a lot of credit, Mickey and Andy would be the first to recognise the biggest single factor for the team springboarding to silverware that season. It was the decision of the supremely talented Danny Grimsdell to become a full-time Wizard, having only played on a handful of occasions over the previous years. It is my genuine belief that Danny should be a household name and that I should know him only as that lad I went to school with who now earns a fortune in the Premier League. Danny is the type of friend who'd do anything for you. A tall man with dark, rugged good looks, he's also a fella you are keen for your girlfriend to meet because knowing him makes you look good, though you do realise she might subsequently want to upgrade.

The omens that Danny would be a great footballer were there from the start. His dad, Mick, was a very talented youngster who played for Tottenham schools, before spending several years at both Arsenal and Leyton Orient, and this despite the fact that as a child polio had left him with one leg shorter than the other. But for the slight loss of pace this caused he might have made a career from the game. Football was in the Grimsdell family genes: Danny's great, great uncle was Arthur Grimsdell who captained Spurs to FA Cup triumph in 1921 in a 1-0 victory over Wolves at Stamford Bridge. His status of being one of the most desirable football cigarette cards to collect was only enhanced when he played for England, captaining his country on three occasions. By the end of his career, he had played over 400 games for Spurs and is considered to be one of Tottenham's greatest ever players, inducted posthumously into the Tottenham Hotspur Hall of Fame. As if this pedigree wasn't enough, Danny was even in the same nursery class as the grandson of Spurs' Double-winning captain, Danny Blanchflower.

Danny's first memories of football are playing with his older brother Aaron in the back garden. Together they watched Paul Gascoigne, who was to become Danny's idol, set the 1990 World Cup alight in Italy. He remembers the Cameroon quarter-final in particular where he estimates he cried multiple times as the scoreline see-sawed back and forth, particularly when Gazza conceded a penalty to put England's progress in the competition in doubt. But then another Spurs legend, Gary Lineker, scored two penalties to send England into the semi-finals against West Germany. When Danny, aged just eight, started to ask his dad to let him play for Chase Side Youth, the local team where his best friend at school played, Mick was initially hesitant. He feared that starting organised football so young would lead to Danny burning out in his teens, falling out of love with the game and getting involved in less wholesome pursuits like smoking or girls. But Danny was determined and Mick relented, so in 1991 he started playing for Chase Side's Under 9s. It soon became apparent that Danny was a precocious talent. Mick explains that one week during a game at Enfield playing fields, a man called Dick Moss approached the pitch. Moss scouted young players for Spurs and was doing the weekly rounds of youth football to find the next potential big thing. Moss had been Mick's manager when he played for Tottenham schoolboys, but they'd only seen each other a couple of times in the intervening 30 years. Once Moss made the connection, he became very excited at the prospect that Mick had a son playing in the game. Almost immediately, as Mick recalls, right on cue young Danny sticks a 'blinding goal' into the back of the net, and Moss immediately asks permission to take Danny to train with Spurs.

Mick was hesitant to allow Danny to go to Spurs at such a tender age and decided it would be better for him to continue honing his abilities in the less pressurised environment of amateur youth football. Mick did however instil the very best parts of Tottenham Hotspur in his young son. As he explains, his own favourite player had been Dave Mackay, whose attitude was to never give up, and on the few occasions he lost the ball to be relentless in winning it back. Mick would say to Danny, 'Always give a simple pass when you have the ball and take a shot when the opportunity presents itself.' Young Danny absorbed these lessons and established himself as the best player in the team which in his second season won the Cheshunt Youth League. In September 1994, Danny moved up to Southgate, the secondary school where I was now in year nine. That season was special to all Spurs fans because Jürgen Klinsmann had arrived at White Hart Lane and propelled us to something very rare: a league finish above Arsenal. (In October of 1996 Arsene Wenger arrived at Highbury and for the next two decades Arsenal never finished below Spurs in the table.)

Danny was finding footballing success much easier to come by than the team he idolised. He was part of an exceptional footballing year group at school out of which several boys had trials with professional clubs, and four went on to have professional careers. Even aged 11, it was clear that Danny was becoming a different person on the football pitch to the mild-mannered, hardworking pupil he was off it. Carol, Danny's mum, always had good reports of his schoolwork and behaviour. It therefore came as a shock to her, proudly watching her son play for the school team from the sideline, when she heard him tell Mr Bolton, the craft, design and technology teacher who had taken on responsibility for running the first year's school team, to 'fuck off'. He had given Danny some ill-informed advice about how to play. Danny's mum was mortified and immediately apologised for her son's outburst. But to his credit, Mr Bolton readily conceded that he wasn't particularly knowledgeable about the game and showed understanding of the mentality of young footballers. 'Not to worry,' he said. 'Danny's in football mode.' This fiery, passionate side to Danny's personality once he's crossed the white line onto the pitch was to become familiar to anyone who had the privilege of playing on the same side as him over the next two decades.

Mick and the other parents of the boys in the school year group, realising what a good set of players they were, decided to set up a Sunday team of their own. They called it the Southgate Saints and it was soon attracting the attention of scouts from all the big London clubs. Matthew Syed, who represented team GB at two Olympic games, talks in his brilliant book, *Bounce*, about his experience as a young table tennis player, and how having access to quality coaching and playing constantly with other good young players elevated several of them who lived within a stone's throw of each other in Reading to become national and international champions. It seems something similar was occurring with the Saints. Mick contacted his old mentor Dick Moss, who was still very keen to take Danny to Spurs, about coaching the team. Within a short time, the Saints were winning everything in sight. Similarly at Southgate School, an actual PE teacher took over the school team. Mick kept a little black leather-bound journal, which he delighted in showing me, where he had lovingly recorded all the achievements of the Southgate Saints and Southgate School teams as Danny's career progressed. It makes phenomenal reading:

1994/95 (Under 12s) Southgate Saints won the league and cup and the school came second in the league and won the cup.

1995/96 (Under 13s) Southgate Saints won the league and Herts County Cup and the school won the league and cup.

1996/97 (Under 14s) Saints won league and cup and school won league and cup.

1997/98 (Under 15s) By this time Danny was involved with the age group teams at Spurs and was no longer eligible to play for the Saints but still played in the school team, which won the league and cup.

As Danny shone for both the Saints and the school team, Mick decided that the time was now right for him to start training with Spurs. Initially this involved going down to White Hart Lane on a Thursday night to train in the indoor ball court in the West Stand. Mick would watch the training from the benches allocated to parents. He recalls being underwhelmed by the coaching offered. As he puts it, the coach who led training could barely move and the sessions were far from inspiring. Danny however was tremendously excited at the prospect of training at Spurs and the £2 he received each week for his expenses felt like the initial instalment in what he hoped would be a long and successful career. There were three age group teams at Tottenham: the Under 16s, which was full of promising schoolboys, the Under 17s and the Under 19s. While Danny was at Spurs, Ledley King and Peter Crouch were making the initial steps in what would be stellar careers on both the Premier League and international stage. During the school summer holidays, Danny was given the chance to play with the Under 17 team. At this elite level, clubs will organise fixtures so that they play each other at the various age group levels on the same occasion. Danny remembers playing for Tottenham Under 17s against Liverpool at Spurs Lodge, the club's training ground in Chigwell at that time. He recalls the game vividly as he started on the right wing and was given the number 6 shirt, two things he wasn't comfortable with.

'Back then if I didn't play centre-midfield I'd get the hump. It was stupid really, you should just play where you are told to play... I only ever wanted to wear the number 8 because of Gazza.' The Under 19s were playing on an adjacent pitch and both games finished 1-1. Peter Crouch had scored for Spurs and Steven Gerrard for Liverpool.

Looking back at this time of his life, Danny reflects that it was amazing experience but also bizarre; players he had on posters on his bedroom wall were now sitting across from him at the training ground canteen. David Ginola and Sol Campbell were the shining lights in the Spurs side of the late 90s. Campbell in particular was an iconic figure who Spurs' fans could legitimately point to at the time of the 1998 World Cup as being world class, as good as any player in his position. Danny remembers one day after training making the long walk down the winding country road, Luxborough Lane, back to the train station when a fancy car slowed down next to him. As the window wound down the identity of the driver was revealed: it was club captain, Sol Campbell, who proceeded to give Danny a lift to the station. 'At that point Sol Campbell was like God to me, so much so that when I was confirmed I wanted my confirmation name to be Sol.' Of all the many things Danny has to be grateful for to his wonderful mum, the fact that she vetoed this request is right up there at the top of the list. The shock waves that followed the decision of club captain Sol Campbell not to accept Spurs' bumper offer of a new contract, but instead move to Arsenal in the summer of 2001, reverberate around London even today.

Danny loved being at Spurs, but was becoming aware that progressing all the way into the first team would be very difficult. As a schoolboy it seemed a long way off. Worried about Danny's prospects and happiness, Mick decided to approach an old contact from his days as a young player. Len Cheesewright was the chief scout at Leyton Orient, and had previously worked at Spurs. He was widely regarded as a great spotter of young talent, having unearthed such gems as David Beckham and Sol

Campbell in the east end of London. Upon receiving a call from Mick to see if Orient would be interested in Danny, he assured them that at Orient Danny would get plenty of chances to play. He promised that Danny could start with a game against Reading that coming Sunday; in fact he would be 'the first on and last off'. The following Tuesday, Danny got a taste of full reserve-team football, receiving praise for an excellent performance. It was boy against men, and the boy done more than good.

The sense of feeling wanted meant a lot to Danny at this moment in his life, as it does to any teenage boy. Leyton Orient seemed willing to nurture him more than Spurs, right down to providing him with a full set of club training gear and tracksuit as soon as he arrived. Setting aside his boyhood loyalty, Danny therefore took the big decision to break away from Tottenham, and signed as a youth training scheme (YTS) player for the O's. It was 1999, the same year he took his GCSE exams. He'd achieved good exam results, excelling at graphic design, but he remembers a careers assessment recommending a career as a fence erector. Little wonder therefore that Danny was only interested in pursuing football.

However, the thrill of formally joining Orient was tempered by the realities of his first full pre-season. The physical demands that summer were huge because, as Danny acknowledges, he was a slim boy and still growing. 'It was just knackering me out… and I struggled really badly my first year.' Moreover, Danny let his competitiveness get the better of him and would try to win the various bleep tests and running competitions that await seasoned pros on their return from their holidays. 'I'd be shattered, and then they'd want you to do a keep ball.' One highlight of this intensive training in the summer of 1999 was a cross-country run the team did at Hainault Forest. Harry Redknapp's West Ham United were on the same mission and as Danny and his team-mates arrived, Frank Lampard, Rio Ferdinand, Joe Cole, Paolo Di Canio et al started to disembark from their coach. Part way into the run through the forest's foliage, Danny came across Samassi Abou, West Ham's Ivorian striker, who'd gotten lost from his team-mates and decided to accompany the young Orient players for the rest of the run back to the car park.

Danny was sometimes included in the Orient Under 19 team, which went an entire calendar year unbeaten. Barry Hearn, Orient's maverick chairman between 1995 and 2014, called the players together at Christmas to praise them and presented each player with an envelope. It's fair to guess that Hearn lost his audience at this point; for the rest of his speech they were all speculating on the contents of the envelope. At last came their chance to see. Inside was £200. It was more than Danny earned in a month as an apprentice.

That January, Danny turned 17 and passed his driving test, and Mick helped him buy a car. 'I drove into Orient for training in my little clapped-out Polo thinking that's it, I'm a Premier League footballer now,' he recalls, 'and the manager calls me into his office and tells me he wants me to go on loan to Norway. The first thing I'm thinking is, I just passed my bloody driving test, all I want to do is drive, now he's sending me to Norway for six months.'

Danny and two other young Orient players, Tommy Morgan and Ray Akontoh, found themselves in a town with a population of less than 6,000 called Kvinesdal. The town's football club played in the lower tiers of Norwegian football, but the facilities were excellent with a great little stadium and training centre all in the same complex. Beyond that there was a petrol station and very little else. The three boys were accommodated in a wooden house also on the club site. At 17 years old, away from home for the first time and unable to speak the language, the boys felt that the comforts of London and home-cooked meals were a long way away.

Nevertheless, Danny immediately set about showing his football prowess to the manager, an English speaker called Glenn, who came to watch the foreign trio play in a youth team match a few days after they'd arrived. Ray bagged a hat-trick and

Danny impressed the manager sufficiently to go straight into the first team for the weekend's league game. He kept his place in the side for all the remaining fixtures during this Scandinavian adventure and his mum and dad came to Norway for a week to watch him play. The strongest memories Danny has of his time playing for Kvinesdal involved a trip by ferry to Denmark to play a cup tie across particularly choppy waters that induced a spectacular bout of seasickness. The boys were put up in a motel that presented them the choice of top, middle or bottom, in a triple-decker bunk bed. Their stay in Denmark was also notable for some unique input from the kit man who at training one day suddenly decided to take all his clothes off. The master of understatement, Danny describes this as 'very weird.'[10] It wasn't clear to Danny why Orient sent the three of them to Norway, and he is not sure that the Kvinesdal first team manager had ever really wanted them. But he does have fond memories of Frank, the man who collected them from the airport when they arrived and who looked after them throughout their stay. 'He was like a director of football for the club… Great person, invited us into his home to eat with his family often. He had a little boy called Jasper who had cerebral palsy; I still think about them a lot.'[11]

Their stay in Norway was shortened to three months as Tommy Taylor, Orient's manager, decided to recall them. After they got back, Taylor called Danny into his office and asked how it had gone. When Danny replied that it had been tough, Taylor seemed to conclude that the experiment had been a success. Looking back now, Danny agrees. 'It was the making of me.'

---

10 It's fair to say that Danny was not overly traumatised by this experience; as recounted in a later chapter, while playing for Wingate and Finchley, he used it as inspiration for some training ground high jinx of his own.

11 Interestingly, some years later, Danny was persuaded by his best friend Ed Thompson to compete in a triathlon. Danny decided to take up the challenge, in so doing raising money for a special wheelchair for a little girl he knew who had cerebral palsy.

As a YTS player at Orient, Danny had regular jobs to do, such as cleaning the first team bus that ferried the players to and from training and 'making the gaffer his morning tea; two tea bags, three sugars. I had it sweet really.' The other major task was cleaning the boots of the senior pros. One of them, Andy Harris, a full-back signed from Tranmere who had been a trainee at Liverpool with Jamie Carragher and Michael Owen, Danny speaks particularly highly of. He always gave him a lot of time and enjoyed telling stories of his time at Liverpool. At Orient, Harris was converted into a centre-midfielder and so later on he effectively was a block on Danny's progress into the first team. In the harsh realities of football at the sharp end of Division 3, where managers' and players' livelihoods are constantly at stake, functionality and experience are often valued over precocious talent.[12] As Danny matured as a player, he felt he could offer more than Harris in central midfield. 'But because he was so kind to me I always wanted him to do well.'

Football is a ruthless business. The reality is that of the estimated 10,000 boys attached to professional clubs in any one season, only a tiny percentage go on to sign that magical, full-time professional contract. Danny was one of the lucky few, but he questions whether clubs did enough to prepare and protect these young boys, most of whom would be 'culled'. He says the boys on the scheme at Orient were enrolled on a GNVQ in leisure and tourism, which involved them attending a class on a Thursday afternoon after training. The teacher, who Danny sympathetically describes as a 'nice geezer', was probably not the inspirational advocate of further education needed by a group of teenage boys whose heads were full of dreams of glittering football careers. 'He loved his football and spent most of the time talking about it. Then we'd read a couple of pages of the text book, sign a few things and that would be it.' This according to

---

12 The fourth tier of English football, confusingly called Division 3 since the launch of the Premier League, was rebranded League 2 for the start of the 2004/05 season.

Danny was the advanced course. 'Some of the boys were doing beginners.'[13]

Danny explains that he never once saw a player told off by the club for not completing his work on the GNVQ course, and there were plenty of boys who 'just showed up and did nothing. The coaching staff really didn't care about the educational side. Thinking about it now, it was a bit of a disgrace how little it mattered. It's not even like if you were a good player they ignored it. It didn't matter if you were fancied as a prospect or not. They didn't care, just so long as you turned up.' In contrast, if you didn't leave the first team's boots immaculate, a task performed in the cold and dark boot room under the main stand, there'd be trouble. 'I've seen pros pin apprentices up against the wall because their boots were dirty or still wet.'

On the pitch Danny was excelling. Through the 2000/01 season, he was an integral part of a very successful youth team that started to rack up trophies. As an ever present in the team, Danny won the Youth Alliance South East league title. But the real highlight came at the Millennium Stadium. With the project to build a new Wembley stadium under way, the FA had moved showpiece games to Cardiff, including the Youth Alliance League Cup Final. Danny's Orient were facing Bradford, who at this point were a Premier League club.

The Millennium Stadium was also hosting the Johnstone's Paint Trophy Final that weekend and so, as the Young Orient players went for a walk after breakfast, there were tens of thousands of football fans in the city, just like there would be for a senior major final.

---

13 See Chris Green's excellent book *Every Boy's Dream*, (A&C Black Publishers Ltd, 2009). During the period Danny was at Leyton Orient, 40% of trainees at professional clubs didn't complete their educational courses, and of those who did, less than 35% passed. Because of this dismal record the government threatened to withdraw funding from football club education schemes in 2003 and finally changes were made. Results improved but there is still doubt about how well these courses prepare trainees who overwhelmingly will not make a career from professional football.

Feeling that he hadn't played his best in the semi-final against Walsall, Danny had some concerns about whether he would start the final. But he hoped the goal he had scored in the subsequent league fixture against Oxford would be enough to see him retain the prized number 8 shirt at the Millennium Stadium. Happily, Danny was given the nod and got changed into his kit in the spectacularly large dressing rooms, which boasted a floor size bigger than a family home complete with huge bathroom and warm-up area. It was a long, long way from Donkey Lane.

Although Orient were underdogs, Danny's dad, Mick, knew his son wouldn't be overawed by the occasion or playing at one of Europe's largest stadiums. 'He just knew he was going to go out and win.' All the same, the perfectionist in Danny was unsettled. It had been decided that both teams would play in their home kit: Bradford in maroon and yellow and Orient in red. As Danny explains, he hated playing in anything anywhere close to a colour clash.

On a sodden pitch, the type which Danny relished playing on as he felt it negated his self-perceived lack of pace and favoured his exceptional passing technique, Orient scored a penalty in front of a crowd of around 5,000, going on to win 1-0. All Danny's family were there to enjoy the moment.

The evidence that Leyton Orient had some high calibre young players on their books was further underlined when the youth team started playing the first team in weekly practice matches at the training ground. Mick smiles as he remembers the calls he would receive from Danny on a Thursday, relaying the scores. 'They seemed to beat the first team every week,' Mick says, '3-0, 4-0, 3-1.'

It was not long before Danny was offered his first professional contract, a massive achievement in itself. Conceptions of what professional footballers earn and the lifestyles they live are very much skewed by the Premier League. Danny's first contract as a full-time pro at Leyton Orient in 2001 was for £300 a week. 'Not money that was ever going to change my life, but when I first joined as an apprentice I was on £47 a week. Jumping from that to £300, I was thinking, this is it! But when you think about the YTS players at Premier League clubs going from, probably about £100 a week, maybe some of them are going from that to £15,000 a week, first contract. How do you deal with that?'

Even though now a full-time professional, Danny wasn't allowed to get too far ahead of himself. During pre-season, the first team squad went to Antigua to prepare for the 2001/02 campaign, but Danny and some of the other new young full-time pros were sent down to Torquay to take part in a tournament. While Devon in the summer is lovely, it's not quite the Caribbean. The Torquay tournament however was not without glamour, featuring sides from around the world. Orient advanced to the final where they'd meet a Brazilian side that had been hammering the opposition in all their games. Ahead of kick-off, the referee came into the Leyton Orient dressing room to wish the boys good luck and deliver some words of wisdom. 'If you lose 6-0, you can consider it a victory,' he said. Then with no sense of irony, he told the players to 'enjoy' themselves. Nevertheless, Orient won the game. One of the youth team coaches, the former Middlesbrough left-back, Peter Johnson, told Danny that if he kept passing the ball the way he had that week, he'd force his way into Orient manager Tommy Taylor's plans and be starting in the first team before long. It was now just a matter of getting a chance at that level to show what he could do.

Looking back at the early stages of a professional footballer's career in the knowledge they made it to the top, it is easy to fall into the trap of assuming that their talent made success inevitable. But the fact is, there is always luck involved. Having signed as a professional Danny now started to play in the reserve team and was dependent on the players in his position in the first team getting injured or losing form. The alternative is having a manager brave enough to take a chance on a talented young player. Danny had exceptional technique; he was able to pass the ball with both feet and score from long distance, but some managers would rather stick with a tried and tested journeyman player who can carry out their instructions to the letter.

One of Danny's team-mates in the reserves did get a break. In a second string game against Reading, in which Danny hit the bar with a shot from a long way out, Nicky Shorey caught the eye of Reading's manager, Alan Pardew, who was in need of a left-back. The next day at training, Orient announced to the players that Pardew had taken Shorey on trial. The move was made permanent for a nominal fee, and Shorey set about establishing himself in a Reading team that subsequently gained promotion to the Premier League. Shorey then made a multi-million pound move to Aston Villa and earned two England caps along the way, both starts at Wembley against Brazil and Germany.

Having taken the club to the brink of promotion in 2001, losing 4-2 to Blackpool in the play-off final in October of the following season, Tommy Taylor lost his job as manager of Leyton Orient. As the team struggled at the wrong end of the league, Danny's former youth team manager, Paul Brush, was appointed as Taylor's successor.

Danny initially thought Brush would champion more of the young players he had worked with and that this would enhance his prospects of making a breakthrough. This turned out to be a false hope. Danny was still overlooked even though the first team's poor results continued into the winter. At this time club captain, Dean Smith, was injured, and so took charge of the reserve team as part of the process of gaining his coaching badges. As the first team conceded five goals at Bristol Rovers on Boxing Day, Danny turned on the style, scoring in a reserve game against Dagenham. Following this, Smith told Danny that he thought he would make the first team for their next fixture against Hartlepool on the final Saturday of December. However, when Danny came to training on the Friday, he found his name again omitted from the first team matchday squad. As he was digesting this disappointment, Smith walked by and consoled Danny, confiding that he had given Brush a glowing report of his performance and urged the manager to play him.[14] Hartlepool 3 Leyton Orient 1.

While Leyton Orient were struggling on the field during the 2001/02 season, times were increasingly bleak for all the professional clubs not on the Premier League gravy train. Hungry for the riches Sky had garnered from subscriptions to watch Premier League football, the newly rebranded ITV Digital decided they wanted a piece of the action. They secured a three-year, £315 million contract to show the Football League. Despite warnings about the viability of this deal, which would hinge on whether viewers were willing to pay as much as £13 a month to watch lower league football, Football League clubs cut their cloth on the basis of the promised windfall. More players were signed to more lucrative contracts than ever before. Once the season started, however, some fixtures attracted television audiences of barely 1,000 and it soon became apparent that ITV Digital had got its sums badly wrong. Who possibly could have foreseen the demand for watching the Football League was not going to be the same as it was for Manchester United against Liverpool?!

Reportedly haemorrhaging £1 million per day, ITV Digital attempted to renegotiate the deal. This plunged many Football League clubs into dire straits as the money they'd committed in advance failed to materialise. Former sports minister, Tony Banks, warned that league football was facing the biggest crisis in its history, and headlines like, 'Debt Ridden Forest Put Entire Squad Up for Sale' and 'Swansea Sack Seven Players to Cut Costs', began to dominate newspaper front and back pages. Danny remembers being balloted by the Professional Footballers' Association (PFA) as to whether the players should go on strike.

---

14 Paul Brush's tenure at Orient proved to be unsuccessful; after two 18th-place finishes he was replaced by another former youth team manager, Martin Ling, who had been in charge when Danny played in the cup final at the Millennium Stadium. Upon taking the top job, Ling made Dean Smith, always a big advocate of Danny's ability, his assistant.

In a vote of its members with a 92% turnout, 2,290 players (99%) voted in favour.[15]

Leyton Orient chairman, Barry Hearn, gave an interview during that season where he forecast 30 clubs in the Football League could go under. 'In the Third Division, 75 per cent of the clubs could go, half of those in the Second Division and 25 per cent of the First. It's been said there will always be someone to put money into a club, but those days are coming to an end... First thing next year we're going down from a 37-man squad to one of 24.' ITV Digital went into administration on 27 March 2002 with a collective debt of £180 million owed to the 72 Football League clubs.[16]

It was in this climate that in the first few days of January 2002, a few weeks before his 19th birthday, Danny was called into Paul Brush's office and told he was being let go. The news came as a cruel shock. Just days before he had believed his first-team breakthrough was imminent.

Danny's mum Carol describes this time as heart-breaking. The dreams Danny had harboured since he first started kicking a ball in the garden with his elder brother were now slipping away. There was an offer to re-join Tommy Taylor, now the manager of Darlington, and talk of a trial at Swindon, but Danny couldn't bring himself to pursue either. Darlington seemed a long way from his family and Mick explains his son's mindset at that point was one of disenchantment with the game. Knowing the talent Danny has with a football, it's easy to wish for him that he had

---

15 These figures are taken from *The Professional Footballers' Association: a case study of trade-union growth* by Dr Geoff Walters, Birkbeck, University of London.

16 Incredibly in 2005, given their experience, ITV struck a deal totalling £175 million to buy Friends Reunited, a website where old school friends could reconnect for a fee. With the explosion of free-to-use social media sites such as Facebook at this very time, what ITV thought to be a golden goose became another investment disaster; in 2009 Friends Reunited was sold for just £25 million, £150 million less than what ITV had agreed to pay for it little over three years previously.

been able to keep pursuing the dream. But thankfully, he was a strong enough character not to let the disappointment ruin his whole life. The depressing story of one of Danny's team-mates from the Millennium Stadium triumph, who was released by Orient around the same time, serves as a grim, cautionary tale. Pitched out of the professional game, this player became a postman. One night he returned to a house on his regular round and forced his way into the home of a young woman whom he violently assaulted and raped. He was sentenced to seven years in prison in May 2006. Within a few months of being released on licence, he was arrested again and found guilty of sexual assault, having put his hand up a woman's skirt in a crowded Holloway pub.[17] Without making any excuses for his former team-mate, Danny wonders if it was the crazy highs and lows of football that tipped the man over the edge.

Immediately upon leaving Orient, Danny joined Arlesey Town, a semi-professional team in the Isthmian League, before joining up with Barnet FC for the 2002/03 pre-season. Danny's time at Barnet was short-lived. He found the manager Peter Shreeves, who had previously had two spells at the helm of Spurs, a difficult character. Danny recounts how another young player asked Shreeves where the changing rooms were to which Shreeves angrily replied, 'I'm the manager of this football club, you don't ask me things like that.' After a few months, Danny left Barnet by his own volition to take up a job as an estate agent in Winchmore Hill. He'd come to terms with the fact that a career in the game wasn't meant to be.

Mick, who acknowledges that he isn't completely free of bias, remains convinced that his son was more than good enough to make it, had he gotten the breaks. It's hard for any of us who played with Danny to argue with this opinion. As a Wizard he scored 92 goals in 113 games from centre-midfield, many of which were of such quality that they would have the referee and opposition players applauding. I maintain that he

17 As reported in the *Waltham Forest Guardian*, 5 August 2010.

is a better technical footballer than many a central-midfielder I have watched playing for Spurs over the years. This may sound like hyperbole, but how many corners do you see hit the first defender in the Premier League? In the six full seasons I played with Danny I never saw him do that once, even when for his own amusement he started to whip them in with his left foot instead of his right just because he could.

Danny is philosophical about his time as a professional and the way things panned out. He occasionally wonders whether if he'd stayed at Spurs his technique might have counted for more there than it did at Orient. When pushed, he says that perhaps he never quite believed in himself enough. As a teenager, he would compare himself to the best players at Spurs and Orient and feel inferior to them, not allowing for the fact he was still developing. Ultimately it's not just about being good enough, it's about believing you are good enough, especially when the knock-backs come. Danny reflects on another of his team-mates from the Millennium Stadium victory, Aaron McLean, who actually didn't make the starting XI that day, and was released by Orient not long after Danny. McLean worked his way back up from non-league football, all the way to playing in the Premier League after signing for Hull for over £1 million. His Premier League debut came as a substitute away at Tottenham. Danny and his brother have season tickets directly next to the dugouts at White Hart Lane and the two former team-mates got the chance to have a chat before the game. Danny explains McLean was not the most naturally gifted of players but he had a brilliant attitude, which enabled him to overcome even a terrible leg break. 'I think I didn't have that mentality,' Danny says now. 'I always worried that other players were maybe better than me... My dad doesn't know that I think like that; even to this day he doesn't know I think like that. You might write it in your book and he'll find out. It just didn't happen for me... It is what it is. I'm happy now and in the grand scheme of my life the day I left Orient is just another day.'

By the time Danny decided to turn out for the Wizards regularly, he had already spent some years playing semi-professionally for Aylesbury United and for Wingate and Finchley, where he was reunited with some of his boyhood team-mates from Southgate Saints. But it was Robbo, another member of the Winchmore Hill estate agent fraternity and someone who Danny vaguely remembers being a couple of years above him at school, who first convinced him to come down and play for the Wizards. Danny is honest enough to admit that when Robbo first suggested this, at a chance meeting in the gym, his initial reaction was, 'Who is this geezer? Does he know where I've played?' However, Robbo enthused about the Wizards passionately whenever he spoke to Danny in the course of work as a fellow estate agent. And then close friend Neil also started applying the pressure. Danny eventually relented and committed to play for the Wizards every week.

'And that was it; from then on I thought, fuck it, I like these boys. Let's just play and have fun.'

Of course we were delighted to have Danny on board. Over the next five seasons he was the crucial factor in the Wizards' success. Only later did I recognise there is a sadness in the fact that we got to live our dream because Danny didn't get to live his.

Chapter Seven

Distractions on and off the pitch

WHILE many people in England greeted the summer of 2006 with great anticipation, believing that the World Cup in Germany would be the stage where England's so called Golden Generation finally delivered, my main worry was about losing our golden boy, Danny. This would become the pattern for a few summers where I would be anxious about him moving on from the Wizards, and we would unashamedly beg him to carry on playing for us. None of us were too proud to recognise that although we were not quite a one-man team, getting the ball to Danny as often as possible was a winning formula. Looking back, I think Danny probably enjoyed being courted by 16 other men desperate for him to spend his Sunday mornings with them.

However, there had been an occasion part way through the previous double-winning season that we feared might lead to our talisman thinking that turning out for us on a Sunday wasn't worth the effort. A routine game at Firs Farm got under way and we started to pass the ball about, probing at the opposition's defence. Suddenly, from nowhere, one of the other team's players said something to a much larger team-mate and the two of them proceeded to pile into Danny completely off the ball, and punched him in the face. There had been no bad tackle or words exchanged between the teams to provoke this. Everyone stood in shock, particularly the referee who had no idea what was going on. The perpetrators were eventually pulled away and both sent off, while Danny with an increasingly angry-looking lump protruding from his face tried to comprehend what was going on. Mickey made the sensible decision to withdraw Danny from the action and he went straight home. It was left to one of our players, who knew the boys on the other side, to explain to the rest of us what had just happened.

Around a year before, Danny was on his way home from a night out, when from afar he noticed a young couple sharing a moment of passion by the side of the road. Keen to share in their joy, Danny gave an encouraging 'Woo Woo' as he approached. The joviality was cut short, however, when he realised that the young lady involved was actually his then girlfriend. Reflecting now, Danny is keen to stress it's not an episode he is proud of. The two young men began a frank exchange of views, from which it transpired the other chap was well aware of who Danny was, realised he had been caught in a compromising position and knew that things would now be settled in the age-old tradition of street-side square-up. It is not clear whether the two of them agreed upon Queensberry rules, but it seems Danny got the better of the poor lad who just a few minutes earlier had been feeling pretty pleased with life. Fast forward 12 months and applying the inexorable law of Sunday League football, whoever you want to avoid in life, you'll eventually find lining up for the other team and we get to Firs Farm. Unfortunately for Danny, not only was it the same fella playing for the opposition that day, but also his brother – his big, big brother. Danny remembers telling the girl at the centre of these events, who at that time he was still going out with, that the bruising on his face was from a stray elbow during the game. He didn't want her to have the satisfaction of knowing she had been the cause of two separate scuffles.

Despite his summer flirtations, Danny became one of the most dedicated Wizards, a player we could count on to show up every week, rain or shine, regardless of how many hours of sleep he'd had the night before. The mere fact of turning up is a much under-valued element of what makes a good Sunday League player, but combined with his propensity to do brilliant things with the ball and also the fact that for the start of the new season he brought along three former team-mates from the Southgate Saints, we felt we'd struck gold. Ed Thompson, Danny's best friend who he had played with since the Under 9s, was a quite magnificent goalkeeper, several cuts above any keeper in the Edmonton League. Ed could also strike the ball more sweetly than the majority of our outfield players. This was demonstrated by the goal he scored that season direct from a free kick on the edge of his own box, that travelled the length of the field before nestling in the opposite net. Jon Leigh, who combined terrific levels of energy with great awareness of where to be on the pitch at all times to receive the ball or intercept it, controlled matches from either left back or centre midfield. Jon also never, ever missed from the penalty spot. Dale Archer, who'd had a spell north of the border with Falkirk, also came on board. He had previously turned out a few times for us as a ringer; he had pace to burn, a hammer of a left foot and the physique of a Greek god. In later years he has made great use of this by co-founding a semi-naked butler service. His glistening torso pops up all over the social media of anyone who is friends with him, leading to some confused questions from many a wife or girlfriend.[18]

In addition an old school friend, Marc Johnson, who had up to this point been playing for another team in the Edmonton League and always gave me a torrid time whenever I came up

---

18 Google: Collars and Buffs – At your service entertainment for booking details!

against him, came over to us after his other team folded. Marc might as well be the footballer for whom the phrase 'great touch for a big man' was coined. Once he joined the Wizards, I lost count of the times I lumped panicked clearances long downfield only to see Marc underneath them, bringing the ball down off his chest or either foot which enabled him to unleash his cannonball of a shot, and me to claim that I had in fact intentionally picked him out with the pass all along. Marc also had a special proclivity for playing his best football when hung over, or more accurately not yet hung over but still inebriated and waiting for the hangover to kick in part way through the first half.

This combination of new boys plus the regulars saw us start the season like an express train. We totted up a 9-2 win on the opening day, two 11-1 wins and an 8-1 victory over the modestly named Studs FC – who judging by that scoreline maybe needed a rebranding exercise – all before Christmas. Mickey Pearce's back condition had also improved sufficiently to enable him to play again, leaving Andy to patrol the touchline. To facilitate his comeback, it was necessary for Mickey to go through a very particular stretching routine that involved lying down on the pitch and rotating his legs in various ways to loosen up the surgically repaired discs that had caused him so many problems. The major challenge he had to overcome was finding an area of the pitch sufficiently free of dog shit to perform these exercises. For some reason, I became the go-to person whenever dog turds were found on any corner of the pitch during the warm-up. It was a role I had no choice but to embrace, bringing a lucky blue plastic bag in my kit bag to use for this purpose. This left me just enough time for my own warm-up routine, which amounted to having my centre-back partner throw up a couple of balls for me to get my heading going. With this extensive warm-up complete, I did the coin toss with the other captain and choosing heads every time I managed to defy the 50/50 odds by almost always losing. Having lost the toss and been made to change ends for kick-off, we frequently found, usually halfway through a first slide tackle, that the opposition had not been as diligent in their dog shit duties as we were.

Our excellent run of results prompted me to invite my girlfriend Mel to watch us play. Ever since we had started going out together, the hours between 7.30am and 1.30pm on a Sunday had been something of a mystery to her. As a Canadian, who had only been in the UK a few years, she had no real concept of what Sunday League football was other than it meant every Saturday night had to end before 10pm, and suggestions for weekends away in the Lake District or somewhere on Eurostar would not be countenanced under any circumstances from the beginning of August to the end of May. I steadfastly resisted her requests to attend a Wizards game for fear that seeing the reality of Sunday League football and my own limitations as a player would lead her legitimately to question why I would let it so completely dominate my (and by association her) life.[19] I carefully scanned the fixture list for a game I thought we'd win comfortably and I'd look half-decent in. Then I arranged with Matt Berou, who was in a similar situation with his girlfriend Sangeeta, that she'd come along too so they could keep each other company on the sideline.

The game couldn't have gone better. We won 5 0 and I imagined Matt and I must have looked magisterial playing in a back four that had never been in danger of being breached. At full time we came off the pitch ready to accept the acclaim we deserved, only to be informed that the womenfolk were sorry that we hadn't managed to win the game. It turned out they had been so busy chatting the pair of them had missed all five goals. Mel said to me no blame could be attached to her or Sangeeta for this as, 'It's not like there is any crowd here making a noise to tell

---

19 Our first ever date had been to romantic White Hart Lane to watch Spurs play the second leg of a UEFA Cup tie against Slavia Prague, Robbie Keane scoring a late winner in a terrible game. Early on in proceedings as Spurs' passes regularly went astray, Mel quite earnestly asked, 'Why do they keep kicking the ball to no one?' I was too busy singing 'We are Tottenham, We are Tottenham, Super Tottenham from the Lane' to answer.

you a goal has gone in.' Neither she nor Sangeeta ever attended a Wizards game again.

Despite the fact we were winning handsomely most weeks, we went through a spell of arguments breaking out on the pitch between our own players as testosterone and male ego soared. If a scientific study were to be performed taking a random sample of these instances, there was always one common denominator, Neil Bower. Away from a football pitch Neil is a hugely sociable, kind-hearted person with a great sense of humour, and is universally popular. Trigger, as he is known to most people, is also someone who enjoys winding people up and is very good at it, particularly as he has a great poker face; people found it hard to determine if he was being serious when he critiqued their performance mid-match. Having spent most of my Sunday mornings with Neil on a football pitch since starting secondary school, and also sat next to him through nearly 20 years of Tottenham's most indifferent history, I was better able than most to recognise that once he laced up his football boots, like so many who play the game, he changed into another person.

Neil acquired the name Trigger, a reference to the character from *Only Fools and Horses*, for a series of comical mishaps that befell him as a teenager where he made an art form out of falling off his bike or getting stuck in unlikely places.[20] Sometimes it felt that he had embraced this role so thoroughly that the scenes of misfortune had been scripted.

There was no way, however, that the timing of the events of 3 July 2001 had been choreographed. On that day Neil found himself a die-hard Spurs fan in a minivan full of his Arsenal mates, including his best friend Mickey, heading for the airport en route to a two-week lads' holiday on the island of Crete. This was the exact moment that the news of Sol Campbell's defection to Arsenal broke. Cue a very long flight and two long weeks for Neil.

---

20 The irony being that Neil is actually a highly skilled and successful financial adviser who has organised mortgages for many of us in the Wizards.

For Neil, me, and a few of the other Spurs fans in the team, it was almost certainly Tottenham's lack of success that made the Wizards so significant in our lives. By your mid-twenties as a football fan you have to be honest about the team you support and we had long since come to accept our place in the north London pecking order.

There was very little we could do about Spurs other than to go on paying them our season ticket money each year despite our better judgement. Much of the time at home games was spent discussing the weekend's main event, the Wizards' next fixture. And if Spurs had a lunchtime kick-off on a Sunday, we would have to scramble in a mad dash from the end of our Wizards game to get to White Hart Lane in time. Interestingly, none of the Spurs fans in the team would ever ask to be substituted early to get away, whereas this became a regular and annoying request from those of an Arsenal persuasion.

It was this burning desire to succeed combined with the reality of being in a team of mates you have known your whole life and are completely comfortable with, that led Neil to become 'more and more vocal' as the years went on. This often took the form of shouting at players if they had made a mistake, which bearing in mind this was Sunday League football was relatively often. 'I was horrendous for that, with I don't want to say everyone but pretty much everyone... It came definitely from the right place, a will to win, but sometimes it went too far. Some people respond to it and some don't and I certainly wasn't clever enough or aware enough to judge the difference... There is an element that as it's your mates you can push it. But that isn't necessarily a conscious decision and doesn't make it right or acceptable.'

It wasn't always clear what would spark Neil to start a row with a team-mate, but he acknowledges that fatigue may have played a part. 'When I go onto a football pitch I am a different person to what I am in any other walk of life, and I think that applies to a lot of people. The way you tolerate situations is different and maybe my fitness levels weren't always where they needed to be. So if you're tired or had a night out before the game, you are more liable to snap. I have often thought if you are running around hitting tackles full of adrenaline and your fitness levels aren't quite there, you are not able to give yourself that ten seconds to think about what you are saying; you just shoot from the hip.'

Credit to Neil, he was completely democratic in the feedback he would give out to team-mates. Most of us definitely didn't want to moan at the more talented players on the pitch if they weren't putting a shift in, for fear of upsetting them, whereas for Neil this was never a concern. Every player, regardless of where he had or hadn't played before, could find himself on the end of a tongue-lashing. It was Mike Angelides, a classy midfielder-come-right-back who brought some much needed quality on the ball to our defence, who would most regularly get involved in 'strong arguments' with Neil. This was all the more amusing to the rest of us as off the pitch they were extremely close friends and both such amiable characters. It never came to blows between them but there were one or two occasions where this seemed close.

Neil was also able to extract the very maximum out of his ability as a footballer. While on occasions it would have been nice to see him taken down a peg or two, this never happened. Instead he would actually assert himself more if the game was already decided. He would suddenly emerge at the front of the queue to take a penalty or free kick within shooting range, miraculously finding the energy to sprint down the pitch and get hold of the ball first, despite having spent much of the match complaining of being tired due to all the work he was doing covering everyone else. Having put himself on free kicks one week, Neil proceeded to hit the woodwork with a great effort, which he then used as justification to have another go a week later. This time his shot bent perfectly round the wall and arched right into the corner of the net for a brilliant goal.

Coming into the season's climax in 2007, we looked set to complete the treble. We had progressed to two cup finals and held a narrow advantage over Attitude, our perennial rivals, in the race for the Division 3 title. We had beaten them 2-1 in the league in February in a bad-tempered game. Both our goals that day were scored by Matt Godwin, who also found time to engage in a bout of actual not metaphorical mud-slinging following a tangle of legs with Attitude's energetic and often angry central-midfielder Chas. Watching two grown men resort to scooping up mud with their hands and throwing it at each other while looking around at their team-mates for approval that never came, will remain one of my favourite memories of Sunday League football.

Matt could always be trusted to wind up the opposition. He would deliver an almost running commentary to their defence as he vied with them for the ball, and has that rare gift of not being remotely affected by whatever they might say back to him; this wound other teams up all the more. Sometimes he didn't even need to say anything. Just his appearance, immaculate hair, white boots and the slight strut to his walk were enough to send opponents into a frenzy. Carlo, the Attitude manager, says about Matt, in what would be music to his ears, 'That forward would have fitted right into our team as well because he had massive attitude; he always used to get into rucks with us, he was pretty full of himself.'

Away from football, Matt had a love of the high life, and inexplicably arranged a trip to Las Vegas over the weekend of our first cup final against Attitude. Worse still, this transatlantic jaunt not only deprived us of certain other key players but also our manager Mickey, who in what can only be deemed a massive dereliction of duty prioritised the glamour of Caesars Palace over the non-flushing toilet of Jubilee Park. Nonetheless, with the four former Southgate Saints still available for selection, we collected the first trophy of what we hoped would go on to be three by winning 5-3. This final only cemented the animosity between us and Attitude. We celebrated that night with a few drinks at the pub, receiving a phone call from the boys in Vegas to whom we relayed the good news and shared a transatlantic chorus of 'Wizards 'til I die'.

However, it was the league title that we really wanted. Going into the penultimate league fixture of the season, we knew that a draw against Attitude would maintain our one-point advantage over them. This would leave us needing to beat the appallingly spelt BG Outsidaz FC, a team we'd put to the sword in a 5-0 win early in the season. Disaster struck in the middle of the week leading up to the Attitude game, when Danny fell ill and was ruled out of what was basically the title decider. One of our players, using his free time wisely, had discovered that Attitude had set up a club website which featured profiles of their players and mug shots of them which we all enjoyed having a look at. More amusingly, however, they also had a message board, open for anyone to view. Some of the posts on there were less than flattering about our team.

There was also a clue that they were going to have some special guest appearances in their starting line-up for the decisive game against us. Being historically well versed in deploying a star ringer or two ourselves, rather uncharitably I took it upon myself to call up the League officials and demand they do a check of ID cards before the game just to make sure Attitude hadn't smuggled Lionel Messi in to their starting XI. (The Edmonton League had by this time caught up as far as 1970s technology, colour photos and a laminator, to introduce photo ID cards.) Attitude had not tried to pull any strokes and I was left red-faced and feeling pretty petty when the League official said loudly in full view of everyone assembled on the pitch that my suspicions were unfounded.

Danny's appearance on the touchline rather than in the heart of our midfield inevitably gave Attitude a boost. Despite not playing well and falling behind, we managed to equalise late on with a brilliant free kick from Mike Angelides. We thought this would be enough to see us home to the draw we needed.

However, in the last seconds of the game a miskicked clearance gave Attitude a throw near our box. I should have won the header from the resulting long throw and cleared the danger. Instead, somehow I only managed to flick it on to the back post from where they were able to bundle the ball over the line, sparking wild celebrations from both their players on the pitch and their friends and families gathered in numbers on the sideline. Up to that point it was the lowest feeling I have ever had from football; I felt physically sick knowing that we had all but mathematically blown the league title, and worse still we had lost out to Attitude. It was Easter Sunday and I phoned ahead from Jubilee Park to give strict instructions that no one at our annual Easter lunch with family friends was to ask any questions about the game, or mention it under any circumstances, such was the severity of the trauma I had gone through that morning.

In the week leading up to the final league game of the season, Matthew Berou and I pored over the league table calculating the unlikely scenarios that might see us come away with the title. It was clear we needed snookers. We had to win our game by eight clear goals and hope Attitude lost to Southgate Rovers. Rovers were a team we had only managed to draw with home and away and included lots of players we had been friends with at school. What's more, the Rovers striker was going out with Mickey's sister. This meant pleas went out to the Rovers boys to have an early night on Saturday. We were optimistic, given their performances against us, that they could do us a favour. And so we came to the final Sunday of the league season. Both the Attitude v Rovers game and our game against BG Outsidaz were to be played at Firs Farm, separated by a few other pitches with games going on. It was like a low-rent version of Sky Sports' final day coverage; instead of split screen, where they would cut from the two games that mattered and put up 'As it stands' league tables as goals went in, we were reliant on one of our subs jogging over to the other pitch to bring back news of what was happening.

We started the game well and set about chasing the cricket score we needed. At the point in the second half when our fourth goal went in, I saw some of our players infuriatingly wasting time in celebrating, and so I ran the length of the pitch to retrieve the ball from the Outsidaz net. As I bent to pick it up, one of the Outsidaz non-playing entourage came behind the goal and kicked the ball away and charmingly said, 'What are you getting the ball for, you lanky cunt? Attitude have won the league.' Having got hold of the ball I looked over to the touchline where our sub was no longer even bothering to make the relay trip, such was the ease with which Attitude were beating our mates Southgate Rovers. It turned out Rovers had been on a massive bender the night before and were missing most of their best players. Thanks boys. And so it was that Attitude won the Edmonton and District 3rd Division by two points. Nevertheless, our second place finish saw us promoted with them to Division 2 for the next season.

Before the summer break we had another cup final to contest, this time in the Edmonton and District Sunday League Challenge Cup against a team called The Boundary. Once again the final was to be played in the auspicious surroundings of the Henry Barrass Surround Stadium where our fortunes had been mixed over the years. As ever the Edmonton League required us to submit our probable starting line-up in the week ahead of the game, and Mickey and Andy had some decisions to make. The whole squad was available for selection except for Ed, who had been magnificent in goal all season.

Mickey and Andy decided to keep the selection under wraps and bring everyone down to the game just in case there were any drop-outs that morning. Having been privy to their selection I arrived at Jubilee Park and started to lay out the kit, hanging it up in numerical order in the changing room before the rest of the boys arrived. One of the earliest through the door was Darryl, a good player and pleasant lad who had been in and out of the team that season owing to other commitments including playing hockey, which in Edmonton was akin to playing polo at a country club and led to some banter coming Darryl's way whenever he returned to Wizards action. I knew that Darryl was not listed in the first XI or among the subs that day, but didn't have the heart to say anything as he started to get changed into the kit. I thought I'd leave it to the management team to break the bad news to him. As the rest of the players arrived one by one and got kitted up, however, I realised that we only had enough shirts for the players that were actually playing or on the bench. I quietly brought this to Mickey's attention, who then had the excruciating task of informing Darryl that not only was he not involved in the cup final but he would have to publicly get changed back out of the kit and give it to one of the other players. I found myself unable to bear this conversation and went and hid in the toilet with my fingers in my ears as the news was delivered to poor Darryl, not my finest moment of captaincy. To his enduring credit, Darryl got changed and stayed to watch the match although he decided to play his football elsewhere the following season.

After the presentation of the two teams to the League's guest of honour, I once again lost the coin toss. As we shook hands, The Boundary's captain handed me a small plastic pendant with The Boundary FC on it as they do in the Premier League. Pondering what to do with it and having nothing to give in return, my mind began to wander back to the Iran versus USA game in the group stages of World Cup '98. Given all the history between those two nations the Iranians had clearly made a decision to go on a charm offensive. The Iran captain embarrassed his American counterpart at the usual coin toss and handshake by presenting him with a massive bouquet of flowers and some sort of giant commemorative silver plate in addition to the customary pendant. Iran famously won the game 2-1, and I nervously thought that this might be a bad omen for us. With events in a random World Cup group game nearly a decade ago plus the Darryl situation playing on my mind, I started the game poorly.

We gave away a free kick close to the halfway line and I was trying to get other players to mark up, completely losing sight of the Boundary striker who had run goal side of me as the free kick was taken.

Helplessly, hopelessly, I put my arm up to appeal for offside knowing my severe lack of pace meant once a striker got goal side of me, they pretty much always stayed goal side of me. But the linesman rightly offered me no mercy. I resolved that I couldn't allow them to go through and score this early in the game because I'd switched off so badly. I started to tug his shirt from behind. He was a big lad and kept going so I started tugging harder, but the ref played the advantage and he continued bearing down on goal. After what seemed like five minutes of trying to pull this guy down, I saw him go over – but to my dismay I realised he was now in the box.

The referee blew up for the penalty and then reached for his top pocket to show me the red card. Coincidentally the referee for this showpiece occasion was a Mr Curbelo, a name familiar to all of us as he was also the father of Attitude's star striker. In fairness to him it was a red card all day long. My only complaint was that had he blown up straight away and not played the advantage, we wouldn't have endured the double whammy of conceding a penalty as well as going down to ten men so early in the game. I took off the captain's armband and put it on Danny and then turned to trudge ignominiously off the pitch. But upon so doing, I was told by a League official that I couldn't stay pitchside and would have to watch the game from the elevated balcony area in front of the changing rooms. As I made my way up the concrete steps I didn't need to look to know the penalty had been scored, the noise from the Boundary fans telling its own story. At that exact moment I honestly don't think I could have felt worse if I had killed someone. Ken Martin, the League's finance secretary, with whom a few years previously we had rowed over the whereabouts of a match card, came over to me and offered a few words of consolation and then in a true act of human kindness made me a toasted ham and cheese sandwich and gave me a cup of tea in a big enamel mug.

It came as a huge relief near the end of the first half when the Wizards were awarded a penalty, which Jon Leigh converted emphatically to bring the game level. As the boys came in at half-time absolutely knackered, having put in a sterling performance on a massive pitch on a scorching hot day, I could barely make eye contact with any of them, sitting slumped in the corner. After Mickey and Andy had said a few tactical bits and pieces, Matt Berou, never one for big speeches, announced suddenly in a loud voice, 'Let's do it for Flynny!' and when the other boys joined in it set me off in silent tears. Even at the time I thought to myself, whatever else in life, I am a lucky bastard to be friends with this set of lads. Yeah, maybe at times we all take playing for the Wizards too seriously, but moments like this are bloody special. The boys then trooped out of the changing room for the start of the second half; I followed behind charged with locking the door while ruminating on the profound emotional breakthrough I had just experienced. Seconds later these thoughts were interrupted by an increasingly desperate knocking sound coming from the inside of the changing room behind me. As I unlocked the door I was greeted by the referee who had earlier sent me off. We exchanged an awkward look and I think it must have crossed his mind that I might attack him in the abandoned changing room where he had snuck in unbeknownst to the rest of us for a clandestine half-time number two in the non-flushing toilet. Instead we shook hands as I let him out and I half-jokingly asked him to even up the numbers in the second half.

The longer the second half went on the more confident I felt that the other boys would dig me out of the hole of my sending off. Mickey had slotted into central defence alongside Neil and the pair of them were colossal, while Danny was magnificent in the middle of the park. Despite being down to ten men we were pushing hard for a winning goal, and just before the end of 90 minutes Boundary had a player sent off for a second yellow card, making it ten versus ten for extra time. Virtually from the kick-off to start extra time, we took the lead with a great finish from Eamon McGarvey. Eamon had played in our first ever game back in September 2002 and was an enigmatic character. He'd acquired the name Foxbat. A small, wiry lad of Irish descent who looked perpetually 18 years old, he was in fact a good bit older than the rest of us.[21] He had come to the Wizards via knowing some of the long-gone original players through work. None of us really knew Eamon away from Sunday mornings; he would turn up in the dressing room wearing a blue Nike baseball cap, change into the kit that was always ridiculously baggy on him, bang in a hat-trick and then disappear for seven days and do exactly the same thing again, with only a one-word text 'In' to confirm his availability for the following Sunday as evidence that he wasn't a figment of our collective imaginations. The *Guinness Book of World Records* has Pele as the scorer of the most goals in a specified period, 1,279 in 1,363 games, but I'm fairly sure Eamon would have eclipsed this comfortably had it not been for a series of broken bones that limited his appearances for us over the years. As he received the ball and started to twist and turn the Boundary defenders until he had worked it onto his right foot, there was no doubt in my mind what would shortly follow, a ripple of the net. With us 2-1 up, the colour finally started to come back to my face, and when our young substitute George added a third, I knew I was out of jail.

---

21 After a good few years of playing together he confided in me that he had once purchased a pair of Glasgow Rangers shorts which he proceeded to wear for a kick-about with his group of fellow Irish Catholic mates. Much to his surprise the other boys quickly informed him that these were not appropriate and the shorts were retired after one outing. This was a story I could relate to as my Celtic-supporting dad took me to Rangers to see what we hoped would be Paul Gascoigne's debut in Scottish football in August 1995 against Kilmarnock. As if to pay penance for this act of treason on the way to Ibrox we stopped off at a sports shop first and he bought me a Celtic Umbro manager's jacket which he asked the lad at the checkout to double bag for fear it would somehow fall out during the game and expose us as not being Blue Noses. As it turned out Gazza was unfit and didn't play.

At full time, having been sent off, I wasn't allowed to go and collect the cup, not that I would have wanted to given my contribution that day. I was told that I wouldn't be eligible for a medal either, as League rules meant players sent off in a final did not receive one. This seemed unnecessarily draconian especially as I had mentally prepared the space for it on my mantelpiece, but then Ken Martin, who seemed to have a soft spot for us as a team, came over and quietly handed me a little maroon velvet box with one of the medals in it. He really was a gent.

Back in the dressing room Colin Cowan, our tireless midfielder, produced two bottles of champagne from his kit bag; we had a little chorus of 'Wizards 'til I die' as had become our tradition on these occasions and agreed to meet at the Salisbury Arms later that evening to carry on the celebrations. It was a particularly sweet moment for George, who was a player we had picked up along the way, and who being much younger than the rest of us was inclined to be quite shy. He often found himself not starting games, which knocked his confidence, though it should be said that this lack of confidence did not stop him having the number plate 'G22 RGE' on his black Ford Escort. George driving away from Jubilee Park that afternoon, absolutely elated having scored in a cup final, was a brilliant sight to behold. He was such a nice lad. There's something special that only Sunday football can bestow.

As some of the other boys said they were bringing their girlfriends, I roped Mel into coming along to the pub. This was useful as I didn't have a car and so needed help to walk a mile along Hoppers Road, carrying the two cups we'd won that season in their heavy wooden boxes. With the drinks flowing that night, spirits were high and none of the boys were remotely concerned about the hangover they'd have to endure at work the next morning. The atmosphere changed, however, when several of the Attitude players appeared unannounced at the bar in the most provocative move since the Montagues snuck into the Capulet ball. Carlo says that this was a spontaneous decision by a handful of his players, but it does seem likely that ever since they had pipped us to the post for the title they'd been looking for any chance to remind us of that fact. Doing it when we were out celebrating a cup final triumph, all the better. As one post on their message board dated 4 May 2007 from champions Attitudes No1 reads: 'Congratulations on winning the league and rubbing it in the Wizards' faces on Sunday at the Salisbury get in there my son LOL.'[22] In fairness to the Attitude players we had to admit it was a pretty amusing stroke to pull. Not being the type of team looking to have a fight, we grudgingly had to laugh it off and admire their commitment to the cause of hating us. We let them enjoy the moment and looked forward to renewing hostilities in September.

---

22 The Attitude website and message board are still viewable online all these years later, a testament to petty rivalries between two sets of 20-somethings that should have known better.

Chapter Eight

The promised land

THE reason our goalkeeper, Ed Thompson, had missed the cup final at the end of the 2006/07 season was that in April his form at Wingate and Finchley, where he played semi-professionally on a Saturday, had been rewarded with a trial at Dagenham and Redbridge. Ed's trial coincided with an important piece of Dagenham history as the club was in the process of being promoted to the Football League. Ed knew that were he to impress during his trial, there would be an opportunity for him to turn professional the following season; the Daggers would need to bolster their squad to face the rigours of League 2 football. Of all the ways for a Sunday League team to lose their goalkeeper, the prospect of seeing one of your team-mates and friends turn pro was by far the best.

Within a few weeks of making his farewell appearance for the Wizards, Ed took part in Sky Sports' *Soccer AM* Crossbar challenge, and subsequently joined an elite group within the footballing fraternity. Every week they would bring cameras to a different professional club training ground and give the entire first team squad one attempt each to hit the crossbar directly from a dead ball on the halfway line. Most players got nowhere near and many totally embarrassed themselves. As it happened, just after Ed joined Dagenham, it was their turn for the visit from Sky.

The recording shows Ed in among his new team-mates, as one by one they shank their shots. Next up he calmly introduces himself to the camera as 'Ed Thompson, Goalkeeper, Dagenham', and then from the halfway line pings the crossbar with a beautiful, arching strike before being mobbed by the other players. In the frenzied celebrations that followed Ed recalls one of his team-mates 'chinned me, I don't think it was on purpose, I couldn't talk for a week. I didn't care though, I was absolutely buzzing... I still have the t-shirt. I should frame it really.'[23]

Ed's long road to the verge of signing a professional contract had started as an eight-year-old at Chase Side Youth FC, which is where he first met Danny. The two started at Southgate School in 1994 in the same class and together became an integral part of the success of the school and Southgate Saints teams. Ed remembers that it was Danny who lent him a copy of *Saves Galore* on VHS where ITV Sport's Jim Rosenthal and Ray Clemence sat in a broom cupboard surrounded by editing equipment they didn't have much idea how to use while they introduced clips of saves from brilliant but clearly overweight goalkeepers like Nigel Spink and Neville Southall playing the previous season in the Barclays First Division. Ed thinks he must have watched this video hundreds of times and can recite most of the commentary to this day.

Despite not being the tallest growing up, he had honed lightning fast reflexes which he attributes to having two older brothers who gave him little choice but to go in goal in the back garden as they squared off in games of 1 against 1. This was a huge advantage, Ed explains, because when he got to playing school and Sunday football in his own age group, no one could kick the ball anywhere near as hard as his brothers.

---

23 YouTube Dagenham & Redbridge Crossbar Challenge to see the magic moment.

I'm sure my requests to my dad to only buy Holsten were purely coincidental.

Competitive dad – penalty shoot-out at Center Parcs.

*Green Lanes,
north London –
paradise awaits
behind the net
curtain.*

*Division 5 winners in our first season – the Pro Star, all-white kit
looked great for about one week.*

When the sun was out I didn't need to use the radiators.

The Cup Final changing room at Jubilee Park – home of the non-flushing toilet.

All the glamour of a show piece occasion. The Wizards and Hop Poles go through a few last-minute stretches ahead of our first Cup Final.

To the victors go the spoils.

The pinnacle of the Edmonton Sunday League – Wizards FC, Division 1 winners, 2009. Back row (left to right) Danny, Shak, Marc, Ed, Neil (Trigger), Ewan. Front row (left to right) Mike Angelides, Matt Godwin, Mickey Pearce, Robbo, Eamon, Matt Berou.

Mike Chisholm (centre) "When you put on that black kit and walk out, whatever level it is, you have a job to do and it's a really important job."

*Ed Thompson,
goalkeeper,
Dagenham and
Redbridge.*

*Ed at full stretch
in action for the
Daggers.*

Roy Chipolina puts in a challenge on Germany's Mario Götze, scorer of the winning goal in the 2014 World Cup Final.

Roy celebrates his team's equaliser at Hampden Park. It was Gibraltar's first goal of the qualifying campaign and I was in the stand with my dad to see it. Final score Scotland 6 Gibraltar 1.

"I think Danny has taken the Spurs manager's job."

Ed remembers football in the garden as being a daily routine; the only interruption came when the old man next door called Dibble became so irate with the constant flight of balls over the fence that he started taking a knife to the balls. It therefore became imperative that the boys climb over and retrieve the balls before Dibble got to them. This foray into enemy territory involved scaling an asbestos shed roof to 'do the Dibbs' and liberate the football so the game could continue. Ed's garden backed onto future Wizards team-mate Marc Johnson's garden, and Mickey Pearce lived just round the corner, so there would always be a game in the street to get involved in as well.

Ed has fond memories of his granddad, who had also been a goalkeeper, taking him to Briggs sports shop in Enfield Town to buy goalkeeping gloves that resembled cotton gardening gloves with strips of pimpled rubber glued onto the fingertips and palms. This started a lifelong fetish for goalkeepers' gloves. Ed admits he spends hours every week looking at gloves online and he still gets the same buzz he did as a kid when a new pair arrives in the post.

His first recollections of playing Sunday football are probably typical of every young goalkeeper who grew up in the era of the four-step rule. This dictated that after a goalkeeper had collected the ball he was only allowed to take four steps with it in his possession before having to release it. 'If I caught the ball on my goal line I could only get to the six-yard box before having to kick it, so I'd barely clear the 18-yard box with my kicks, especially if there was a strong wind.

'The four-step rule was a killer; I used to regularly take five or six, and give away a free kick the other team would score from. I used to get so upset conceding any goal because I felt I had let people down and I would cry.' Ed explains that it was hard to assess how good he was at that age as he was making mistakes and learning all the time. But it was clear to the parents watching from the sideline and to his young team-mates that he was a special goalkeeper.

By the time Ed started playing for the Southgate Saints, his mum and dad had divorced. He remembers that Danny's dad, Mick, would often ferry him to training sessions and games in order to help out his mum. Ed frequently stayed at Danny's house on a Saturday night before games on a Sunday morning, and the relationship to this day is that of brothers. It was while playing for the Saints and having been selected to play for the county that Ed was identified by Dick Moss as a potential professional footballer, and invited down to train with Spurs a couple of times a week. It was often Mick who took him to these sessions. As Ed says, 'Danny's family were always very good to me.' He remembers Mick buying him his first proper goalkeeper's top with his name and the number 1 printed on the back, a silver Umbro kit worn by lots of the teams in the early years of the Premier League with the diamond-shaped logo forming a purple pattern over it. Ed says he monitors eBay regularly trying to find a vintage replica of this shirt.

It was at Spurs that Ed received his first proper goalkeeper training as opposed to one of the dads smashing some practice shots at him a few minutes before kick-off. While he recognises his time at Tottenham helped his development, his abiding memory is not a happy one. He recalls a trial game where he did not know any of his team-mates and came on in the second half against Arsenal, the team he supports. The final score was 8-0, and Ed's impression was that every goal had been a lob over his head. 'It was a horror... a harsh lesson... no one really spoke to me afterwards.'

At training the next day, Dick Moss put an arm round Ed and tried to pick up his confidence, but although Ed would go on to win the goalkeeper of the week prize a few times while at Spurs, he remembers being demoralised about his height and thinking that unless he had a growth spurt, his hopes would be dashed. In the end Spurs released Ed, citing as the major reason his lack of height, perhaps seen as the barometer for a goalkeeper's future prospects more a generation ago than it is now. As he explains,

'Perhaps they looked at my mum and dad and concluded I'd never grow tall enough.'

Ed remembers feeling much more comfortable playing his football for the Saints and school team, thinking deep down perhaps he wasn't quite good enough to make it. As some of his best friends finished school and signed with professional teams, Ed started playing semi-professionally for Wingate and Finchley while studying in the sixth form. He recognises that while he was thrilled for Danny, who seemed to be living the dream they had shared since they were eight years old, it was hard to see him go off to train with Orient, while he himself had to continue in the classroom.

At Wingate, Ed was quickly promoted from the Under 18s and thrust into the reserves. He highlights that jump to playing the men's game as being the best education possible for a young goalkeeper: 'Getting streetwise, taking high balls and getting smashed by opposition players who target you as a young goalkeeper because they think you're the weakest link.' That's when you need mental fortitude, especially if you make an error. 'There is nothing worse than when you make a mistake early in a game and it's like all of a sudden, "let's put it on the keeper, he's dodgy". That's when it really tests your mettle. I've played in games where I've made a mistake early, dropped a cross or whatever and then you get bombarded. That's where you really have to grit your teeth and say to yourself, "Come on!" I've played games where I've made three or four mistakes, especially when I was younger, and you do question yourself afterwards, "Am I not good enough?" But you go to training and go to the next game and nine times out of ten you do all right.'

The saves must have been far outweighing the mistakes though. When Ed moved up to Lincoln for university, he went straight into the university first team. Then during his second year, Wingate and Finchley asked him to come back, which meant a commute for training midweek before the game on the Saturday. By this time, Danny had been released by Orient and Sam Sloma, another former Saint who had been signed by Wimbledon, had also been let go. All three converged at Wingate and Finchley for a couple of glorious seasons.

The main impression Ed gives of this time in his life is that these were happy years spent playing winning football with his best mates, getting paid a bit of money to do so and enjoying the dressing room banter that was a feature of the club. One story from those years at Wingate has achieved legendary status among the players who were at the club at that time. The team would train midweek under the floodlights, and on this particular evening all the players had gone out from the dressing rooms to the training pitch and started to warm up. As balls zipped about on the wet turf, suddenly a figure emerged from the changing room, completely naked except for a blacked-out motorcycle crash helmet. The unidentified man proceeded to run around the pitch much to the amusement of all the players. The manager however was less impressed as his training session plan did not include any nudity, although I'd wager it crossed his mind that sending on a naked man in a crash helmet could be a more effective tactic when chasing a late equaliser than the traditional approach of pushing a centre-back up front. After several minutes of hilarity, the manager deduced that one of his players was not accounted for and that this player must be the culprit. Danny was asked to take off the crash helmet and sent inside.

I think most people who have been lucky enough to share a football changing room with their best friends rather than just a group of random team-mates will say they mourn the silliness and banter before and after games as much as the football itself. That is certainly the case for those of us who played for the Wizards.

Ed still harboured hopes of moving up the non-league ladder and having won player of the year twice during his time at Wingate, his aspirations were realised. Sam Sloma had left Wingate to play at a higher level with Thurrock and had subsequently come to the attention of Dagenham and Redbridge, who signed him. Dagenham's first choice goalkeeper was the legendary former QPR and Wales international, Tony Roberts, who despite still performing excellently was in the twilight years of his career and for whom cover was needed. Sam mentioned to the staff at Dagenham that he knew a good goalkeeper that they should take a look at, and so it was that a scout came to watch Ed play for Wingate. With hindsight, Ed reflects how playing Sunday football for the Wizards right up to the point his trial started at Dagenham was pretty reckless. He shudders slightly as he considers how easy it would have been to pick up a serious injury on Sunday, given that his body was already tired and sore from playing on Saturday. This could have torpedoed his chance at Dagenham before it ever began. However, as he says, 'At that stage in life you think you're invincible.'

At the time Dagenham showed an interest in Ed, he was 24 and working as a warehouse manager for a broadcast hire company called Gearbox, where fellow Wizard, Mickey, also worked. Ed had received a promotion and he was earning good money. After his trial, Dagenham invited him to carry on training with them but had not yet offered him a contract. In order to pursue the opportunity Ed had to quit his job, which was a big financial sacrifice at that stage with no guarantee of the outcome. Consequently he had to take a shift at the Salisbury Arms, the scene of the Wizards' post-cup final celebrations, to ensure he had a bit of money coming in. When finally he was offered a contract by Dagenham, it was for significantly less than he had been earning at Gearbox; contrary to the conventional wisdom about professional footballers, going pro actually meant some tough financial decisions and a change of lifestyle. Ed remembers calling his mum, Deborah, to discuss the offer Dagenham had made, and her supporting him by letting him move back home. She recognised that although the money wasn't good, the opportunity to play professional football was one Ed had to seize.

To make ends meet, he continued working at the Salisbury Arms right through the summer. He thinks he even worked a shift behind the bar the night before Dagenham played their first league game of the 2007/08 season against Stockport, such were the financial constraints. Living the dream wasn't all that it was cracked up to be. Naturally he didn't tell the club, but as he says, 'I needed the money.' Players' contracts were heavily loaded towards appearance money, difficult for Ed as he was signed as back-up to the established goalkeeper. At least to begin with the opportunities to play would be limited. 'It was a foot in the door... so I got, maybe not taken advantage of, but I was going in there as a number two and Tony Roberts was still the number one. But we knew he couldn't play forever, so I thought I'd get a chance.'

Ed explains that Dagenham manager John Still was a master at plucking players from the non-league game and moulding them into a team. The Dagenham side contained lots of players who hadn't previously been at a professional club but instead were working day jobs, one on the market, another as a teacher, before the Daggers earned Football League status. And so the team still had that feel to it. Ed liked the fact that there were no big egos among the playing staff, just a desire to train and succeed.

He found his first pre-season as a pro surreal. The jump from playing for Wingate and Finchley to suddenly coming on for the final ten minutes of Tony Roberts's testimonial against West Ham, sharing a pitch with household names and England internationals like Scott Parker and Robert Green, was a mental challenge for him on top of the physical challenge of now being a professional athlete and training every day. Three days after West Ham came another game, against Premier League Fulham, where Ed remembers he played really well in front of lots of his friends who had come down to watch. They witnessed him make great saves from the likes of Simon Davies and Diomansy Kamara. 'After that game I remember seeing a forum on BBC 6.06 saying, "Who is this lad in goal for Dagenham? Where did he come from?" and people saying "He's a prospect" ... I was buzzing seeing that, and I got a really good write-up in the match report on the Fulham website.'

The dynamic between goalkeepers at a football club is unique. The reality for Ed was that for him to play regularly, he would need misfortune to befall the established keeper, Tony Roberts, whether it be a loss of form, injury or suspension. However, Ed says this was never something he hoped for. He has nothing but respect for Roberts, a Dagenham legend who made over 500 appearances for the club and who always took the time to encourage him and share his wisdom. The two goalkeepers also shared another connection, one that Ed explained to Roberts when they first started training together at Dagenham. Ed is a huge Arsenal fan and was in the stands at Highbury on a rainy day in December 1994, when Arsenal met Queens Park Rangers. This game holds a special place in Arsenal folklore because after two years of trying John Jensen scored his first goal for the Gunners. Arsenal actually lost the game 3-1, but Ed's disappointment was tempered by the fact that at one point, when Arsenal had a corner, Ian Wright cheekily went into the young QPR goalkeeper's net, pulled down the towel he had hung up there to dry his gloves off (regular practice by goalkeepers in wet conditions to guard against mishandling), mopped his wet face and threw the towel into the crowd. Tony Roberts's blue towel sailed straight into 11-year old Ed's arms as he sat in the stand behind the goal! It was a memento he hung over his bed for years, and he still has it to this day. As Ed recounted this story to Roberts 13 years later, his new team-mate and mentor remembered the incident vividly and recalled being pretty 'pissed off' with Ian Wright.

Ed explains that even by the time he arrived at Dagenham, he was still very raw as a goalkeeper, though capable of making brilliant reflex saves that defied goalkeeping conventions.[24] But

---

24 He confesses that Bruce Grobbelaar was his hero as a boy; perhaps some of the Zimbabwean's style had rubbed off on him, although thankfully this did not extend to his dress sense.

under Tony Roberts's tutelage, he worked some of the rough edges from his game and improved immeasurably. During the latter part of his career playing for Dagenham, Roberts was also doing goalkeeping coaching at Arsenal in his spare time, which Ed says illustrates how knowledgeable Roberts was. 'I hung on his every word, I was so eager to learn… He was always about getting the pure goalkeeping technique into me. He was the only person who took the time to point things out to me, more than anything he was just good for my confidence. Even at that level of football, managers and assistant managers don't really understand about goalkeepers. So the games I played, he studied the DVDs with me. "Work on this; you did that well." He sort of had my back, which was reassuring. It's nice to have someone who really knows what they are talking about to guide you.' Ed adds that as well as imparting goalkeeping wisdom Tony Roberts was also a generous, regular source of new goalkeeping gloves. Given Ed's lifelong glove habit, this was an act of kindness he'll never forget.

It wasn't until midway through his first season as a professional that Ed got to make his competitive first team debut, in unusual circumstances in an FA Cup third-round tie at Roots Hall against Southend. With the Daggers trailing 3-2 in the dying embers of the game, Tony Roberts had left his goal and gone up for a corner. Rather than heading home an equaliser to force a replay he instead got involved in a scuffle, headbutted one of the Southend players, and was sent off. Ed was therefore thrust on by manager John Still with minutes to go to full time, and had to scramble to get his shin pads and gloves on, entering the field with the number 30 shirt on his back. Although he recalls being really nervous at taking this first step into professional first team football and it coming in the world's oldest cup competition no less, Ed was grateful that he didn't have any time to think about it and get worked up.

With all the stoppages there was still time left in the game. Inevitably, Dagenham poured forward leaving the back door open, and Southend picked them off for two more goals. Final score Southend 5, Dagenham and Redbridge 2. The next day, Ed remembers seeing that the *News of the World* gave him a mark of three out of ten for his cameo performance, which in the circumstances he thought a bit harsh.

Roberts was now suspended for three matches, which meant Ed would claim his place in the team, first up against Morecambe, away from home. The coach trip up to Lancashire seemed to last an eternity, Ed fearing all eyes would be on him. Nevertheless, playing in the pouring rain, there was a fairy tale moment when Ed saved a penalty and was all set to be the hero of the piece, until in the 94th minute he conceded a late goal and Dagenham made the long journey home empty-handed.

Next came his full home debut, against Grimsby. While this was an amazingly exciting time in Ed's life, there is also a sadness to his memories of those weeks. Ed explains that ever since childhood he'd had a difficult relationship with his dad, particularly after his parents went through a horrible divorce where his dad experienced some sort of emotional breakdown. 'He was never really part of our lives… he was never really into football, he never took me to games, never watched me, never showed an interest from whenever I started. And he never used to come on holidays with us. I remember saying to my mum when I was young I don't really know this guy.' Despite this, Ed explains how his mum, whom he describes as an angel, tried to facilitate a relationship between father and son throughout his teenage years and into his early twenties. Ed reflects that his mum, knowing the huge importance of the occasion, had tried to get his dad to go along to the Grimsby match. However, when the day came around, 'He made up some excuse why he couldn't make it. I knew she'd asked him, and I thought maybe he would turn up, but when he didn't I was disappointed not surprised… It's hard; you just want to look to the sideline and see your dad.' Sadly, when we talked, Ed said he hadn't spoken to his dad in three years and didn't envisage that changing.

Against Grimsby, Ed was outstanding and the game ended in a goalless draw. He confirms with a rueful smile that there was no 'clean sheet' bonus in his contract: 'I should have negotiated one.' Ed did however get a good write-up the next day in *The Sun*'s match report.

The final game of Tony Roberts's suspension saw Dagenham travel to Sincil Bank to play Lincoln. This was a homecoming of sorts for Ed, returning to the city where he'd been a student. During his three years at university, he had grown an affinity for Lincoln and even went to watch the Imps' play-off final in Cardiff in 2005. He says coming back to play there was a dream. Lots of his Lincolnshire-based friends were in the crowd and there was an article about him in the local press, but the game ended disappointingly for Dagenham who suffered a 2-0 defeat.

Ed was fully aware that Tony Roberts would now come back into the side and resolved to work hard in training, keep improving and wait for his next opportunity to come. But as the season went on, the rigours of training prompted a historical knee injury, initially sustained playing for Wingate, to re-emerge. His knee was swelling up each time he trained and on a couple of occasions it actually locked. Whereas the original injury had never been properly diagnosed, Dagenham had the resources to get an MRI scan done. The club physio judged that Ed could make it through to the end of the season, but would then need an operation to tidy up the wear and tear in the joint. The operation was successful and the surgeon said that although there was a slight bone abnormality it was not serious; Ed would be fine to resume training when pre-season came around.

He recalls coming back from his knee operation feeling strong, ready to work hard and build on the experience he'd had of playing in the first team. His form in training that summer was good. But such are the vagaries of goalkeeping, during a pre-season friendly against Erith and Belvedere, he explains he had a nightmare match. Blaming himself for the goals conceded, he says his confidence melted away faster than an ice cream on a hot day by the Essex seaside. In most walks of life when an employee has had a knock to their confidence, you'd hope for a manager who could put an arm around them, literally or metaphorically and help lift their spirits with an offer of support or extra coaching. In football, however, there remains a certain old school 'wisdom' that the way to get the best out of people is to hammer them. What Ed recalls straight after his dip in the Erith game is John Still, shouting in front of all his team-mates, 'Fuck off, you're not good enough. You're never gonna play, too quiet. Fuck off, don't bother coming in tomorrow!'

While Ed laughs in recounting this, it is clear by how accurately he can impersonate Still's voice that those words are burnt into his memory. 'It broke me. I was devastated and took it badly... For a spell of games after that I was terrible.' Opposition players would be in his ear during games after any sort of mistake, again testing him mentally, and he recalls his own belief in his ability to play at this level was being 'annihilated'.

Although Ed says what Still did was wrong, he is quick to add that he owes him a great deal for giving him his chance at Dagenham. One of the players who had worked under John Still for many years explained that all the players had received this treatment at one time or another. The key was to take it on the chin, not let it affect you and show a positive response. 'But unfortunately for me it went the wrong way. The next game I was a nervous wreck and I made another mistake. We played a friendly against Gillingham and I had a shocker; a ball went over my head. After the game, I spoke to the manager and said I don't know what's going on.' Still responded by saying that there had been a scout from another club watching Ed that day having enquired about taking him on loan, but on the basis of his performance they would not be following up their interest.

Ed recalls feeling so low at that point that he even suggested that a loan to a non-league side might enable him to regain his confidence. 'It wasn't a nice place to be, you just want to disappear, you dread going into the training ground. Although probably the other boys aren't talking about you, you feel like they are. As a goalkeeper you need your players to believe in you, you get your confidence from that. If they are thinking, "He's going to throw another one in," you go into training trying not to make eye contact with people. I remember going to training during that spell and I wasn't even playing in the practice games, I was on the side watching as the keeper behind me would play and had sort of taken the number two role. I think that was part of the test as well. Maybe John Still wanted to take the pressure off me. I wasn't loving the game at that point. There are dark times as a footballer.'

The sense of relief is still palpable today as Ed explains that things turned round for him in the next friendly game he played when he suddenly hit good form again. 'It was all new to me; it was hard learning, but in the end it makes you tougher and as a keeper you have got to be strong mentally.' Ed credits John Still for always being honest with him and teaching him a lesson that he feels applies to both football and life in general. 'He said something that has always stuck with me: "Never get too high if you win, or too low if you lose." The more you mature the more you realise that's right.'

Ed's contract with Dagenham didn't pay enough for him to live on, and over the summer he was having to do some driving work for Danny's dad to supplement his wages. He explains that during his first year as a professional he had racked up serious credit card debts. He is quick to point out this was not due to excessive spending or a glamorous lifestyle. It was in order to pay for the basics, like putting petrol in the car to get to training. Ed feels that people have the wrong perception of professional footballers because of what they read about those at the top clubs. In fact, he says, in the lower leagues it is a hard living. 'I'm proud of having been a professional footballer, and in a way it was great; but from a financial standpoint I realise now that I sacrificed a lot.' It got to the stage where he had no choice but to approach Still to ask for a rise and thankfully he was offered an improved two-year contract. The thinking was that the contract would take him to 2010, at which time Tony Roberts would likely retire. Ed was hopeful he would establish himself as the long-term successor. When asked why the club had not paid him a living wage from the start Ed says, 'I don't know really. I think they try and get away with it.' When I suggest that really they are exploiting people who are pursuing a dream, he doesn't disagree. 'Pretty much, I wouldn't argue with that. Everyone I spoke to there was the same. But I saw boys start on that and then move on to really good money, so it was the chance.'

Cruelly, fate intervened before Ed could see exactly how far that chance would take him. As the season got under way his knee started locking up again. He was sent for another scan where it was determined that there was no cartilage left in the joint, two bones were rubbing together and fragmenting. He underwent surgery a second time and immediately started to do the rehab work, but just as he'd resumed training, the problem recurred. This time the specialist who examined him confirmed that there was nothing that could be done to stop the knee periodically locking. Ed explains he was having to ice his knee every day after training and there was no prospect of getting a move to another club as he would not pass a medical. 'So I knew I was a liability… I couldn't see any silver lining.' In theory, he could have sat out the remainder of his two year deal, but mentally he couldn't face it; and so he went to see John Still and they mutually agreed to cancel his contract. 'That was it. A day later I wasn't a footballer anymore.'

Now in the second half of his twenties, Ed had to go about finding something else to do. He says it was a tough time, with no job and lots of debt. 'For a couple of months I was down, I was probably depressed without realising it.' Understandably he says he felt cheated by circumstance. 'I gave up a lot, put a lot into it and it got snatched away from me. I felt bitter for a while, didn't want to play, didn't want to be around football; and then I started playing Sundays again [for the Wizards] and got back my love for the game. I still think about it, what might have been. You can't too much as you'd go crazy but I had a bit of a raw deal. Who knows what might have happened? I don't think I would have necessarily gone a lot higher but I would have had a good run of games in the lower leagues and been there at Wembley for the play-off final Dagenham got to, which would have been an amazing experience.' While it's clear that Ed has come to terms with the way his professional career ended, the fact he knows how many games Chris Lewington, the goalkeeper who replaced him, and then succeeded Tony Roberts, played for Dagenham (143) shows just how close he feels he was to that breakthrough. But as he says, 'Looking back, I had the chance to play in the league and the FA Cup and proved to myself I could do it.'

For a time after leaving Dagenham, his financial circumstances were so difficult that he had no choice but to ask the Professional Footballers' Association for some financial support, for which he is very grateful. It was to his best friend Danny, someone who could relate to that sense of mourning a career in professional football, that Ed turned as he tried to figure out what to do next. The result was that the two of them went into business together, creating what has become a very successful company, Green Planet Logistics. Each of them has a young son of his own now and if I were a Premier League scout, I'd be sure to go and watch the pair of them once they are old enough to start playing Sunday football.

Chapter Nine

Roy of the Red Imps

ONE member of the Southgate Saints team we never managed to bring into the Wizards' fold was Roy Chipolina. Danny remembers Roy, the schoolboy footballer, as a Gary Lineker-type goal poacher who for the Saints and school team would regularly clock up 50 goals in a season.

Roy was born in Enfield, north London, but aged four moved to the British Overseas Territory of Gibraltar, where his family is originally from. Roy remembers playing youth football there, which given that the population of Gibraltar is around 30,000, consisted of just six teams in the league and wasn't particularly competitive. As a 12-year-old, Roy moved back to north London, initially going to school in Wood Green before moving to Southgate School. Here he joined the same year group as Danny and became a mainstay of the school team and the Saints. 'I loved every minute of Sunday League… every game in the Cheshunt League was competitive and enjoyable.'

Being part of two successful sides as a schoolboy, Roy was selected to play for Hertfordshire County and was another of the Saints who attracted attention from professional clubs. He had a trial period with Luton Town and trained with them for three months. He then spent a week at Leyton Orient and played in one trial game, but regrettably for Roy, that was as far as it went. Aged 18, he decided to move back to Gibraltar to live with his nan; he recalls finding the relaxed lifestyle and sunny climate very attractive. Reflecting on that decision, Roy has a slight tinge of regret at giving up on his dream of playing professionally in England. 'It's disappointing really; I would have liked to have had at least a few more opportunities. Maybe I should have stayed a bit longer in England and tried at the lower leagues... to be honest, I was a bit too young, and I suppose naive, in giving up and moving to Gibraltar.' Comparing his own talent to that of those Saints who did get to turn professional, and seeing the challenges his friends subsequently faced to establish themselves, Roy is under no illusion about how difficult it would have been to make a career in the game.

Even while still at Southgate School, Roy would spend holidays in Gibraltar, and so he started training with the youth side of Lincoln Red Imps, one of Gibraltar's leading teams. When Roy moved back to Gibraltar permanently it was natural for him to reconnect with the Red Imps. All football in Gibraltar at this time was amateur and like all the other top-flight sides, they played in the Victoria Stadium. Space in Gibraltar is very much at a premium as the entire peninsula is contained within 2.6 square miles. A football stadium has a very significant footprint. Roy explains that the Victoria Stadium has one of the most spectacular vistas of any football stadium in the world, with the iconic Rock of Gibraltar behind one goal and Gibraltar Airport and the planes taking off and landing on its runways behind the other. Over the course of the next decade Roy was converted into a rock-solid centre-half and became captain of the team that in the 2015/16 season won their 14th consecutive league title.[25]

---

25 At the time of writing, according to the records kept by the Rec.Sport. Soccer Statistics Foundation, this is the best ongoing run in any top-flight domestic league in world football, and the joint best ever run of consecutive league titles in Europe held along with Skonto Riga who won the Latvian League 14 times between 1991 and 2004.

It was through his performances for the Red Imps that Roy was selected to play for the Gibraltar national team. Despite having a tradition of playing international football since 1923 and a Football Association founded in 1895 (pre-dating such footballing powerhouses as France (1919), Germany (1900), Italy (1898) and Spain (1909)), Gibraltar had been unsuccessful in gaining UEFA membership. This was largely due to resistance from Spain, which scuppered Gibraltar's applications to UEFA in 1999 and 2007. For political reasons, Spain went so far as to threaten to withdraw all its teams from UEFA competitions in 2007 should Gibraltar's bid succeed; Spain feared that Gibraltar gaining recognition as an independent football team undermined the Spanish claim to sovereignty over the territory. Gibraltar had been ceded to the British under the terms of the 1713 Treaty of Utrecht, which ended hostilities between the two powers in the War of the Spanish Succession. Potentially even worse from Spain's point of view, was the possibility that Gibraltar gaining UEFA membership would create a precedent for Catalan or Basque 'national' teams.

The Gibraltar national team, although not hailing from an actual island, was therefore confined to playing against the likes of the Isle of Wight, Jersey and the Isle of Man at the biennial Island Games, a multi-sports event first held in 1985 and organised by the International Island Games Association. Roy scored two goals against Orkney in his Island Games debut in 2001 and went on to represent Gibraltar multiple times in this competition over the next ten years. He was an integral part of the 2007 side that won the gold medal by defeating Rhodes 4-0 in the final.

Although Roy was aware of the Gibraltar Football Association's continuing efforts to be admitted into UEFA, he had been told that the chances were remote. As he was in his late twenties by this stage, it seemed that his appearances in the Island Games would be the high point of his international career. Roy recalls, however, that after 2011 the landscape had shifted; people he knew involved in football administration and the media started to express a new optimism that there was now a real chance that Gibraltar would attain UEFA status. Since the unsuccessful 1999 vote, Gibraltar had taken its claim to the Court of Arbitration for Sport (CAS). Its case hinged on the fact that it was only after Gibraltar had submitted its application that UEFA changed its statutes to confine membership to those countries that are sovereign states. This was despite the fact that non-independent states such as Wales and Scotland were afforded UEFA membership in 1954 (its inaugural year) and the Faroe Islands were admitted as recently as 1990. In an interview with Charlotte Simmonds in the *New Statesman* in spring 2014, Dennis Beiso, the chief executive officer of the Gibraltar FA, explained, 'It became very clear to us through subsequent conversation that UEFA's rules had been changed precisely because of our application and the difficulty this created for Spain.'

In the interview, Beiso explains the Gibraltar FA's position. 'It was unfair, immoral, even illegal for our case to be considered with a new set of rules.' Doggedly determined, Gibraltar went to CAS three times.

On the first occasion, CAS ruled that Gibraltar was entitled to membership of UEFA, but this failed to move UEFA. On the second appeal in 2006, CAS said that Gibraltar's membership must be considered at the next UEFA congress of members. Despite this, in the vote at the 2007 congress only three UEFA nations supported Gibraltar's application, thanks to the clout held by Spain in European football. This prompted Gibraltar to go back to CAS a third time.

'The third [ruling] in 2011 was the strongest of all – it stated that not only was Gibraltar entitled to membership; it should be admitted at the next congress.'

It was with this judgement that Roy's life in football really changed. The Grosvenor House Hotel in London, rather than the Victoria Stadium, was to be the scene of Gibraltar's greatest footballing triumph, as on 24 May 2013 the 53 UEFA national federations voted to make Gibraltar UEFA's 54th and smallest member.

The news of the decision, although anticipated, was greeted with delirious scenes back home. According to Roy, people in Gibraltar follow football to an 'unbelievable' level and because of the territory's geography and history, many people also follow a team in both England and Spain. Roy however has no split loyalties; he is Arsenal through and through. A parade was organised in Gibraltar to mark the UEFA announcement, and all Gibraltar FA-registered junior and senior players and officials assembled in the main piazza. Dressed in their kits, they walked en masse to Casemates Square, where a large stage had been erected. Here speeches were made by the mayor, the president of the Football Association, and the chief minister of the territory. Roy and his team-mates of the senior Gibraltar men's team, many of whom were veterans of past Island Games campaigns, took to the stage to a huge ovation from the jubilant crowd, as the realisation sank in. From now on, the team's fixture list would swap matches against small islands like Guernsey for full UEFA European Championship qualifiers against the best national teams in Europe. Roy would now be sharing a pitch with world-class players he had spent so many years watching on TV plying their trade in the Champions League, European Championships and World Cup.

He admits he felt a certain sadness that the decision had not come a few years earlier. He was fully aware of the positive changes that would now flood through football in Gibraltar, the forging of links to professional clubs and the opportunities for young players to develop their game in UEFA Under-17 and 19 tournaments. It is only natural for him to wonder where this might have taken him had this happened ten years earlier. But he quickly snaps out of that line of thought. 'That's looking at it negatively I suppose. I am very lucky that it happened before I retired.'

Gibraltar would not be able to play their European Championship qualification games at the Victoria Stadium as it does not meet UEFA's criteria. Given that Spain had opposed Gibraltar's right to play as a UEFA nation, using a Spanish stadium to play 'home' matches[26] was out of the question. It was therefore to the other Iberian footballing powerhouse, Portugal, that Gibraltar turned.

A deal was reached to allow them to play their home qualifiers at the Estadio Algarve in Faro. This stadium had been built for the European Championship tournament hosted by the Portuguese in 2004, and with a capacity of 30,000 was capable of holding the entire population of Gibraltar! Less than six months after the UEFA announcement, this was the venue for Gibraltar's first full international, which was against Slovakia, giving them crucial experience ahead of the European Championship campaign due to start in September 2014. 'So from May to November we went literally from playing Sunday League football to playing Slovakia. When you look at it like that, it's just mad!'

The extent of the challenge faced by the Gibraltar FA in building a team to take on a nation like Slovakia is perhaps best illustrated by the fact that there are only 600 registered footballers in Gibraltar, about the same number of players as in the Edmonton and District Sunday Football League. As skipper of the all-conquering Red Imps, Roy had been made captain of the Gibraltar team after their last appearance at the Island Games, and for manager Allen Bula he remained the natural choice to wear the armband. 'It was just unbelievable; to be honest, being captain of my club team here in Gibraltar didn't really mean that much.

'I'm just the captain and that's it. But then when you are told you are going to be the captain of your nation against countries

---

26 A well-established practice for footballing minnows like Andorra, who played several qualifiers in the Olympic Stadium in Barcelona, the former home of RCD Espanyol.

in UEFA, for me that was like a dream come true. It was a lot to take in, a lot of pressure, especially when the manager took me to one side and said, "There is a lot expected of you, things are changing," and how I had to be a role model for the youth of Gibraltar and so forth.'

Just like the players, Bula was on a steep learning curve. Having been at the team's helm since 2010, he was now charged with leading a group of amateur footballers into the ultra-professional cauldron of international football. It was the news that Bula had approached his nephew, Danny Higginbotham, that really brought the Gibraltar story to the attention of the press in the UK. Higginbotham, the former Manchester United and Stoke defender, who by the 2013/14 season was winding down his playing career, would be able to bring to the team a wealth of experience of playing in big games in big stadiums.

In Gibraltar this sparked a debate in sections of the media, the kind of debate that many a Sunday League team faces, namely the need to balance loyalty to the regular players there from the start with the desire to be as competitive as possible. It would be unfair to say that Higginbotham was a ringer as he met the eligibility criteria set out by football's governing bodies, but some in Gibraltar were not happy.

Their concern was that the Gibraltar national team, an important symbol of their identity, was being diluted. Several UK-based players were selected whose only affinity to the territory came through their parents being born while their grandfathers were stationed on the rock during service in the UK armed forces. The call-up for Scott Wiseman, at that time plying his trade with Barnsley in the Championship, and who had previously represented England at Under-20 level, was another case in point.

Roy's view was a pragmatic one. 'At the end of the day there are criteria players have to meet and if they do then I suppose people have to lump it really. You only have to look at Spain – they even have Diego Costa, and that's Spain, so why wouldn't

Gibraltar do the same thing?[27] Spain have got the best players in the world and even they bring in some extra ammunition. To be honest, those players have improved us already, the knowledge they bring to the game. In Gibraltar we are sort of raw talent, not tactically minded... being in UEFA will bring better coaching.'

Roy says he was hugely impressed by Higginbotham, who went on to make his international debut for Gibraltar in the game against Slovakia a month shy of his 35th birthday. In particular Roy remembers Higginbotham giving a little pep talk to the players in the dressing room ahead of the game. 'I thought, blimey, look how professional he is when he is talking and how far behind I am.' In fact for Roy it was all a case of learning on the job. As captain of a UEFA country, he was now required to answer questions with statesmanlike diplomacy at official press conferences covered by both print and television journalists. Unlike the other national team captains, most of whom had graduated through the ranks at some of European football's biggest club sides, Roy had not had the luxury of media training. He remembers not feeling that comfortable with his media responsibilities as skipper, although he can laugh about it now. 'To be honest, I get a bit embarrassed. I look at myself and I think, what the hell am I doing here? I am just a Sunday League player sort of thing... I shouldn't be here, do you know what I mean? As the last two years have gone by and I have done a few press conferences and so forth you start coming to terms with it and start settling down, but the first few interviews and press conferences with all the cameras and stuff like that, it was just too much really.'

Despite perhaps some natural feelings of inadequacy off the pitch, on it Roy and his team-mates battled their way to a

27 Costa was born in Brazil and represented them at full international level, but following his omission from the 2013 Confederations Cup squad, and having been granted Spanish citizenship, he took advantage of FIFA's rule that players who had only played in friendly games could switch to play for another country provided they were eligible. Costa went on to play for Spain in the 2014 World Cup, ironically held in Brazil.

remarkable 0-0 draw in the friendly against Slovakia. 'For us that was like a victory. We were expecting to get hammered. Let's face it, we had our backs against the wall the whole game and it was just unbelievable to get a draw.' Perhaps the only thing that could have made this result sweeter would have been had the team's maiden match been held on the rock itself, rather than in front of a largely empty stadium in the Algarve. Nevertheless, 500 fans had travelled to Portugal to see history being made.

In February 2014, Roy and the other members of the squad gathered, wearing their official red and white Gibraltar Admiral team tracksuits, in a large suite of the Rock Hotel to watch on television as the draw for the 2016 UEFA European Championship qualifying groups was made in Nice. This was a particularly special moment for the Gibraltar players. As Roy explains, 'Most of us had been playing together since we were 14 and a few since we were six or seven years old, so it's been a long journey.' Perhaps more than any international football team in the world, the sense of togetherness resonates through the Gibraltar squad. 'One of our stronger points as a nation is we have known each other such a long time we are like a family.'[28]

Gibraltar were to be drawn from pot six, which featured all of European football's minnows: Luxembourg, Kazakhstan, Liechtenstein, Faroe Islands, Malta, Andorra and San Marino. Ironically, when the draw was made Gibraltar were placed in the same group as Spain; but it had already been determined that the two could not be in a group together, giving the lie to the oft-used phrase 'politics has no place in sport'. And so Gibraltar were switched into Group D, which would pit them against Georgia, Poland, the Republic of Ireland, Scotland and the most illustrious team of all in the European game, Germany. The delirious reactions of the assembled squad were recorded on camera as part of a documentary film being made about the team. Roy explains his thinking at the time of the draw: 'People

---

28 Not just a figure of speech – the squad includes three brothers, Lee and Ryan Casciaro (both police officers) and Kyle Casciaro (a shipping agent).

asked me, "Who do you want?" And I said, "The strongest teams!" With no disrespect to the smaller nations, you want to play against Germany. England would have been fantastic, but those are the nations you want to be facing. Chances are we are going to get beaten in almost every game, but at least you get to play against the best players in the world. Not only did we get Germany, but if you look at the groups we more or less got the strongest team out of each pot. Apart from us, it's going to be a very competitive group.'

In the month following the draw, Gibraltar played their second ever full international friendly, this time on proper home soil against the Faroe Islands at the Victoria Stadium.[29] It was in this game on 1 March 2014 that Roy recorded another remarkable piece of personal history as he became the first man to score a goal for Gibraltar in an official UEFA game, stooping to head home a corner at the back post. 'I think everyone was too busy trying to mark Danny Higginbotham and no one marked me. It was just a free header – I was surprised to be left in so much space.' Although Roy's goal put Gibraltar ahead in the game, the final score was a 4-1 defeat, which served as a severe reality check for everyone involved. The prospect of the likely scoreline teams like Germany could run up against them began to bite. A few days later some pride was restored in a spirited performance against Estonia, which ended in a 2-0 defeat. This was Danny Higginbotham's last match for Gibraltar; having decided not to play in the qualifiers, he retired from international football. In June, Gibraltar achieved their first victory, beating Malta 1-0 in Portugal in their fifth official game.[30]

---

29 The Victoria Stadium pitch is an artificial surface; the 'soil' is made up of small bits of black rubber that leave a breadcrumb-like trail to wherever the player and his boots have gone after the game.

30 Until Gibraltar's election to UEFA, San Marino had been the smallest nation in European football; it took them 14 years and 65 matches to record their first win (a 1-0 triumph over Liechtenstein) having played their first official game in 1990.

8 July 2014 was a particularly memorable day for Roy. Lincoln Red Imps were playing the second leg of their UEFA Champions League qualification tie against HB Torshavn of the Faroe Islands. As champions of Gibraltar, now part of UEFA, the Lincoln Red Imps had proudly become the first club side from the Rock to play Champions League football. But disappointingly for Roy, the famous Champion's League music is not played while the players line up before kick-off in the first qualifying round. 'We were looking forward to just standing in line while the music played, but at that stage of the competition they don't do it.' Following a 1-1 draw in the first leg, the Red Imps lost the away leg 5-2. Had they progressed, they could have met teams of the calibre of former European Cup winners Celtic and Steaua Bucharest, but it was not to be.[31]

On the day his club team lost out, the eyes of the footballing world were elsewhere as the World Cup built to its climax. Football fans will remember where they were on 8 July 2014 as Germany demolished Brazil 7-1 in the World Cup semi-final in Belo Horizonte. Of course for Roy and the whole of Gibraltar this result had extra significance. Roy recalls his reaction to the scoreline – aware that he would be leading the national team onto the pitch away in Germany in less than six months' time. 'You are thinking, "Oh my God!" It's very scary. Everyone in Gibraltar was thinking, "If they can do that to Brazil, what are they going to do to us?" It's going to be a cricket score.'

Ahead of Gibraltar's first European Championship qualifier against Poland in September 2014, manager Allen Bula had defiantly been talking up the team's chances of making the play-offs by finishing third in the group. The reality for Roy, however, was that he was going head-to-head with one of the

---

31 Roy was not to be denied for too long. At the start of the 2016/17 season, having narrowly seen off Estonia's Flora Tallinn, the Lincoln Red Imps advanced to the second qualifying round of the Champions League where they met Celtic. Remarkably, the Red Imps beat the Glasgow giants 1-0 in the first leg of the tie but were eliminated from the competition following a 3-0 defeat at Celtic Park a week later.

best goalscorers in world football, Robert Lewandowski. It was a difficult period for the players, as Roy explains. The domestic league season in Gibraltar hadn't yet resumed and so some of the squad hadn't played any competitive matches in the run up to the tie. 'Our preparation wasn't the best, let's put it that way. You go from having your summer holidays, a few BBQs and the rest of it, and then you get on the pitch and you are playing against Lewandowski and Poland.'

As captains, Roy and Lewandowski were required to perform the customary coin toss and exchange of pendants as equals, despite the gulf between them. Lewandowski had become a Bayern Munich player that summer on a five-year deal earning a reported 11 million euros a season. Roy, on the other hand, explains how he has had to fit his career as an international footballer around his day job as a customs officer. 'It's been very hard. I used to do shift work but since UEFA membership I have moved into the office on regular hours. Whereas before if I was on night shifts it was impossible to train, now I am in the office it makes things a lot easier.' As a government employee, Roy was initially granted ten days' special leave a year to represent his country, but this only went so far with the training and international travel required, even for their home games. It has therefore been necessary for him to take unpaid leave to play for Gibraltar. 'So I lose money to play basically. But let's face it, you'd pay money to play these teams!'

Against all odds, during the first half of Gibraltar's maiden competitive game, Roy was able to keep Lewandowski at bay and off the scoresheet. At the interval Roy and his team-mates left the pitch only 1-0 down. Any chance of an upset result, however, was swept away in a tidal wave of Polish attacks at the start of the second half, which yielded four further goals in 11 minutes. With the Gibraltar players out on their feet, by full time it was 7-0 and Lewandowski had scored four. Roy explains what the experience of trying to mark a player of that quality had been like for him. 'Lewandowski, whatever I did I couldn't get the ball off him; if

I got too close to him he'd take one touch and be away; if I gave him two yards he'd keep it. He never made the wrong decision and I think that's the difference between the top players and us. They make the right decision every time, and you make it maybe one out of ten sort of thing... They make the decision of what to do with the ball before they have received it, whereas you make the decision once you receive it; by the time you have got the ball under control you have four men around you... It's just an honour to be on the same pitch as him.' Roy remembers as the final whistle blew he was close to the Polish skipper and found a last reserve of energy to beat his team-mates when it came to the exchange of shirts. 'Everyone wanted Lewandowski's shirt but I pulled rank on that.'

Gibraltar's next outing a month later saw them travel to Dublin to take on Martin O'Neill's Republic of Ireland. The opening stages of the game again reflected the harsh realities of football at the highest level. Before the amateur players in the Gibraltar team could adapt to the atmosphere of playing in front of 35,123 people, they found themselves 3-0 down inside 20 minutes with Robbie Keane netting a hat-trick. A further burst of four goals in 11 minutes soon after half-time left Roy and Gibraltar on the end of another seven-goal defeat. The goals conceded are hard to watch and resembled Sunday morning football far more than a competitive full international. Gibraltar goalkeeper, Jordan Perez, a fireman by trade, endured a particularly difficult afternoon where he conceded a penalty, scored an own goal and faced the humiliation of being substituted immediately after conceding the seventh goal of the game. Whether it be in a brand-new, world-class stadium or the local authority-owned pitches in north London, there is nothing worse than seeing a goalkeeper go through the mill. No words can console you.

Watching Perez trudge off the pitch when his number was held up transported me back to my 12-year-old self, where after one game in which I had dived over a ball and made a mess of a back pass I came off the pitch in tears, preparing myself to answer that most embarrassing question when I walked through the front door and saw my mum: 'How did you get on at football?'

After running himself into the ground, Roy was also substituted around the hour mark in Dublin, and soon found the Ireland captain whom he had struggled to subdue on the pitch joining him on the sideline. This gave Roy the chance to jump to the front of the queue at the final whistle and again acquire the most high-profile shirt from the opposition. Roy describes captain and record goalscorer, Keane, as he does Lewandowski. 'They were very down-to-earth; I didn't think they would have time for me, but they were good guys.' Roy explains he hasn't yet decided what to do with the shirts he has collected, and has resisted framing them thus far. Ideally he would have liked to get them signed at the return fixtures, although he concluded, 'I think I'd better just frame them. It would be a bit too amateur to say "Robert, I got this shirt off you last time, would you mind signing it for me?!"'

While humouring my fascination about how he has rubbed shoulders with star players, Roy also makes it clear that for him the inevitable initial feelings of being star-struck, experienced by all the Gibraltar squad, had to be overcome with increased professionalism both in their preparation and during matches. 'Now we just accept, let's get on with it, we're here to play football not to meet anyone famous.' Three days after the chastening Republic of Ireland game, a much more competitive Gibraltar lost only 3-0 at home to Georgia. Gibraltar even managed to get the ball in the net for what would have been their first-ever competitive goal but Roy explains it was wrongly disallowed. A foul was given against Roy as the ball came in from a corner. 'I don't know what the ref saw.'

Despite this improvement in the margin of defeat, there was a clear sense of trepidation among the squad as they prepared to meet the world champions in Nuremberg in November 2014. Immediately following the Georgia game, tensions between the manager and the Gibraltar FA began to show, leading to Allen Bula publicly stating that he was being pushed out of his role. Originally, there had been plans for Danny Higginbotham to join his backroom staff but this had not materialised. Disagreements over the levels of funding and what could be expected of the team surfaced.

Even as the squad assembled in the days before the game, the documentary cameras captured a row between Allen Bula and his assistant Davie Wilson, who voiced concerns that the players were not being prepared properly for facing the world champions. The cameras captured him telling Bula to do his 'fucking job', and promptly being ordered off the training pitch. This atmosphere could not have been ideal for Roy and his team-mates about to play the biggest game in their lives. Roy recalls his feelings on the eve of the game as he unsuccessfully tried to sleep. 'A lot of us stayed up chatting, you are so nervous, it's so exciting to be given this opportunity, but you are terrified at the same time.' The German media were speculating about how many goals their team could put past Gibraltar. Even Joachim Löw, the Germany manager, broke the normal protocols of international football by allowing himself to get drawn into a discussion at his pre-game press conference, about whether his team could eclipse the 16-0 by which Germany had beaten Russia at the 1912 Olympics in Sweden. Löw was quoted as saying, 'If the team play like I imagine, then we can set a new record.'

Any notion that Germany would put out a weakened side for the game was dispelled when Roy, as captain, signed off the team sheets ahead of kick-off. All the big guns were starting. He remembers reporting back to his team-mates in the dressing room that the Germans were not mucking around. Allen Bula's team talk before kick-off, filmed for the documentary, is all about the players enjoying themselves and playing with a smile on their faces.

For me as a player who found even an 'important' Sunday League game would set my stomach churning, this seems an impossible instruction to follow. But as the television cameras scroll along the line of Gibraltar players during the national anthems, somehow Roy manages a smile. He reflects on how moved he was by the fact that both national anthems were performed live by a brass band. 'It was an incredible moment, hairs standing up on the back of your neck.' Roy remembered the German anthem being powerful and intimidating even when he'd heard it from behind the safety of a television screen. Now here he was facing the fittest, most experienced big-game players and current world champions, in front of a capacity German crowd of over 44,000. 'So much to take in, you just forget where you are; but once the game has started you are so concentrated, focused on not getting turned inside out. You sort of block it out, but the atmosphere is incredible, you can't really hear, you are screaming but people can't hear you. Unbelievable really. But the excitement takes over and you just run until you can't run anymore.'

Roy explains that for the Germany game he had been moved from his normal position in central defence in order to play the holding-midfielder role. 'You call it centre-mid, but it's actually an extra defender. Their centre-backs were playing on the edge of our box.'

When I asked at what point the reality dawned on him, Roy replied with a laugh. 'There were moments to be honest when Toni Kroos received the ball, and for that split second I was thinking, bloody hell that's Toni Kroos! It's so surreal, so much to take in, when actually you have just got to be concentrated on playing football.' It is indicative of how serious Roy is about his football and his position as national team captain that when I ask him if he has a favourite pass or tackle he made as an individual during the game, something every Sunday League player can take home and focus on even after the worst defeat, Roy instead stresses it was the team's overall performance and the way they collectively stuck together that night in Nuremberg. Incredibly, despite conceding a very soft first goal, late in the first half Gibraltar were only 3-0 down. Just before the break they took a quick throw-in, and Liam Walker hit a looping half-volley from well outside the 18-yard box on the angle, which sent the world's best goalkeeper, Manuel Neuer, furiously back-pedalling to claw away the ball from under his crossbar. Roy recounts how during the half-time interval Mario Götze, the scorer of the winning goal in the World Cup Final in Brazil a few short months earlier, 'knocked on our dressing room door asking for Liam Walker's shirt at the end of the match. Unbelievable!' Gibraltar held Germany to a solitary goal in the second half. The 4-0 defeat was a result that felt like a victory to the Gibraltar players and to put the cherry on the cake, Roy was able to secure Thomas Müller's shirt at full time. 'My thinking was in the long term he might end up the highest scorer in the history of the World Cup, so I'll take that one just in case.'

Such was the scale of what Gibraltar had achieved in that 90 minutes, by the time the post-match interviews began, all talk of record scorelines had been banished. Roy found himself being asked by one journalist whether the result in fact meant Gibraltar were better than Brazil, to which he jokingly replied, 'Yeah, that's what the scoreline says.'

Roy's involvement with Gibraltar afforded me the chance to do something with my dad I had always meant to – watch Scotland play an international at Hampden Park. Gibraltar's visit to Glasgow coincided with changing the clocks to mark the end of winter. It was Sunday 29 March 2015, although as dad and I made the trip from his house in Edinburgh on the train the sun was nowhere to be seen. The wind and rain whipped down as we arrived at Hampden two and a half hours before the game. We sussed out where the team coaches would pull in so we could wave at Roy. As the rain poured down, numerous coaches came and went. We stood marvelling at the number of Scotland and Gibraltar fans who had come to the game in only a replica shirt and kilt in defiance of the weather. Eventually the Scotland team arrived all clad in Beats headphones and Scotland Adidas red polo shirts with team sponsor, Vauxhall, emblazoned across the front. We shared a laugh along the lines 'shit cars for a shit team', which tapped into my dad's very genuine anxiety that Scotland were going to be humiliated by Roy and his team-mates. Thoroughly soaked by the Glasgow rain and no longer able to feel our hands and feet, we realised that the game was due to kick off in 20 minutes and noticed through an emergency exit that both sides were already out on the pitch warming up. The Gibraltar coach must have gone in through a different entrance.

We took our seats, which happened to be at the end Gibraltar were warming up, and I set about telling everyone around me that I had gone to school with the Gibraltar captain. Given that we were sitting in the home end and I have a clear London accent, this did little to endear me to the Tartan army. I was absolutely transfixed watching Roy go through the series of drills known to every footballer from Sunday League clogger to top international star: keep ball, one two, then shot on goal. The surreal nature of the occasion for me was only added to when a severe gust of wind took hold of the Vauxhall inflatable, dragging the two poor fellas it was tethered to around the pitch before getting lodged behind an advertising hoarding, much to the delight of the 34,255 crowd. I hoped Roy had not noticed that on the big screens where they beam up a smiling picture of each player to show the starting line-up, the caption read, 'Number 6, Ray Chipolina'.

For this game Roy was again stationed just in front of the Gibraltar defence, patrolling an area the width of the 18-yard box. Gibraltar held out for the opening quarter of an hour before conceding a penalty. Only a minute later, though, Gibraltar stunned Hampden Park. Following a lovely passing move, Lee Casciaro drilled a low shot across the advancing goalkeeper and into the corner of the net to equalise. I felt particularly chuffed as when I'd talked to Roy ahead of the match, he'd mentioned that his work colleagues had been bantering him about when the team would score their first goal in the qualifying campaign. I'd said to him half-jokingly but half-knowingly on the basis of years of watching Scotland on television, that the moment would come for sure at Hampden Park. As the ball crossed the line, I couldn't help but jump to my feet. On the pitch, the Gibraltar players entered into some of the most joyous goal celebrations I have ever seen, while in the stands, the sizeable contingent of their red-clad fans took a break from ironically singing, 'We're from Gibraltar, we brought you the sun,' to revel in another bit of national footballing history.

All in all, Roy had an excellent game. He stifled waves of Scotland attacks as well as showing good quality on the ball before being withdrawn in the 74th minute with Gibraltar 4-1 down. By full time, Scotland had scored six and Steven Fletcher had completed the first hat-trick by a Scotland player for 46 years, a statistic that perhaps explains my dad's lack of optimism about his country's national team. In the queue for the train back from Hampden, we got chatting to a man who had come over from Gibraltar to watch the game with his son and grandchildren. He beamed with pride at what Roy and Gibraltar's other footballers had achieved. For the thousandth time that day, I waited for the opportunity to throw in how I went to school with the captain, but so thick was the man's accent that when I did it wasn't clear whether he had understood me. Dad and I demolished the only food available at Glasgow Queen Street at 9pm on a Sunday, a Burger King. I sat bemused as one set of Scotland fans on our train back to Edinburgh Waverley regaled the carriage with a chorus of 'Fuck the Pope'. My dad knowingly leaned over and told me that they'd be getting off at Falkirk, which they did.

For the train back to London on Monday, I bought a copy of *The Herald* newspaper because it had a big picture of Roy, celebrating the Gibraltar goal with his arms outstretched showing his blue captain's armband ready to hug the life out of Lee Casciaro. I was annoyed to read a patronising report of the game, where the journalist 'joked' that following their equaliser the Gibraltar captain didn't know how the game would be restarted as it had never happened before. I uttered to myself the word 'knob' rather too loudly for the liking of the woman next to me. As I scanned the paper for more remarks on the Gibraltar performance, I liked to think Gordon Strachan the Scotland manager had Roy in mind in particular when he said, 'All the credit should go to them today. They made my life a misery for periods of that game.'

Unfortunately for Roy, now in his thirties, it seemed the completion of the European Championship qualifiers would mark the end of his time as an international footballer. The world football governing body FIFA still did not consider Gibraltar to be an independent territory, having turned down their application for membership in September 2014. While Gibraltar took the all-too-familiar step of appealing to the Court of Arbitration for Sport on 21 May 2015 to try to overturn this decision, no ruling had been made in time for the FIFA Congress held a week later in Switzerland.[32] Gibraltar were therefore the only member of UEFA excluded from having the chance to play in the 2018 World Cup qualifiers. Roy told me at the time what this meant for the Gibraltar national team and for him personally. 'Who is going to want to play a friendly against us? Those two years will kill me off, I think. Time's not on my side.'

Nevertheless a year later, just days before the 2016 annual FIFA Congress was due to convene in Mexico City, the Court of Arbitration for Sport ruled that Gibraltar should be admitted as a full member and without delay. And so Gibraltar became the 211th member of FIFA, and will compete in the qualification campaign for the 2018 World Cup after all. Even had this late reprieve not arrived, Roy is fully aware of how fortunate he has been. 'To be honest with you, if you had told me three years

---

32 As it transpired, the 65th FIFA Congress in 2015 turned out to be a seminal event in the history of football, setting off a chain of events that eventually resulted in Sepp Blatter relinquishing his vice-like grip on the presidency of the game's governing body. Following investigations made by the FBI, and a series of dawn raids, nine FIFA officials were arrested two days before the Congress started, on suspicion of receiving bribes.

ago that I'd be playing against the world champions and I'd be captain of my nation, I would have thought you were crazy.' It's a real Roy of the Rovers tale.

Chapter Ten

Football, bloody hell!

WITHOUT Ed between the sticks, goalkeeping became a major issue for the Wizards at the start of the 2007/08 season. In fact in the course of our first five games we had five different people in goal. But rather than spending the summer trying to resolve this potentially season-defining issue we had instead decided that what we needed more was a new kit. Upgrading from Prostar to Nike. This time the new kit even came with matching socks, and not just any socks but orange ones with black trim that we soon discovered were impossible to replace once ripped. Luckily Mel was accomplished with a sewing needle.

Having spent the farm on kit, we had very little left in the coffers for anything else. This wasn't helped by the fact that there were always a couple of players, the same couple of players, who would 'forget' to bring their £5 subs every week.

For our first game of the season we had two balls to warm up with, one that did not bounce and another that you could only generously describe as round. I therefore turned to eBay to see if we could find a deal on a job lot of practice balls and found a set of 12 FILA footballs, a manufacturer far from synonymous with footballing excellence, with no bids on them. By the end of the week I ended up paying £20 for the lot, plus a bag to carry them in. Bargain. Or so it seemed until they arrived. The balls needed to be inflated, so that Saturday night I spent a lonely evening pumping up ball after ball with a little hand pump. What struck me about the balls as they expanded was how cheap they looked and also the undeniable fact that they stank. Not just a little bit. They absolutely overwhelmed the room with an invisible toxic cloud. Assuming this problem would wear off in time, I put my boots on and did a few kick-ups in the front room, knocking over a lamp and nearly taking out the TV screen in the process, and became aware that these balls were assaulting another of my senses: they were really painful to make contact with. Nevertheless, the prospect of graduating from having to play imaginary passes to each other in the warm-up the next morning was greeted with excitement from the boys. Secretly crossing my fingers, I tipped out the new balls onto the wet grass. After a few minutes, it was clear that the balls were absorbing a large amount of water and as they did so they became like boulders. They were so hard, we were risking injury even before the game started. A couple of weeks later, it was not difficult to decide what to do. We abandoned the balls strategically by the side of the pitch, hoping that one of the teams we didn't like very much might decide they couldn't look a gift horse in the mouth, and then live to regret it.

A new addition to the team that season was Daniele Cannas, one of the few good footballers from school who had up to now, whenever there was a social get-together, resisted our nagging to come down and play for the Wizards. I had played with and against Daniele in various teams since the age of ten and knew that he was a talented player in centre-midfield, who could win the ball back and then use it very efficiently. What I had forgotten was how much he enjoyed the verbal side of football. From the very first time he pulled on the orange shirt, Daniele exploited his gift to infuriate opposition players, delivering sly comments insinuating that their technique perhaps was not the best, or failing that, straight abuse accompanied by a smile, which only enraged them further. Such were his abilities as a communicator, language itself proved no barrier. One team we played that season had several players who spoke hardly any English, but this seemed no obstacle to Daniele. At one point in the game, the opposition's non-English-speaking number 8 seemed to reach breaking point, picking up the ball, running up to Daniele and booting a powerful volley up his backside. He may have been a team-mate and a friend, but it was hard to feel any sympathy since we knew more than likely he fully deserved it. Perhaps in a homage to this incident, upon scoring his first goal for us, an exquisite chip over the goalkeeper, reminiscent of Philippe Albert's against Manchester United for Newcastle, he ran into the goal, pulled his shorts and pants down and patted his bruised buttocks repeatedly. Both sets of players and referee looked on temporarily stunned by what they had witnessed.

As Christmas approached, our league season was going well. We were in contention for the title with a team called Clavisque, which made our first meeting with them all the more significant. This was a game that threw up something hitherto unheard of for us in Sunday football, the need for an away kit. Clavisque were the only other team in Edmonton who wore orange. Consequently, I had to scramble round to find an alternative for us to wear and managed to borrow a terrible dark blue set of shirts, styled straight out of 1995, from Alex, who had himself borrowed them from someone else as an away kit for *his* new team. The fashionistas in our side were quick to point out as I unpacked it from a black bin bag in the dressing room that the yellow sleeves and massive Cantona-style collars did not chime at all well with our orange socks, but I placated them by explaining how in fact the yellow brought out the colour in their eyes. And so we took to the pitch with a team of the bare XI and beat Clavisque 5-2.

Our title charge stalled in February, however, as we threw away a two-goal lead against Attitude to draw 2-2, and then the following week narrowly lost to a side called The Bull. The Bull were a big, powerful team and featured several players from the north-east and north-west of England. Their teammates had seemingly let their imaginations run wild in thinking up nicknames for these exotic imports. The big blond centre-midfielder from Newcastle, who was a decent player and a master of the acerbic one-liner, was inventively called 'Geordie'. The bad-tempered centre-forward from Liverpool was known as 'Scouse'. He was one of those players you come across in Sunday football who has zero sense of humour and seems to channel a week's worth of frustrations into 90 minutes of out-and-out aggression. Scouse spent the whole game kicking lumps out of me and mocking my subsequent protestations to the referee. At one point he attempted an overhead kick from the edge of the 18-yard box, and as I headed the ball clear his boot followed through into my face. Clearly contrite, he consoled me by offering the following words of wisdom: 'Don't put your fucking head in the way next time, you prick.'

I never resorted to having a cheap shot at someone like that off the ball, largely for fear of what might happen to me next. But the temptation was often strong given some of the characters we came up against. I had long ago concluded that fighting was not for me and I was confident I would be terrible at it. The game of football sometimes offers its own glorious opportunity for retribution nonetheless, particularly when you are playing centre-half. You find yourself praying for a short pass or loose touch which gives you the sweet opportunity of a 50-50 ball with your principal tormentor where you can launch yourself with absolutely everything you can muster into a slide tackle. Even if it means starting the slide from the other side of the pitch and ending it in the opposition's half. The key is to win the ball cleanly and not foul the opposing player as that would sully the beauty of that feeling of hitting a big tackle, something which I would say is comparable to the joy of scoring a goal. While I liked to think I was fearsome in the tackle, our player-manager,

Mickey, was a level beyond me. Again he always took the ball, but his tackling was so ferocious that opposing players generally opted out after their first interaction with him. If you were ever in earshot of Mickey as he went to ground in a tackle, as I often was when he partnered me in central defence, you could hear a guttural growl emanating from somewhere deep within him as he slid into the poor bastard in possession, and then a noise like a thunder clap as he connected with the ball. Chemically I think winning tackles did something to his brain; he was addicted to the feeling it gave him. Sometimes he would play on the right wing – he also moved like a runaway train and reinvented the conventional method of playing in that position. Countless times, rather than beating the opposing left-midfielder, left-back and anyone else who came across to that side of the pitch to cover, his first, second and third touches would all be tackles, one after another, until he had bulldozed himself the length of the pitch, leaving bodies strewn in his wake. Mickey would be the first to admit that having made these advances his final ball or shot was not always the most composed, but no matter, he would just get back in position and win the ball again. What a player he was!

That February of 2008, Spurs reached a cup final at the new Wembley stadium for the first time, against Chelsea in the League Cup. My joy at this prospect was diminished by the fact that the Wizards were due to play Attitude that morning in our second league meeting in a matter of weeks. I knew a few of our Tottenham-supporting players, including Danny, would want to savour a Spurs cup final appearance and make a day of it as reasonably they concluded the opportunity might not come round again soon. I decided to set a captain's example saying that I would play the game regardless and then go to Wembley directly in full, soiled Wizards kit if needs be. But my hope that this would prick other players' consciences was misguided, as Neil and Danny still said they were going to skip the Wizards game that day. My next move was to take a calculated risk. I contacted Carlo, the Attitude secretary, to see if he would agree to moving the kick-off forward by half an hour so that people had more time to get to Wembley after our game. I thinly tried to disguise that this was to ensure that some of our best players could play, which I imagined would be grounds for him to turn me down. As it turned out lots of his players were Spurs fans too, so he agreed. I felt like I had just solved the Cuban missile crisis, only for the other Spurs boys in our team to say they still weren't going to play. In the end, I gave up guilt tripping them and we took to the pitch that day against Attitude with the highest percentage of Arsenal fans in our starting XI ever. Happily we won the game 3-1, although already strained relations with Attitude took a further turn for the worse when, at 2-0 up, we put the ball out for an injured player to get some treatment. Instead of returning the ball to us in the time-honoured fashion, they launched a long throw into our box and scored, setting up a nervous finish to the game before we sealed it with a third goal in the final minutes.

The day had the perfect ending as Spurs came from behind to win the League Cup via a scruffy Jonathan Woodgate header in extra time.

Another landmark in the history of the Wizards was reached that season when club institution Matthew Berou scored his first goal in 128 appearances. Matt was an outstanding right-back who loved defending. Very much of the old school, his boots were always black with minimal design gimmickry and he viewed the phrase 'wing back' as a dirty bastardisation of the noble art of defending he had practised his whole life. If Matt ever crossed the halfway line he resembled a learner swimmer who had somehow found himself in the deep end when the wave machine was switched on. He would frantically back-pedal to the shallows of our own half. While his instincts played a huge part in our defensive solidity, it limited his chances for personal goalscoring glory. Whenever we got a corner Matt was stationed on the halfway line to ward off any counter attacks. Essentially the only way he would ever score would be if we were beating a side so emphatically that the outcome was certain, and then we got a penalty that he could take. This scenario had actually dawned three years previously in a game where we were seven goals to the good: the ref had pointed to the spot and I had used all my authority as captain to manoeuvre Matt into position for taking it. I must confess this came from a sense of curiosity as to how he would approach taking a spot kick as much as it did from benevolence towards my oldest friend. On that occasion, Matt scuffed his shot so badly the ball bounced about eight times during its anaemic 12-yard journey from penalty spot to goalkeeper's hands. It seemed Matt was destined never to score a goal for us, but then finally the circumstance arose again. Right at the end of a game against Haringey Athletic, where the points were already in the bag, the ref blew for a penalty. Immediately a cry went up from the touchline where Andy stood, 'Let Berou have it!' Matt stepped forward with the confidence of someone who had spent the intervening three years practising in his bedroom for this very moment. He clinically dispatched the ball into the corner of the net, sparking wild scenes of celebration where everyone in an orange shirt, subs and management piled onto the pitch and on top of him, much to the bafflement of the Haringey Athletic players, who just wanted to get home for Sunday dinner. Matthew Berou was christened BeRooney and was never allowed anywhere near a penalty ever again.

The points we had dropped against some of the weaker sides in the league meant Clavisque were just out of reach in the run-in and beat us to the title by two points, despite us beating them home and away. We were secure in second place though, which meant being elevated to the top division in Edmonton for the coming season, our third consecutive promotion. For the first time in what seemed like a Sunday League lifetime, Attitude would not be joining us as they had finished fourth behind The Bull and 13 points down on our total. It was probably a good thing that the rivalry would be put on ice for a season as it had started to turn spiteful, and there was a danger it would spill over were we to play them several times again the next year. However, as it turned out, both teams had again reached the cup final and so there was a chance to say a not-so-fond farewell to Carlo and the Attitude boys. Our cup final record against them was one victory each, but going into the game the consensus among our players was that we very much owed them one from the year before and their impromptu appearance at the pub.

From the start of that final we tore into Attitude and were 1-0 up inside five minutes, thanks to a typically smart finish from Eamon. I then got to enjoy a sweet moment of redemption. We had developed a highly potent long throw routine where I would stand parallel to the post on the six-yard box and Colin, who could throw the ball as far as most people can kick it, would put the ball on my head to flick on for one of our players to arrive and finish from close range. Very rarely would an opposing team put a player in front of me to stop me getting the flick; I usually didn't even have to move, and we scored a lot of goals this way. In the first half of the match we had several opportunities to deploy this sophisticated weapon. It may not have been to the liking of the footballing purists, but we knew it worked and we stuck at it. On about the fourth attempt my flick-on led to a scramble and the ball broke to the edge of the Attitude box, from where I retrieved it, cut inside a defender and drove a shot into the corner of the net.

It was a great personal moment for me. I had made amends for my sending off in last year's cup final. But the reaction of the Attitude players indicated trouble in their camp; words were being exchanged between their goalkeeper and the rest of the team. He hadn't been at fault for either goal, but it seemed some of his team-mates had said some things to him that he wasn't happy about. There was a lot of finger-pointing and even a bit of pushing. It was a bit like a replay of Bruce Grobbelaar versus Steve McManaman that time in the Merseyside derby, but without the handlebar moustache and beaded rat's tail, sadly. Attitude didn't have their usual intensity that day and seemed angry with the world, even more so than usual. They went down to ten men after one of their players threw a punch at Neil having been dispossessed of the ball. Although they did pull a goal back we felt comfortable in the game, which was very unusual playing against Attitude, and Eamon sealed victory with another clinical finish. It's fair to say we overdid our celebrations on the pitch at the full-time whistle which, while perhaps not being very sportsmanlike, felt good – especially as we knew what we would have endured had the roles been reversed. Finally, having collected the cup and our winners' medals, we exuberantly made our way to the changing room. Although we weren't to know it at the time, this was to be the last time the Wizards played in a cup final.

Events then took a strange turn. The Attitude goalkeeper who 12 months earlier had posted on their message board his whole-hearted endorsement and delight at their attempts to gatecrash and spoil our cup final celebrations, now came up to Mickey and asked where we were going for a celebratory drink and whether he could come along. Most of us had not heard this exchange, so when we later arrived at the Salisbury Arms, as was our tradition, it was bizarre to see him there already slightly the worse for wear having a beer with Robbo. As the afternoon turned to early evening and the drinks flowed, he started to say how he had fallen out with the other Attitude players in the week before the cup final. Daniele, who had not been involved in the last month of the season owing to injury, suggested to him that perhaps having a photo with the cup would cheer him up. A few drinks later Daniele had talked him into having another photo, this time using the lid of the cup as an impromptu hat. Having known Daniele for so many years I could guess where this was going. A few more drinks and he had convinced their keeper to give him the mobile phone number of Chas, one of the more combustible members of their team. The picture was sent, and with seemingly impossible speed lots of the Attitude team arrived at the pub, understandably irate about their own goalkeeper's actions hours after losing a cup final.

Up to this point the situation had been curiously amusing, but I feared now that things were going to get out of hand as they were insisting that the goalkeeper step out into the car park with them. A few of us intervened at this point and said he wasn't in a fit state to go anywhere, and eventually their players left. The prospect of getting beaten up by his own team-mates in a pub car park had obviously sobered him up a bit and he took himself home, leaving the rest of us to try and figure out what had happened. The idea of one of our players joining in an Attitude post-match celebration was beyond the realms of possibility, yet for some reason one of their players had taken it upon himself to come along to ours.

Seven years on, the treasure trove that is the Attitude FC website with its message board helps to shed some light on these strange events. In the build-up to the final the Attitude goalkeeper, who Carlo recalls was always 'untrustworthy', had been telling his team-mates he was leaving to play for the Wizards the next season. It seems there had been a falling-out in the squad after he had let them down by no-showing for a couple of big league games. The grounds for his claims were that apparently on a night out he had bumped into Robbo, who had drunkenly suggested he could come and play for us. (This is a type of throwaway comment often deployed in the Sunday League fraternity to defuse potentially awkward meetings with disliked opposition players away from the relative safety of your own team and referee.) It seems that the goalkeeper took this offer at face value, and when it appeared he might lose his place for the cup final against us, he decided to go on the offensive by announcing to the rest of the Attitude players he would be leaving to join their hated rivals, or as one of them put it on their message board, the 'Scummy Wizards'. The same player elaborated further, 'We stick to the 442 formation so we can get one over the soon to be Wizards goalie (fucking traitor) Lets all get r heads on the game lads and av no fights wit each other on the pitch I fink we all need to put R commitment on the field and not let it com out of our mouths. Lets fucking av it com on.' This rousing battle cry was echoed by another post: 'Come on lads lets fucking smash these wankers up.' It seems to have transpired, however, that the goalkeeper who was supposed to deputise dropped out in the run up to the game, and so it was that despite the acrimony they were forced grudgingly to play the 'fucking traitor' who after they lost the game was the focal point for their disappointment and who decided to throw petrol on the fire by joining us at the pub. Mystery solved. Yet again our cup final celebrations were overshadowed by Attitude, but this time it seemed a fitting way to say goodbye to them, the end of the Attitude era.

With the season over, Daniele's dad Toni was good enough to allow us to have our end of season awards night at his restaurant, La Scala, in Finchley. Danny had won the players' player award for the third season in a row; his 21 goals in 21 games from centre-midfield that year meant that, like in a FIFA presidential election, the vote was a foregone conclusion. I was delighted to win the runners-up prize of manager's player. The gloss was slightly taken off this in that as secretary it was my job to organise the trophies ahead of the awards night, including ordering my own. The Edmonton League had a partnership with LRS Engravers. Each year towards the end of the season a friendly chap called Steve, who looked like he should have been playing bass guitar for Chas and Dave, would come to the monthly league meeting to promote his wares. We put our trophy orders in, making sure that the trophy I chose for myself was fractionally smaller than the one for Danny to ensure that no one thought I was getting above my station.

LRS Engravers were located at a residential address in Palmers Green a short drive from my house, and given that time was tight, once he had done the engraving on them, Steve kindly let me pop round to his house to collect them. There were also 16 runners-up medals presented by the League to mark our promotion to the top flight. My mum gave me a lift to the address

I'd been given, and as we pulled up to the house with a scruffy front garden I spotted a wooden LRS sign. I rang the doorbell and Steve beckoned me in as he gathered up everything marked 'Wizards'. It was like walking into a pirates' cave of treasure, but instead of Cortes' cursed coins the hallway and house as far as the eye could see were filled with polystyrene crates holding small gold-coloured plastic statuettes of distinctly 1980s-looking young footballers affixed to faux wooden plinths forever frozen mid-scissor kick, towering header or sprawling save, ready to be re-homed depending on what position a given team's player of the year played in. I thanked Steve, took the boxes marked Wizards, and stowed them in the car. On the way home I was musing that in place of years spent earning these trophies by dint of effort on the football pitch, cold hard cash could bring you all the trophies and medals you ever wanted. I bet there are more than a few Sunday League footballers out there with a medal haul they impress the grandkids with that bears no relation to games won and lost. This chain of thought was interrupted as my mum reversed into our driveway a little too fast, misjudging our proximity to the sharp corner of the ledge on the front room bay window, which smashed through the rear windscreen, showering the precious trophy cargo in tiny pieces of square glass.

At the awards night I did my best to act surprised as Mickey and Andy announced to the rest of the boys that I was that year's manager's player. It meant a lot to me that this was happening at Toni's restaurant with him there to watch it. I hadn't seen Toni for years, and even deep into my twenties it felt special to me that he was there to see me being recognised as a decent centre-half in a good team all those years on from when he used to pick my chin up off the floor as a 12-year-old on the drive home after yet another nightmare in goal for Winchmore Hill.

Chapter Eleven

Robbo

OUR first game in the Edmonton top division in September 2008 was against Clavisque, the other promoted side, and it meant another airing for our away kit. Secretly I had my doubts about our ability to compete at this level; we certainly had good players, but the majority were reaching their late twenties and it wasn't clear whether getting up on a Sunday was still going to be a priority. As people worked their way up the career ladder they also began to take longer summer holidays to more exotic destinations, which meant getting a team together for the early fixtures of the season was getting progressively harder each year. When booking a trip to Malta for a friend's wedding that summer, I had ensured that Mel and I returned 24 hours before the Sunday morning kick-off against Clavisque, 11am at Firs Farm, and had also looked into how to get back on time by boat should there be any issues with the plane. I like to think I was always fun to travel with.

Despite my best efforts, however, at one stage on the eve of the season opener we only had eight players confirmed, one of whom had to leave at half-time. By the morning, having lit the beacons to call in anyone we knew who had ever played football, we had a full 'team' and even one sub. I remember a lad called 'Tank' came down, presumably not his actual name but I can't be sure never having seen him before or since, but thank you 'Tank' whoever and wherever you are. We assembled at the changing rooms but as the minutes bled away before kick-off it became apparent that Robbo was missing. This was totally out of character because although he enjoyed a night out more than most and would often arrive for a game off the back of very little or no sleep, he would never let the team down altogether by not showing up. The missed calls from me were piling up, and when eventually he answered his phone the speed and excitement with which he was talking suggested that whatever he'd been doing the night before hadn't fully worked its way out of his system. Robbo picks up the story.

'I remember going out to Warehouse [a nightclub in north London based in an industrial site], and I did too many pills and had a really good night. A really good night. I got in about six in the morning. I was dying. I knew I was not getting out of bed for half nine, and I remember you calling saying, "Robbo we need you, we are at Firs Farm, you have to play." I remember buying lots of Lucozade, getting down there and we were playing Clavisque, who I'd had some problems with before. I was still high and in love, I remember the ball came to me, the keeper miskicked it and I just remember kicking the ball from the halfway line and it went in the net! I just started telling all their players, "I haven't slept mate, I've done three pills," and I was loving them, cuddling them, and normally I wanted to kill them. Most people would have turned the phone off and not answered, but I couldn't ignore your call so I got out of bed and played and that hopefully showed my true love for the Wizards.' We beat Clavisque 2-1, and with Robbo flying high and scoring to secure another win a week later, we were off to a great start in the league.

Despite the challenges Mickey and Andy had dealing with his dad in the early period of their time managing the team, Robbo had been a mainstay of the side from day one when we played as the Winchmore Arms. His enthusiasm for Sunday football was infectious, and he was always meeting people on nights out or at work and talking them into signing up. He is quick to acknowledge how important playing football was to him. 'I have made some friends for life through Sunday football. Some people don't realise what playing football can bring, or moan about people who see it as the be-all and end-all, but men like to have that social inclusion, you meet friends. Men are different to women, they can't understand it, don't try and understand it. I'm all for it. Football… it's important socially.'

While Robbo felt that women would never understand his unwavering love of playing Sunday League football, this never proved to be a hindrance in his ability to charm them. As the house I lived in with my mum was located on the route from Robbo's house to the playing fields that hosted all our fixtures in the Edmonton League, Robbo would often be my source of a lift to the game. Regularly there would be a different beautiful girl in the back seat who had sufficiently enjoyed his company the previous evening to spend the night and was now to be treated to a morning standing on the sidelines watching him run around a football pitch. Robbo explains the quandary he faced each Sunday morning. 'Some of them were sorts,[33] by the way, some of them, I don't know how I left behind for you lot. It was difficult, but that's how much the Wizards meant to me and still mean to me today; I'd still kick a worldie out of bed if I was called upon by you boys.' Robbo estimates that during his twenties he spent the night with in excess of 200 women, a fact that he is keen to have recorded in print.[34] There was a hotel he would go to

33 'Sort' or 'a right sort' is London vernacular for a very good-looking woman.

34 Robbo explains simultaneously the key to his potency with women and perhaps where the rest of us were going wrong; he didn't spend his Friday and Saturday nights,'sitting in a pub talking about the latest results in the Premier League and that bollocks'. His mantra was to seek out the best-looking woman and 'enjoy' himself.

in Enfield, checking in in the small hours and leaving without breakfast, where the doorman got to know him by name and would drop him in it by saying, 'Hello Robert, here again?' But this lifestyle did not come cheap and, as he explains, between 21 and 28 he racked up in the region of £25,000 of debt. 'I was living beyond my means and I was still living at home until I was 30. I never got close to girls because I couldn't give them the flat or flash car; I was a bloke living at home with my mum. One-night stands suited me, I didn't have to open up to them. That was a big part of it.'

Although we'd been to the same school, it was only when we started playing Sunday football together that I really started to know Robbo, and he appeared away from football to be this larger-than-life playboy. However, as we talk now he explains that those years at school were a tough time for him and shaped how he lived life in his twenties. 'I don't have the fondest memories of Southgate School because I was bullied and I never felt accepted. They used to call me "Steroid" because there was nothing of me because I was running competitively. Elise, my first girlfriend at 18, broke my heart when she later went off with an older boy. I felt she was the love of my life and it broke my heart. She knocked my confidence, and football helped me find it again, I could reinvent myself, I could put this act on and I think a lot of the time it was that, an act. I think deep down I always had those insecurities and I never wanted to have a girlfriend again who would run off with an older guy, because when you're 20 and your girlfriend is leaving you for a 26-year-old it fucking hurts. I wasn't brave enough to start a fight with him but the football gave me that release. It was all the making of me. I didn't want to get too close to any girls, I didn't want anyone to do that to me again. And looking back, there were girls I should have stayed with… and I'll admit it was always me that would end it. I think it was protection, you know, people protect themselves.'

While this insight puts some of Robbo's exploits in a different perspective, I think all of our team would say the time spent with Robbo in the dressing room before the game was just as much fun as, if not more than, the football itself. He would have us in stitches recounting the 'complications' of his life where sometimes he would have 'four or five women on the go' at the same time. He was like a character from a sitcom. One week he started to unpack his normally meticulously prepared football bag to discover a woman's leopard-print thong in among his boots and shin pads. Seconds later he was wearing it and dancing around the room wearing nothing else; he then proceeded to put his kit on over the top of it and played the whole 90 minutes with it on. 'That was my way of expressing myself, and I used to love people taking the mick out of me and being the centre of attention. I loved making everyone enjoy it. And if people didn't want to turn up and play and enjoy it I didn't like them that much because they weren't part of the team. People who enjoyed my banter and the laughs are the people that stuck with us through thick and thin… When the whistle went it was serious, and as you have seen it meant the world to me and it wasn't a joke.'

Since our days playing Sunday football have come to an end, Robbo's life has completely changed direction. He has managed to pay off all his debts and settled down in his personal life having been happily married for four years. All the same, the fact that he ends our conversation by asking me to have a quick word with his wife on the phone to confirm where he's been tends to suggest his reputation follows him to some extent.

Robbo was an excellent footballer. Years of competitive running at different distances meant he was probably the fittest player in our team if not the whole league, with genuine pace to get up and down the wing. He was also very strong with both feet. Quite early on in playing alongside him, I became aware that he didn't enjoy being tackled very much. He would often turn up the pace to skip past a player who could not stay with him and so would bring him down. The first few times this happened, Robbo's screams of pain would lead me to think he had broken both his legs simultaneously; however as team-mates reached his prone body fearing the worst, he would suddenly pop up and it was apparent no lasting damage had been done. Sometimes the screams of agony would be pre-emptive, before the opposing player had made any contact, in which case even if he was fouled the rest of us and the referee would usually carry on with the game. As Robbo explains, 'I didn't like being tackled, I don't know why but I always thought I'd been fouled, or maybe I just felt pain too easily and I'm a bit of a wimp. But there were some occasions where I felt that was a bad foul and I'd look up and you lot were like, "Robbo that wasn't a foul." I'd be like, "Fucking hell, that was a yellow card, surely?" I think I learnt from the reaction of you boys. I remember I got some guy sent off one time, he didn't even hit me, I just went down screaming and got the guy sent off. It was a game of football and I'm competitive. But that was the evil side of me, the bitter side, twisted. I needed to toughen up, maybe I still do.'

Unsurprisingly these antics made Robbo a less than popular figure with the opposing team's players who having seen his over-the-top response to a genuine attempt to win the ball would then actually target him both verbally and physically. Robbo's appearance was also a source of ire to opposing players and acted like a target on his back in the largely conservative confines of Sunday League football. 'Everyone else was pale and I'd have a sun tan in the middle of December… it was all to do with getting the women.

'So my routine of getting my hair done [blond highlights] and having a sun bed, looking pretty, was all geared towards Friday and Saturday night and it just so happened come Sunday morning I couldn't manage a rugged look.' This was topped off by a love of football boots in 'rascal colours' which only served to enhance his reputation as a pretty boy asking to be rattled with a few tackles to test his mettle. 'I think that was the era when boots were getting a bit lairy and I was partial to a lairy boot. Gold Nike Vapors. I loved boots. I had a boot for every occasion, four or five pairs a season, minimum.'

As the years went by, Robbo picked up some genuinely bad injuries on the pitch as a result of heavy tackles, broken bones in his hand, and damaged knee cartilage. He started to play with more of an edge. Now as well as going down screaming he would get up angry, leading to confrontations which deep down he didn't want and the Wizards weren't up for. Almost on a weekly basis Robbo would end up tangling with the other team's self-styled hard man, and this became a distraction. 'I can honestly say it was like a red mist that came down over me. I think if you have a look at the players I had a problem with, they were bullies, and that was a problem. I knew they were bullies, I knew they were horrible and I couldn't resist it. And they probably couldn't resist it as they knew I was an easy target.' Thankfully it never went much further than pushing and shoving; we had enough calm heads on our team to get Robbo away from trouble before it escalated into anything more serious.

It was a paradox that Robbo struggles to explain. By nature he has never been an aggressive person and it was clear to everyone on the pitch he didn't relish the physical aspects of the game, but out of a sense of not wanting to be intimidated or bullied he would then put himself directly into potentially aggressive situations. 'I just thought I was right and they were wrong and I got fixated on that. I couldn't switch off, re-evaluate, count to ten. Really it was just two idiots on a Sunday morning pitch. I was their outlet, they were my outlet.'

At one point Robbo makes reference to Luis Suarez. This is instructive given an incident Robbo was involved in after the Wizards had folded and he started to play for Zenit St Whetstone in the Barnet League. A player had fouled him badly, and from the resulting free kick the ball hit the wall and spun out to the edge of the box where Robbo ran to retrieve it, only to by scythed down again by the same player. 'So I got up and that was it, the red mist. We were head to head, he was quite a big guy and I was thinking he's going to hit me here, so I just bit his nose hard, he swung a punch, I ducked and then everyone jumped in. He got sent off, I didn't… I wouldn't have done that if he hadn't have fouled me twice in the space of 30 seconds. I just reacted… when you are up close with a man who wants to hurt you and you can see in his eyes the hate, what are you going to do? I don't know. Maybe natural instinct kicks in, a defence mechanism. Maybe throwing a punch was too slow, he'd see it coming? I do not know what possessed me to bite his nose, but I did bite it hard. He showed the ref the teeth marks after the game.'

Later Robbo received a text message from an unknown number. The message purported to come from the Barnet police and said, 'We are urgently trying to contact you regarding a complaint about a nose-biting incident.' Robbo began to panic and decided the best course of action would be to call Barnet Police Station immediately to give his account of events. After an animated detailed description of what had occurred he finally took a breath, which allowed the police officer on the other end of the line to interject by saying that he had no idea what Robbo was talking about, no such incident had been reported to them, and they were not in the habit of contacting people by text message. It turned out that the message had in fact come from Alex, Zenit's manager and Robbo's old team-mate from the Winchmore Arms years. Alex had recently come across some software that allowed him to send anonymous text messages.

While biting someone's nose certainly crosses way over the line of what is and what is not acceptable on a football pitch, and I am glad that the incident didn't occur while he was playing for the Wizards, having played with Robbo all those years I'd say this definitely was a departure from his normal conduct. But I remember an incident that occurred when we were in the First Division of the Edmonton League that perhaps fed into his reaction to bite another man's nose a few years later playing for Zenit.

Early on in an important game when we were chasing down the First Division title, a loose ball fell between our striker Matt Godwin, who by this stage was engaged to Robbo's sister, and the opposition goalkeeper. There was a bit of a coming together and a few words were exchanged, the type of incident that happens in almost every game. For some reason the goalkeeper went up to Matt and headbutted him as hard as he could. It was a truly shocking moment, and for all the years of empty threats and the occasional punch or kick our players had received, this was on another level. Robbo was particularly affected by this incident. It played into his sense that certain players in Sunday football were only there to intimidate and hurt him or Matt – who he was always looking out for. Shamefully, once Matt picked himself up and got cleaned up and we established that no lasting damage had been done, my immediate thoughts were that as the perpetrator had been sent off and they would now have to play about 80 minutes with no proper goalkeeper, winning the game shouldn't prove too difficult. However Andy, who was very close with Matt, and there on the sideline, was outraged. He says he doesn't remember making the call, but other people who were there that day, including Robbo, are certain he immediately contacted the police; at all events, they quickly showed up while the game was going on. The goalkeeper had fled the scene as soon as he'd received his marching orders from the referee, and in the end Matt decided not to take the matter any further. As soon as the final whistle was blown, the other team's secretary came up to me and apologised for what had happened. Apparently the guy had never played for them before and had been drafted into their team at short notice. He was 'doing them a favour' that morning.

Chapter Twelve

It was the season of light

MY initial fears about us struggling to compete in the top flight in 2008/09 were calmed by our first outing, the 2-1 victory over Clavisque, but that victory had come at a terrible cost. Once again our big problem was turning out to be goalkeeper-shaped.

After the trouble we'd had at the start of the previous season, we had found an able replacement for Ed in goal. Gary Bedford was a policeman and good mates with Daniele. Unfortunately in our very first match in Division 1, one of the Clavisque forwards went in very high and late on Gary, crashing into his leg. Despite heroically seeing out the rest of the game more or less on one leg, he was so badly injured that it ruled him out for the rest of the season, horrible bad luck for Gary, and a terrible blow to the team. We roped in a keeper a few of our boys knew called Anthony, but he was only available about one game in three. This meant most weeks, especially when we were low on numbers, we had to put in goal whoever was carrying a knock. We'd then try to attack teams from the off, before they realised we had a pretender between the sticks.

Coming into our first league meeting with Elm Athletic, I'd begun to dare to dream that not only could we compete in Division 1, we could actually win it. Both sides had won all their league games going into the match and so it had extra significance. This time Matt Godwin, our centre-forward, did the goalkeeping honours, having pulled up injured in the warm-up. The referee was Mr Curbelo, who I hadn't seen since my cup final sending off. As we renewed acquaintance before the kick-off he discreetly said to me, 'I hope you have big shin pads.' It seemed having refereed Elm before he knew we were in for a bruising 90 minutes.

For once, I won the toss and elected to scale the hill that was Elm's prominently sloped home pitch in the first half. My thinking was that by the second half they would tire and we could use gravity plus their fatigue against them. Having had that very pitch for our own home games in the past, I had contacted the league at the end of the previous season to plead that we'd done our time on its rugged incline and deserved a move to the flat pitches of Church Street rec. Church Street wasn't without its own hazards; the branches of the massive trees behind the goal overhung the crossbar, sometimes intercepting crosses that came into the box, making mugs of strikers and defenders alike as they rose to meet a ball that never came, as well as testing the referee's knowledge of the lesser-known laws of the game: subsection, Trees and Shrubbery.

Elm took the lead in the first half with a fortuitous, mishit cross; Matt Godwin could only watch helplessly as the ball looped agonisingly into our net. They were all over us in that first half but we managed to keep the deficit to one. At the break, Andy gathered the players together to deliver a rallying cry, which was increasingly his job since Mickey had returned to playing. But soon after the restart our spirits sank again. Matt had bravely hobbled from his goal to intercept a long ball over the top, wiping out the onrushing Elm forward and Neil in the process. As the three of them untangled themselves, the ball popped loose to another Elm player who simply couldn't miss. So now we were two goals down. Internally I was panicking. I knew that we were getting older, each week it was becoming more of a challenge to get a team together, and with people getting married and having children this was only going to become more of an issue in the future. If we were ever going to reach the summit of Edmonton Sunday football, this season was our chance. It's amazing how quickly such anxieties can manifest in your mind on a football pitch, but also just how quickly they can disappear. We forced a corner, which was cleared to the edge of the box, where Danny met it with a stunning volley that flew into the top corner of the net, one of the best goals I have ever seen at any level of football. Inside the last ten minutes it was game on; the Wizards were storming downhill, piling everyone forward, and at last a goalmouth scramble resulted in Mr Curbelo awarding us a penalty for handball.

This sparked a mass pitch invasion from the irate Elm bench of about 20 shouting people and one angry-looking Staffordshire bull terrier. Unfazed Jon Leigh coolly placed the ball on the spot and dispatched the penalty with minimal fuss, prompting a further outbreak of scenes on the sideline. We seemed to switch off after this madness and inexplicably we allowed Elm to walk through our defence from the kick-off. It was only a brilliant last-ditch tackle from Robbo – reminiscent of Darren Anderton's against Argentina in World Cup '98, where half the England team were off celebrating Sol Campbell's non-goal, neglecting that ancient Sunday League maxim of playing to the whistle – that stopped Elm breaking our hearts.

Then, deep into time added on for the minutes it had taken to get their entourage off the pitch following the penalty decision, substitute Eamon, who'd been on the bench after arriving late for the game, picked up the ball and drove towards the Elm box. He committed and beat one defender after another. Then much to everyone's surprise, he declined the chance to shoot and instead squared the ball to Dale who fired home an unlikely winner with the last kick of the game.

Danny, Jon and Dale, three former Southgate Saints, who had played together for so many years, had led us to salvation. Unlike some of the more famous saintly miracles in history, this time there was a referee and there were witnesses. Scenes of unbridled joy burst out from our side at the final whistle. Matthew Berou, who had been unable to play owing to injury, jigged his way onto the pitch, channelling David Pleat's reaction to keeping Luton Town up all those years ago. The 12 players plus Andy and Matt cuddled each other in an orange and black pile of humanity in the north London mud as if we had won the Champions League, until we were the only people left out on the 12 pitches of Firs Farm and the realisation that our goal net wouldn't take itself down kicked in.

Before making our way to the car park, we all resolved that we owed it to each other now to see out our remaining league games and win the title. It seemed that the desire and passion that the core of the team had always had for the Wizards had now spread through everyone. From that moment, I no longer had to beg people to defer their weekend away with their significant other and we all knew that Sunday morning, 11am, under the slate grey skies of Edmonton was where we wanted to be.

A couple of weeks later, we played Elm again in a cup tie. This was a game notable for half the team having a go at taking a reasonable goal kick and failing miserably. Such was the level of ineptitude of the rest of us at getting the ball off the ground that day that eventually Mike Angelides, who was this week's injury-selected goalkeeping incumbent, resorted to taking them with his wrong foot. The game was 1-1 at half-time but then Danny was sent off for dissent following what he perceived as poor refereeing decisions. From there we caved in, 7-1. The game ended in animosity when one of the Elm players, having exchanged pleasantries with Dale, threatened to get a gun and shoot him, which seemed a little bit dramatic. But the nature of some of the Elm players meant that such a claim couldn't be dismissed entirely as idle talk. As I tried to reason with the gentleman concerned to allow Dale to make his exit, the player told me repeatedly not to touch him and that we didn't know who he was and that prison held no fear for him.

We decided to take a week off and therefore forfeit the tie rather than playing the second leg of what was a lost cause. I'd be lying if I said it didn't cross my mind not to tell Elm in advance, so that their players would have to get up early and go through the process of getting geared up for the game only to find us not there, but in the end my conscience got the better of me and I made the phone call. It seemed our next league meeting with Elm might be a little tetchy.

Before that game came around, we had to make sure that we didn't slip up against any of the other sides in the First Division; we knew if we won all our games we could afford a draw against Elm and still win the title. I became obsessed with my pre-match routine, making sure to replicate everything as closely as possible at each of the grounds where we played. The changing rooms at Firs Farm during the winter were always so cold that players' teeth would actually chatter as we sat waiting for late comers to arrive, conducting a game of bluff to see who would be the first to take the thoroughly reckless step of stripping off the multiple layers of fleecy clothing they had worn for the journey to the playing fields, and settling into what was essentially nylon shorts and a t-shirt. Interestingly, the sub-zero conditions seemed not to bother certain well-endowed members of opposition teams at all. These were the players who would take a shower both before and after their game, just in order to stride through the communal area between showers and changing rooms with their manhood on display with the intention of out-psyching the players on the other side. Never one for public nudity pre-match at Firs Farm, I always kept my head down and made my way to the second cubicle from the left to complete my own pre-match ritual, trying as hard as possible to make minimal contact between my body and the toilet seat which best-case scenario would have someone's piss all over it that you would have to mop up with toilet paper before sitting down. This was very much best case. It was part way through the season where our undefeated league run meant I had to maintain my pre-match routine to the letter at all costs that I realised someone must have been using the same toilet cubicle for a little pre-match ritual of his own, judging from the porno mag tucked behind the cistern.

This routine seemed to be working as we continued our 100% record in the league. A further omen that this season would result in something special for us occurred in another cup tie at Firs Farm. On a filthy day where those two bad weather titans, wind and rain, decided to form an unbeatable tag team, we triumphed 5-4 over a side from a lower division called Thames North. More remarkable than yet another hat-trick from Danny was the surname of the referee for that day, Mr F. Ardiles.

While people from all countries and cultures have made north London a home over the years, Ardiles is a name that means only one thing: Tottenham Hotspur royalty. From first sight it was clear that the young referee resembled the great Ossie Ardiles, but the question remained. Why, if he was indeed the son of a Tottenham and Argentina legend, would he be refereeing Sunday football in the pissing Edmonton rain? Not wanting to come across like a giddy schoolboy, I decided not to ask him any questions about his family tree as we shook hands and flipped the coin. He was an excellent referee and, interestingly, none of the players on either team so much as queried one of his decisions, let alone swore at him as the rain continued to stair-rod down for the entire 90 minutes. Any doubt about his identity was resolved at the end of the match, when I made out the figure of a long-haired, tanned, handsome, bearded, older man walking towards us. At that exact moment, as if by magic, the sun broke through and illuminated his path across the pitch to greet the referee.

IT WAS THE SEASON OF LIGHT

It was Ricky Villa, scorer of the greatest goal ever in an FA Cup Final, and a World Cup winner – two moments he shared alongside our referee-for-the-day's dad, Ossie Ardiles. That vision of the great Ricky standing on the football pitch I had just been playing on will stay with me for as long as I live. I just hoped he had been looking the other way during my attempt to control a long high ball just before the full-time whistle.

We were massively buoyed going into our last 11 games of the season by the return of Ed, who despite going through a difficult time coming to terms with his departure from Dagenham was quick to put himself forward for Wizards duty. This crucial run of fixtures included what was to be the key return league encounter with Elm. Since our last-gasp victory over them earlier in the season both sides had won all their league games, and so if they turned us over when we met again they'd be level with us in the table.

We started on the back foot, intimidated by their forceful tackling and massed ranks of supporters, accompanied as ever by their canine mascot, which I am sure should have fallen foul of the Dangerous Dogs Act. I felt for Andy that day on the touchline, completely outnumbered as he was and the subject of some very unpleasant abuse. For what it's worth, Andy is no wallflower, well over six foot tall, very broad shoulders, a big physical presence who you wouldn't want to be on the wrong side of. But on these occasions he had no choice but to stand there and take the abuse that was directed his way. 'In the Edmonton League there were some nasty teams and in a sense we were a bit out of our depth because we didn't have that streak ... When it kicked off with Attitude, I thought it was almost playful. It was a football rivalry style banter, we don't like each other but no one is going to pull out a knife and stab someone. With Elm, I was worried because had they really gone for us, full throttle, we would have got battered. It was a concern because we had some players who would run their mouths; I used to look around our team and think we're all nice guys and with all due respect, people like Berou, Trigger and you, aren't boys you'd choose to have beside you in a 22-man ruck… Sometimes I'd think, "We've done well to get out of that without a pasting." I had visions of us sometimes, running.'

Personally I wasn't fully aware of what was going on at the side of the pitch. I do remember however that every time I went forward for a corner I would hear their centre-half, who looked remarkably like John Terry, tell Matt Godwin that he was going to break his legs if he touched the ball. Elm took the lead with an excellent long-range strike before Robbo made a great run from left-back and took a dramatic tumble in the area, which won us a penalty for Danny to convert. At half-time the game was locked at 1-1. But soon after the interval we found ourselves 4-1 down. As each of those goals went in, the Elm substitutes took to running down the sideline and celebrating right in Andy's face, complete with hand gestures.

On the pitch things were turning really nasty. Robbo went down saying he had been headbutted. While none of our players saw it happen and taking into account his proclivity for overreacting, the way he played thereafter suggested something serious had happened. That strong sense of injustice seemed to have taken Robbo's game to a level none of us had ever seen from him until that moment. He pulled the game back to 4-2 with a superb left-foot half-volley from the edge of the box that beat their keeper all ends up, lifting our whole team in the process. But within ten seconds of the restart and with just ten minutes to go, I mistimed a tackle and the ref blew for a penalty. It's hard to describe how instantly the old doubts and disappointment crowded back into my head as I envisaged them restoring their three-goal lead. If they converted at this stage, we'd have no chance to come back.

Before the penalty could be taken, however, a confrontation had broken out between Danny and half their team who had circled round him like sharks. Danny, never one to back down, exchanged blows with their most vocal player. Both were sent off, and unhelpfully Matt Godwin had also gotten himself sent off for dissent after swearing at the ref for not protecting Danny. So now we were down to nine men against their ten. You couldn't really blame the referee though; the game wasn't really controllable and he would not have been human had he not felt intimidated by what was going on. Fortunately, by the time those who'd been dismissed had left the pitch and things had calmed down sufficiently for the player I had fouled to take the penalty, about ten minutes had elapsed. Now too much thinking time before taking a penalty is never beneficial. It looked like their player changed his mind about four times on his run-up, before missing tamely.

Suddenly the momentum of that game completely changed and without our talisman Danny, it was Robbo who drove us on. The way he played in those closing stages made it feel like we had the extra man rather than Elm. He smashed in an identical shot to his first to make it 4-3 with minutes remaining. Elm were completely gone by this point – screaming at each other now instead of at us; both sides must have been remembering what had happened at the death of our first meeting. I can see it now, as if in slow motion: Robbo striding down the left wing, looping a cross over, the ball hitting the top of the crossbar, the ball then dropping, gradually dropping, onto Mickey's boot from where he sent it crashing into the net 4-4.

We had done it to Elm in the closing moments once again. There was even still time for Eamon to go through one-on-one with their goalkeeper, who came charging out to meet him. Eamon took the ball round him and sent it towards the unguarded goal from 30 yards out. Just as it appeared we would seal the most remarkable of comebacks with a winner, the ball slowed down as it travelled across the mud-covered 18-yard box, eventually coming to a stop agonisingly short of crossing the goal line. One of the Elm defenders cleared the ball away, sliding in dramatically even though there was no longer any danger of the ball going in, and then expectantly looking round to his team-mates as if he had just saved the day. As the full-time whistle blew, handshakes were not exchanged. Despite now feeling a bit disappointed that we hadn't taken all three points, we knew we had taken a huge step to the title. Reflecting back a fair few years on from these events, there is real emotion in his voice when Robbo says, 'I did myself and the boys proud that day and my dad was there on the sideline to see it.'

The transition from winter to spring in 2009 seemed to be on hold. There was a spell of several weeks in which every game was preceded by a pitch inspection where a referee would do some less than scientific tests to establish whether the frozen pitch was safe to play on. These tests involved flamboyantly bouncing the ball on the ground a couple of times and then dribbling it across the halfway line at walking pace, to cheerful shouts of, 'I can see why you don't play football ref!' While conducting the pitch inspection, the ref would usually be flanked by delegates from both teams trying to influence his decision according to their own agendas. I remember at times suggesting the game should go ahead as the pitch was 'a carpet' if we were at full strength and the opposition appeared to be short of players, or conversely arguing that it should be called off as it was unsafe to play on and 'rock hard, dangerous' when I knew our line-up wasn't as strong as it could be. More often than not, though, the key factor was probably that since the referee had already got out of bed, put on his kit and ventured down to the ground, he understandably wanted to get paid. Game on. On these mornings we looked for all the world like we were wearing stiletto heels, tottering on top of the icy surface, until it had thawed sufficiently for our studs to dig into the ground. I also figured out why you don't see too many slide tackles in ice hockey.

Sometimes, however, the need for a pitch inspection was a secondary consideration. First you needed the opposition to turn up. Nothing led to more moaning on our side than when we would bravely exit the shelter of the changing rooms to put up the net in the bitter cold in a cup game where we couldn't actually progress, only to find the opposing team had decided to stand us up for a lie-in and full English. The prospect of being awarded the victory by forfeit proved little consolation to most of the Wizards, who seemed to enjoy the actual process of playing football far more than I did. For me at this stage, as we pushed onwards for the title, the 90 minutes was something to be endured: all that mattered was the three points at the end of it.

My biggest anxiety in the run-in came when Spurs reached the League Cup Final for the second year running, but such was the sense of purpose among the Wizards this year that there was no need to adjust kick-off times; everyone said they would play our league game against Southbury on the morning of the cup final. We won the game 6-2, despite being the object of some banter from already well-oiled Spurs fans on the top deck of a chartered blue-and-white-clad Routemaster bus that passed by our home pitch on its way to Wembley. For the first week in years I left it to some of the other boys, one sat on another's shoulders, to unhook the net from the crossbar and collect in the kit, which was supposed to be dropped off to me later that evening to be washed. We raced back to Danny's house to make ourselves presentable for Wembley before Danny's dad, Mick, drove us to the game with time to spare. I remember saying to Neil on the Saturday night that as long as we won our game and went on to win the league, I could live with Spurs losing that cup final. Having kept our side of this equation it was never in doubt once the game went to penalties that Spurs, despite performing well on the day, would keep theirs. They lost to Manchester United following one of the most inept spot kick displays English football has ever seen.[35]

It was coming off the pitch at the end of winning a cup game against the Green Dragons at Church Street rec that Robbo received a phone call from someone whose identity is to this day unclear, but who had been at Firs Farm that morning and relayed the news that Elm had dropped points in their league game

---

35 This was part of a sequence of seven consecutive penalty shoot-out defeats for Tottenham lasting nearly 20 years.

with Rio; also, Travellers in third place had lost to Southbury. According to the Edmonton Sunday League's version of Deep Throat, this meant it was now mathematically impossible for us to be caught and we were champions. I immediately set about pouring cold water on this information, firstly because I thought the phone call was likely a wind-up, secondly because I'd been working out all the permutations myself for weeks on end. I was insistent that we needed at least another win from our remaining three league games against Travellers, Rio and Southbury. Obviously I was concerned that erroneous information would result in some of our players assuming that they were now free to 'no show' our remaining fixtures and end up costing us glory.

The protocol in Edmonton was that at full time the home team had to ring in the score from their game to the League. A fella called Gary Brooke, who ran the Bricklayers, was the one who collected and collated all the scores. Usually when you called Gary's number, it was his wife who answered. As I informed her of our scoreline, she saw the funny side of a game of football played between the Wizards and the Green Dragons. Having built this magical rapport over the phone I felt empowered to ask her all the results from the first division that day, which I furiously scribbled down.

The results Robbo had been given were accurate, but my terrible maths plus years of conditioning as a Spurs fan that football usually bites you in the arse, meant I was still convinced we hadn't yet sealed the title. Eventually Mickey called me to say he had done the sums and we were definitely champions. While I agreed his working out seemed solid, I still wanted the confirmation of Matt Berou, the chartered accountant in the team, before informing the rest of the boys. Trouble was, Matt was halfway around the world in Mumbai on holiday with his girlfriend and not answering his phone. I therefore sent him the longest text message in the world with all the scores and asked him to corroborate. As I waited for a reply, Mel convinced me to go with her for a walk round Broomfield Park, a park I had been going to all my life and where I probably first kicked a football. For some reason, that day we decided to go into the Garden of Remembrance, which is tucked away in the south-east corner behind a wall, and which many people would not realise is there. The garden commemorates the young men from north London who lost their lives in the two World Wars.

It was while sat on a bench in this remembrance garden, surrounded by plastic poppy wreaths and rows of names, that I received a text message from Matt Berou. All the way from India. Confirming we had done it.

Matt is someone I had known since I was four years old; I'd stood next to him on a football pitch for the Wizards and other teams over the years more than any other person. It made me think, being there in front of the names of all those other north London boys; some of them had probably played in the Edmonton Sunday League. This had never occurred to me over the years when the League asked teams to observe a minute's silence before games on Remembrance Sunday. It somehow didn't seem appropriate to forward Matt's message to the other lads until we had left the garden and got back to the main section of the park by the football pitches. Matt remembers being sat with Sangeeta in a restaurant called the Delhi Darbar in Mumbai, when my text with the other teams' results came through. He is only half-joking when he says the euphoria of knowing that we had won the league led him to propose to her, his now wife, before they got back to the UK.

In the immediate weeks before and after the league title was secured, the team had been regularly updated by Neil about holiday plans of his own. He had proposed to his long-term partner, Julia, and being a romantic had planned an exotic trip with her to Goa on the Indian coast where they would enjoy the beautiful surroundings and get an excellent deal on an engagement ring. Triggs took great delight in reminding the rest of us, particularly on the Sundays when the British weather was at its worst, that in a few short weeks he'd be basking in the sunshine on a beach thousands of miles away. Unfortunately, although he had swapped notes with Matt Berou whose trip to India ended a few weeks before his own was due to start, the issue of visas never came up. It was only when Neil arrived at Heathrow for his flight that he realised that the whole trip was a non-starter. I was absolutely gutted for him, but as he willingly admits, the incident is a classic example of why he is known as 'Trigger'. It was hard not to have huge respect for the way he handled coming to the changing room, where he knew sympathy would be in short supply, before our game the following Sunday when he should have been sunbathing with a cocktail in each hand. 'The one thing you know about a football changing room, especially if you enjoy the banter, is you reap what you sow. You have to take on the chin what you dish out, otherwise you get very quickly found out… It was a case of manning up and facing the music. I was always quite vocal in taking the piss out of most people about most things. I'd be the first to take the piss if it happened to someone else. You can only do that if you then accept it back.'

My aim was now to go the whole season unbeaten and in a small way reclaim the term 'Invincibles' for those of us who weren't Arsenal fans but had endured hearing about their 2003/04 team being the greatest of all time ever since. It wasn't to be. Prior to securing the title, we had won every game except for the one glorious draw against Elm. Now we were confirmed champions, however, getting several of the boys to turn up proved impossible, and our three remaining fixtures resulted in two defeats and a draw. This slightly took the gloss off our achievement before we received the actual trophy. Often times winning leagues doesn't afford you the immediate feeling of jubilation that lifting silverware at the end of a cup final does, even though league triumph is infinitely harder to come by, especially in Sunday football where it is such a battle to keep players turning out week after week. However, when we finally did get hold of the league title and were presented with a huge wooden shield which is impossible to lift above your head in the time-honoured fashion, I really did feel like our lives had changed. The front of the shield was silver-plated and engraved with the names of the best teams in the whole of the Edmonton League dating back to its formation in 1925. To see the name Wizards 2008/09 immortalised there was a feeling I couldn't get enough of. For the next few weeks I managed to work it into every conversation I had, almost taking offence when people who probably didn't even know who had won the Premier League that year failed to recognise the team captain of the Edmonton and District Sunday Football League champions. I can't honestly say that the feeling of euphoria has completely dissolved even now. I'm not sure it ever will.

We again congregated at La Scala restaurant for our end-of-season celebration and awards night. I had gotten 'E.D.S.F.L Division 1 Winners' printed below the badge on one of our shirts, which every player signed that night and I subsequently had framed. Financial constraints meant I couldn't afford to replicate this for the whole kit, much to the disappointment of the other boys. Everyone, including Danny who'd had a monopoly on the players' player award, was thrilled that Robbo took that particular honour for the season. Receiving that recognition is something that deeply affected him, as he says today. 'It was huge and I'm proud to be part of the Wizards… I'd do it all again tomorrow without even a question.' For me, writing this a fair few years after we stopped playing, there is now a sadness remembering what was one of the happiest nights of my life, a sense of mourning that my best footballing years are now very much behind me. But much more poignant is the fact that that night was to be the final time I spoke to Daniele's dad, Toni, save for a wave and mouthed hello across a large function room at a wedding. For me, the news of Toni's death during the run up to Christmas 2012, in the most sudden and tragic circumstances, seemed like the end of a special era in which my life had been completely dominated by football.

Chapter Thirteen

Who would be a Sunday referee?

ALTHOUGH we had failed to go the whole league season unbeaten, Danny had made a different kind of history himself by the end of the campaign. He had completed a hat-trick of red cards for dissent, the final sending off coming at the hand of Mike Chisholm with whom he'd exchanged barbs earlier in the year. Looking back, Danny regrets some of the things he used to say to referees, particularly Mr Chisholm. 'I'm ashamed... I know I used to give referees a hard time. If it wasn't for them we wouldn't be playing.'

Reflecting years later on the challenges Sunday League refs face, I was interested to find out why any of them do it. I contacted Mike, hoping he would remember the Wizards. He did, and we arranged to meet up for a chat.

Going to meet Mike in a pub in Waltham Cross having not seen him in the years since he last refereed us, I don't recognise him at first without his referee's kit on. Now he's in jeans and a checked shirt. Initially it feels like bumping into a teacher you never got on with at school when they are out shopping with their family, which makes you see them as a human being for the first time. As a player it is hard to get away from the 'us and them' mentality with referees, and not to judge them as all being the same. I know I always struggled to view them as individuals. It was hard to stop negative experiences with one week's referee from clouding my opinion of the next one before a match had even started; or to allow for the fact that we may previously have caught this particular referee on a bad day, the sort of day I had often enough on a Sunday League pitch.

But as we start to talk, I find Mike to be a really likeable character with a great sense of humour and lots of interesting opinions on the game and refereeing in particular.

So, I asked, what could possibly possess someone to make them want to become a Sunday League referee? Mike explained that he started refereeing in 2005 when he was in his forties. 'I was rubbish at football. I was a typical "you're only a referee because you're useless at football".' Mike says refereeing was always something he had fancied doing, but being a police officer and working shifts and at weekends it wasn't possible until he became senior enough in the police to get off shift work, and start studying to qualify. All refs start at the same level and have to work their way up from there. Mike explains that once qualified as a referee, he had three years at grass-roots level before he started to move up the ladder. It takes a particular type of character to deal with the stresses of working in the police, and I find it amazing that someone in that profession would want to spend their free time 'relaxing' by officiating games of amateur football. It strikes me as one of the most thankless tasks imaginable. But this was never the case for Mike, now ten years into his refereeing career. He tells me, 'I didn't find refereeing stressful. I used to go home on a high, I got a buzz out of it. I wanted to keep fit but going to the gym bores me, and I wanted to find something where I could get some exercise and really enjoy it, and I ended up with a bit of beer money on top. There's not many sports where you can do that and get paid for it. I used to really look forward to it, still do. It's not a job you can do properly if you don't enjoy it. If you're there and you're just wanting the 90 minutes to disappear, for 30 quid it's not worth it.'

Mike explains that the process of qualifying wasn't the most rigorous preparation for those taking their first fledgling steps in the world of amateur football. 'We had to go to a class every week where you test each other on laws of the game and then sit a final exam. But if you get to the end of the course you usually pass because they are very short of referees, especially at grass-roots level. So unless you are completely useless you are going to make it.' He remembers that upon qualifying he was recommended to contact the Edmonton League as a good place to cut his teeth as 'they run a good league in Edmonton' and Mike lived nearby in Winchmore Hill. He admits his first game was a step into the unknown; he hadn't even played Sunday football. So he didn't divulge to the players that he was making his refereeing debut.

'The first time I set foot on the field I had no idea what was going to happen or how I would react. You hear horror stories about people turning up drunk or under the influence of god knows what, giving refs a really hard time, even violence. But to be perfectly honest I wasn't worried about any of that as I've dealt with that all my life in my job. When they said, "We haven't seen you before" I told them I'd come from another league, and being the age I was, 40, I strutted about as if I had done it for years. It was only at the end of the game when I had done a half-decent job that I said, "I have something to tell you, that's my first ever game." And they said, "You've done all right."'

Mike's experience as a policeman clearly stood him in good stead to handle the pressures that come when controlling a group of 22 men and those on the sidelines, many of whom use the 90 minutes as an outlet for any unhappiness in the Monday to Saturday part of their lives, with no linesmen, fourth official or video technology to support him. 'It's like the police training at Hendon. Nothing really prepares you for that first time on the street.' While Mike took all this in his stride, looking back now it is painfully obvious why of the select group of people inclined to try their hand at refereeing, many don't come back after their first taste of a real match. As Mike talks I find him debunking a lot of the preconceptions I had about being a Sunday League referee and it comes across just how much he came to enjoy it. 'People said to me, "You must be mad – why do you do it?" but there was nothing I hated about it.'

Before talking to Mike, it had never occurred to me that the banter and camaraderie that makes Sunday football so special for players can also be valued by a referee. 'The banter, some refs think they are above it, but I can have a laugh and a joke especially with people I found in previous games had been problematic.' Mike's view is that referees need to give as good as they get. 'Lots of amateur and maybe even pro players struggle with this concept. They think they can say whatever they want to a referee but if you say something back it's like the worst thing you can do, and they'll say, "I'm going to report you."' However, some of Mike's favourite memories of refereeing in Edmonton are of the exchanges he would have with players. He remembers one occasion where a player had been chipping away at him all game questioning every decision he made. Despite initially trying to encourage him to just get on with playing the game, it eventually reached the point where Mike decided it was time for the player to go into his book. As he reached for his yellow card the player said, 'You can't book me today, ref, it's my birthday,' to which Mike replied while handing him the caution, 'Well there's a birthday card for you!' 'The player and both teams pissed themselves laughing and he didn't say another word to me all game.'

Another favourite recollection from his time in Edmonton involved a player called Ganja, who at half-time went off the pitch for a 'funny fag'. 'People were asking "Where is he?" when a plume of smoke started coming up from behind a bush. As we were about to start the second half I said, "Which of these balls should we use?" (Mike was only holding one ball in his hands). He looked at me and didn't have a clue.'

Mike recounts refereeing a cup final at Jubilee Park, where one of the teams had a really talented but 'gobby' player he had encountered before. Mike was keen not to have to send the player off in a showpiece game, so prior to kick-off approached him and struck up a bargain where if the player stayed on the pitch for the whole game Mike would buy him a beer, whereas if he didn't the player would be the one buying. 'We shook hands on it and for 85 minutes he was brilliant, didn't say a word; he scored and his team were winning. Five minutes from the end of the game he got injured and stretchered off. So I went up to him on the stretcher and said, "You owe me a beer." He laughed and said, "Ref, you're a fucker." I did buy him a pint after.'

Mike would try and build a rapport with players as a technique to manage the game. 'It's really important to ref each game with a clean slate. It's nice to know some of the players. If you have had dealings with someone before, go up to them with a smile. If it's been really nasty in the past, walk across the pitch with your hand out and say, "How are you? Have you had a good week? I'm looking forward to the game." He'll be saying to his mates "This ref's a wanker," then I walk up and I'm as nice as pie and it disarms them. There is a lot of psychology to it. You could start the game off by saying, "Two weeks ago you did XYZ and I'll be watching you," which puts someone's back up and makes him say to his mates, "See I told you," and could lead to a mass confrontation, and abandoning the game. That's the last thing you want; you have failed then haven't you?'

Mike believes that some referees don't always apply the rules: perhaps feeling intimidated makes them shirk making the difficult decisions; maybe they think they are doing players a favour. To Mike this is misguided; it just causes a problem for yourself next time round or for other referees, if players think there are things they can get away with. When Mike applied the rules, he says, players would complain that refs weren't consistent. The thing that he takes most seriously on the pitch is any accusation that he isn't being impartial. 'Swear words on their own don't mean much to me, but being called a fucking cheat… well, if anyone questions my integrity then it's a red card. Questioning a ref's integrity is far more offensive than calling me a wanker, we are all wankers aren't we?' Mike explains that he would interpret instances like this on the basis of 'was anyone offended?' 'I can manage someone calling me a tosser. I might reply, "You're a tosser for missing an open goal. Don't say it again and let's get on with it." Whereas saying that what I am doing is bent in any way, that is offensive to me.' He recounts one time in the Edmonton League, refereeing a game, where the mother of one of the players had recently been diagnosed with a terminal illness and that it was common knowledge among both teams. Following a tackle an opposing player made reference to this. 'He didn't swear, but talk about offensive, that was it! No one complained when I sent him off; his own team were disgusted by him.'

Mike thinks that referees in the professional game don't always do their counterparts further down the ranks any favours. In games shown on television you can see they're brilliant at keeping the game flowing for the viewers. 'But there are tackles that should be straight reds and don't get given, and dissent goes unpunished. In the Premier League if they sent off every player who swore at the ref, they would be criticised for ruining the game; but when you are out on the parks if you let players get away with this you are making it very difficult for the ref the next week.'

Mike's technique when things seemed to be getting out of hand was to call the two captains in and warn them that the next incident, whether a player swearing at him or a bad tackle, would result in a red card. Normally this would calm things and bring the game under his control. He recounts a conversation he had with Howard Webb, a fellow police officer and perhaps England's most respected referee, which made him think that Webb should have adopted this technique during what he described as the two most difficult hours of his life, the 2010 World Cup Final between Holland and Spain. Holland put in a number of X-rated challenges early on to try and disrupt Spain's fluid passing, but Webb did not act decisively enough to rein them in. Although Mike clearly has great respect for Webb he says, 'He needed to stamp his authority on the game but he didn't, and he admits that himself. The ref gets blamed for spoiling the game when they send someone off, but the way I see it is, I haven't spoilt the game, the player has. He's the one who's made a bad tackle or told me to "fuck off". I'm just doing my job, and if I don't do it properly I have let everyone down.'

Mike says he's always prepared to hold his hands up and admit if he has made a mistake or missed something he should have spotted. 'I think it's a big problem at all levels that refs don't do that. It takes the wind out of people's sails. Say, "You're absolutely right, I'm sorry," and they've got nowhere to go.'

As a player, one thing that I found very frustrating about the referees we encountered was their propensity to discipline players for swearing, or other more petty types of dissent like kicking the ball away, while on occasion turning a blind eye to some really bad tackles. I can appreciate that a ref could be intimidated out in the middle of the pitch on his own when a team was really aggressive, but understanding a referee's predicament did little to ease the pain of the player who'd just been clattered. Our team liked to play football, and so this was something I was particularly conscious of. Mike says, 'I would try and protect the teams, within the laws of the game, who wanted to play football against the teams that just wanted to kick the shit out of people. One of the reasons I joined the police was my hatred of bullies. A lot of these teams tried to intimidate and bully other teams and they probably got away with it with other referees, but I wouldn't let them. The first few times I tried to referee these teams I would have battles with them; six or seven yellow cards, sendings off and rows with the coach. But as the season went on, that would change because they knew I wouldn't have it. I would always want to be on the side of the team who wanted to play football. If someone ever went out to try and hurt someone they would be off the pitch. The Wizards had some gobby players and moaners, but you were all nice guys and you wanted to win fairly. The Wizards is the team I remember the most about; the rest blur into each other.'

My other major gripe with Sunday League referees was that they never would send a player off for a 'professional foul' (unless it was me in that cup final). Week after week our forwards would get brought down when through on goal, and no further action would be taken. Mike's explanation finally shone some light for me on referees' thinking at amateur level. 'There is no such thing as a professional foul or last man, the offence is denying an obvious goalscoring opportunity. And what I think it boils down to is ability. If you are 20 yards out and fouled in the Premier League, the chances are pretty high that it's a goalscoring opportunity because you're fit and running through on goal. Whereas in the Edmonton and District if you're 20 yards out and get fouled, what's the likelihood you'll have a chance to score? Not massive. You probably fall over, it's bobbly or something like that. Refs are taught to look at the conditions and the ability of the players. Watching games on TV, you can see he is through and a world class player, whereas in Edmonton he has got to try and get through the ruts in the pitch and try and control the ball, a dog could run on. Even if he wasn't fouled, was that going to be an obvious goalscoring opportunity? Probably not.'

In putting me right about professional fouls, Mike highlights one of the other areas of tension that emerge between amateur players and referees: the fact that in Mike's view players only really know about 70 per cent of the laws of the game. He says this is only exacerbated by rule changes like those in recent years to the offside rule, challenging enough for referees in the top flight let alone at Sunday League level. Even so, Mike never asked the teams to provide him with a linesman to help out. 'They're more trouble than they're worth. They don't understand offside rules, and they are going to be biased. They flag for offside on a goal kick or give the ball going out in the wrong direction half the time… Lots of refs do ask teams to get a sub to run the line so they have someone else to blame for mistakes, whereas I would rather be accountable to myself.' He says the most common rule players get wrong is handball. 'Handball has to be deliberate. Everyone screams "handball", but nine times out of ten it's not handball as there is no intent. That's a problem from top level to bottom.' When I suggest that perhaps better education of players on the laws of the game might help referees, Mike's view is that this wouldn't make much difference as 'it's an instinctive and passionate game'.

He is also honest in confirming something I always suspected was occurring in our games but could never be sure of, the phenomenon of referees using the players' reaction to determine a decision when they hadn't seen the incident for themselves. 'In the training for referees they can't say look at player reaction, but it's something you learn. When a ball comes off two players and you are not sure, unofficially you are taught to go with the defensive team as even the players don't know who touched it last. But when you have just missed seeing it, hold on and see who goes to take the throw. I didn't learn this straight away. Serious injury from a foul is the same. If a player is really hurt then his team-mates usually go to him, whereas if he is not they go to the ref. Players do know, they have taught me a lot. Player reaction is a wonderful guide for referees at all levels. If you are not sure, just wait two or three seconds and player reaction will help you make up your mind.'

As he talks, Mike's enthusiasm for football and the seriousness with which he takes his role as a referee are apparent. He explains how he learned a valuable lesson at the start of his career, which cemented this sense of responsibility. 'I reffed a game early on when I'd been out the night before. I turned up the worse for wear and I wasn't in a state to referee. You hear the term, "You're not fit to referee" and I wasn't that day. But I thought, "I can't let them down by not turning up." I was dreadful. I was annoyed with myself because you have 22 players plus subs and coaches, plus the man and his dog watching, and I felt I had let them all down. I suppose as a player if you turn up in a state you are letting your team down, but you aren't letting the opposition down, they're pleased. But when you put on that black kit and walk out, whatever level it is, you have a job to do and it's a really important job. It's not just a kick-about on a Sunday morning. Thirty players, coaches, training during the week, a few supporters, girlfriends, kids have turned up and referees have got a responsibility. What's so important is the integrity. And to be fit enough to officiate at the level you are refereeing at and to be able to deal with people. If you have got those three things you make a half-decent referee.'

Moreover it is clear just how physically and mentally demanding the role is. Again something that connects a referee who wants to be the best he can to the players in teams like ours more than I had ever realised: 'You are making decisions every couple of seconds. It would be interesting to work out how many decisions or non-decisions you are making in a game. It's constant – you can't switch off for a second. You run something like 10km in a game, and afterwards you're buzzing, but when that subsides you are shattered. The next day I'm absolutely knackered, and it's not from aching legs, it's the mental exhaustion. Unless you've done refereeing to a decent standard you don't appreciate that. If you're passionate about being the best ref you can be, then it's bloody hard work. Not like your fat guy who spins round and round in the centre circle or some other referees I have seen who are just there for the money.'

Given the nature of some of the players we came across on a Sunday morning in Edmonton, I assumed that Mike might have had prior dealings with them in his capacity as a local police officer. Mike says this was never really the case and has an interesting theory as to why. 'Do you know what? Yes a few of the guys may have had a few scraps, but I think if you are truly a villain, a nasty person, you are not the sort of person who is going to get up on a Sunday morning, discipline yourself and play in a team game. The bad people I have to deal with are very selfish and they wouldn't be a part of a team, wouldn't think about other people, only themselves. So I think you don't really get "wronguns" in Sunday morning football. I worked at Edmonton Police Station so I would have known. That's why I think sport is such a wonderful thing for young people – a sense of belonging, of camaraderie. If everyone did it I think the world would be a much better place.'

While I can't say I fully agree about there being no 'wronguns', there is definite merit to what he says. Surprisingly, the worst thing that happened to Mike as a matchday official occurred after he had left grass-roots football behind. Having done his time in the Edmonton League, he worked his way up to semi-professional games, officiating in the Spartan South Midlands and Ryman leagues. 'I was running the line at Tilbury, 85 minutes in, next thing I know I am on the floor. I'd been rugby tackled. Basically this guy, pissed, came out of the crowd from behind me. He's got up and looked at me, then dropped his trousers and mooned in my face and then jumped over the barrier back into the crowd. I didn't feel threatened at any point, I don't know if it was a dare or a bet. He was arrested and banned from that club for the rest of his life. People were laughing. I was sitting on the floor with my flag and pressed my buzzer. The referee has come over and said, "I couldn't see you, Mike. I thought you'd disappeared!" Nothing ever happened at the parks, but for that assault to happen where people pay to get in, where there are stewards and barriers, was weird. I told the arresting officer, this never even happened to me at Firs Farm.'

Mike concludes that overwhelmingly his experiences in the Edmonton League were positive. 'You are disappointed at the end of the game if the majority of players don't come up and shake your hand because you have done your best; you've been honest, turned up and got them through. It's nice to get that, you have been lonely for 90 minutes, you are looking forward to that gesture. If they come up and say, "Thanks, good game ref," or even "Thanks, you had a shit game," at least they said thanks… It's when the team that's lost come and shake your hand you know you have done a decent job. I went home on a high. If I felt I had done a good job it's probably the same feeling as players get after a victory; I felt like I had won.'

At the time we spoke, Mike was recovering from a knee injury that has prevented him refereeing for a while and checked his further progression up the refereeing ladder. 'I am one of the oldest Level 4 referees in the country. I think my time at that level is finished. Level 4 is the top 5%. But I really miss it and next season I will see how the knee goes. A Level 4 referee has to take a fitness test and I probably won't be ready for that, so I will drop down to senior county level. So you go up and then you drop down and down; I will probably end up back in the parks in a few years and I'd do it as well. I will carry on doing it until the day I go, absolutely for the love of the game. I miss those Sunday mornings, I mean it's nice having neutral assistants, being in a ground with people paying to watch, but there is something special about Sunday League football. That's where I learnt my trade and you don't forget it. I'd do it again, I will do it again… if you ever need a referee you've got my number.'

Chapter Fourteen

The magic runs out

W HEN a player was sent off you could hope that the referee would take pity and decide not to put the paperwork through. This happened occasionally, but unfortunately for us and Danny, this was never the case for him, such was the impression he was making on the match officials at this time. As Mike Chisholm told me, Danny was a good challenge for a referee. Even before the game started he'd take the ref to task if he felt the ball wasn't inflated to the optimum level. 'I didn't think for one minute he was a nasty person. I could see the frustration in him, he just couldn't bite his lip.' His talent on the pitch made Danny stand out, but for our part we felt that referees weren't protecting him sufficiently when other teams targeted him with bad tackles. More often than not it was this that led Danny into arguing with the ref.

Each time Danny was given a red card, a few days later an envelope emblazoned with the light blue crest of the London Football Association dropped through my door because I was acting as club secretary. Inside would be a concise description of the incident from the referee's perspective, which as you can imagine didn't usually tally with our own recollection of events and then a form saying how long the suspension would be, what the appeals process was and the amount of the fine. I think the need of club secretaries to pay Football Association fines was one of the main reasons banks kept chequebooks in existence. A look through the stubs in my drawer reveals that every single cheque I wrote for a period of five years was to the London FA for 'fines'. A yellow card was in the region of £10, a red card £30 which included a £10 administration fee. Those LFA branded envelopes don't come cheap.

There was an option on the forms you had to send back to refute the charge and even request a personal hearing for a player who had been sent off (another £50 plus £10 administration fee) but it was never clear exactly how you were supposed to prove what had happened, given the lack of video footage of 99.9% of our games or impartial observers. Other than devising some sort of one bark for yes, two barks for no for the dog of the oft-mentioned man and his dog who might be on the sideline for a few minutes, you basically had to tick a box marked 'guilty' but then plead for leniency. Danny and I, like a crack legal team, would turn the incident over and over, recalling the things said and done by the opposition players in the build-up to him losing his rag. I took real pride in crafting our responses to the charges. I still have a folder on my computer called 'Danny appeal letters'.

Several times we were able to get the length of his suspension reduced owing to mitigating circumstances, such as the threats made by player X, or the referee missing a chest-high tackle on Danny that bordered on assault. I also worked out that, depending on what stage you sent the reply back accepting the charges (there was a window of a couple weeks before further 'administration' fees were levied for tardiness) you could postpone the start of any suspension. This delay was especially useful at the end of the season when a key player like Danny could play in a big game and defer his suspension to the start of the next campaign.

Cunningly, at the start of the 2009/10 season, I asked the League that we start our campaign a couple of weeks late. The reason was that the FA operated a system where players' suspensions were determined by dates rather than by a fixed number of matches. This seemed a ridiculous rule to me. Nonetheless, that was how it worked and so if you had no match during the suspension period, your ban lapsed without you missing any games. While this seemed like a stroke of genius on paper, and demonstrated how much as a team we felt we needed Danny on the pitch, in reality my cunning plan backfired. In fact due to the number of cup games scheduled in the early part of the season and a particularly bad spell of weather, it was a disaster. Come February, we had only played three of our league games, meaning for the first time ever we were going to have to play double headers, where you play the same team twice on the same Sunday back-to-back in order to complete all your fixtures.

The season had turned into a long slog. The old adage about defending a league title being harder than winning one first time round certainly rang true for us, although I doubt whoever coined this piece of wisdom in the professional game faced the challenge of some players simply not wanting to get out of bed and play football anymore. The summer after winning the top flight, several of the boys felt it was the perfect note on which to bow out. Andy, who was such a driving force for the team off the pitch, had also voiced his intentions to pack it in. It basically took a two-line whip that summer, Mickey and I phoning him on alternate nights over the course of a week, to put on the pressure to give it one more year. Neil, however, was the first to actually hang up his boots and being one of the players I was closest to, and someone you could always rely on to be there and give his all, this was a major blow. As he explains, 'I felt the spark was gone after we won that league. It was definitely harder getting players to turn out. I had been involved in making sure people played and the recruitment side of things, picking people up and ensuring we always had an 11, and that was aggravation and I remember thinking "I have outgrown this".'

I secretly admired Neil for being honest enough to walk away and go through with it. Part of me wanted to do the same as I had found the previous year of chasing down a title all-consuming and genuinely stressful, and now felt anything but winning it again would be a failure. But I knew that if I were to jump ship the team would fold, and since there were just about enough players who wanted to keep going, I felt I had to carry on. As the season unfolded, I think more of us began to realise that Andy and Neil's instincts had been right. The spirit just wasn't the same as it had been; people's lives had gone off in different directions and they weren't able to give the team the priority it needed for us to sustain the standard we'd set ourselves. Seeing us struggling week after week to get a team together and out of a sense of duty, Neil actually agreed to come back and play the last six weeks of the season. 'Coming back into it part way through that final season was because the team was short and because my mates were saying, "Why aren't you playing? You're not an old man!" I got dragged back in because you sort of feel you are letting your mates down. When I came back maybe I felt I'd missed it; but two weeks in, I felt like I'd made the right call first time round, and "Why am I doing this again?"'

Danny was sent off, for dissent, against The Bull. This time the suspension that came through proved to be particularly punitive as his prior misdemeanours were taken into account and the ban extended. I immediately took to writing an appeal letter pointing out that as we were now to play double headers most weekends during the time Danny was suspended, this would effectively rule him out of double the number of games he could normally expect to miss. Shamelessly, having used the anomaly to our benefit at the start of the season, this time I argued that the London FA should consider changing its rules.

I can see now that my 'good' ideas, based on no experience of running a Sunday League, were bound to cut no ice with men who had been successfully running amateur football in London for decades. The first of the double headers we were to play was against Attitude, who had been promoted to the top flight at the end of the season we'd won it. At the League meeting that was held the week before the fixtures were due to be played, I suggested that as there were other double headers being played at Church Street that weekend, after the first game the referee should swap pitches so that the ref was not having to officiate the same fixture and players twice. For example, if a ref had given a dubious decision in the first game the pressure on him would be relentless if he then had to referee the whole match again immediately afterwards. Similarly, given the history of the fixture, I suggested that this measure would also alleviate the issue of a player being sent off in the first game and then being back on the pitch for the second with the same referee. For reasons that weren't clear, this suggestion was deemed a non-starter. The League officials suggested that teams would need to be sensible and self-policing: although there was nothing to stop a player who was sent off in game one turning out in game two, club secretaries should prevent this happening. Unsurprisingly this judgement was greeted by a chorus of laughter, winks and elbow-nudging among the assembled club secretaries at the meeting, who knew that noble intentions and gentlemanly behaviour were unlikely to win out over the desire to take three points.

A year apart had done nothing to dilute the antagonism between Attitude and the Wizards, and now we were due to face each other in two games on the same morning, back-to-back. It was the week in April when volcanic eruptions in Iceland had created an ash cloud that shut down airspace across the continent for several days. And so the first game kicked off under quiet Edmonton skies unusually free of air traffic.

Midway through the first half of the first game I tackled one of their more skilful players, 'Skinner', who was a combustible character, and as soon as I had played the ball forward he turned round and booted me as hard as he could without a single exchange of words between us. Perhaps the referee had come up with his own way of avoiding tensions in the second match by just ignoring anything that went on in the first. At least that's how it appeared as he didn't even give a free kick, let alone reach for his top pocket.

Shortly after this, Attitude broke into our box and Ed came rushing off his line and got fingertips to the ball as their striker tried to go round him. Having seen the ball diverted away, the striker went down and his team-mates all called for a penalty. Adrenaline pumping, I ran over to the player and 'politely' encouraged him to get up as he writhed on the floor, even trying to drag him to his feet as this went on, which understandably was not well received when it transpired he was genuinely hurt. My mind immediately went to Alf Inge Haaland who had done a similar thing to Roy Keane when playing for Leeds against Manchester United; Keane had actually torn his cruciate ligament and would be ruled out of the game for months. Thankfully the Attitude player wasn't seriously hurt, but I regretted what I had done. Ironically, a matter of minutes later a ball went over my head around the halfway line; as I turned to run after it the rubber studs of my Puma King moulds locked in the hard ground causing my right knee to stay facing forward as the rest of my body turned and faced the other way. The pain was immediate and intense as I crumpled to the floor. However, having just lambasted the Attitude forward for faking injury, pride made me get up and try to play on, which I did for a few minutes until half-time, knowing something serious had happened. I was substituted at the break with the game at 2-2, and watched the second half unfold sitting on the ground next to Andy. We conceded a late goal to lose 3-2. With no further subs available, and with only a short rest for water, the same 11 Wizards then took to the field for the second match and produced a 4-2 win. In a way this confirmed just how well matched the two teams were. Over the years our games with Attitude were always tight and as this showed, on any given Sunday we could beat them and they could beat us. Literally.

That was to prove my last ever start for the Wizards as it later turned out I had torn my cruciate ligament, completing a set of injuries made famous by professional football. A couple of weeks later, when two of our players had to come off injured, I did come on as sub and played the last 15 minutes of the second game in a double header against Southbury, but it was at walking pace as I physically couldn't run. It was to be my final appearance in an orange Wizards shirt. I watched us play out our remaining fixtures sat on a fold-up garden chair by the side of the pitch. The double headers were killing us as we limped to the end of the season. Infuriatingly, we finished the season second in the table, narrowly behind Clavisque, who won the title, even though each time we played them we were significantly the better team. Our final game of the season was the second game of another double header played, as the final fixtures of the season always were, on a pitch where the grass was now so long it partly camouflaged the ball and had some rogue daisies sprouting out from it, waiting to be culled any day by a man from the local authority on a ride-on mower.

At full time, we congregated at the side of the pitch and the inevitable question, 'What are we doing next year?' was asked. There were a handful of players who said they wanted to carry on – Ed and Mickey were particularly vociferous – but although I didn't want to be the one to say it, it was clear that the fire in the team had gone out. We didn't have 11 players willing, and Andy said there would be no talking him round a further time. I knew we were done and Sunday mornings would never be the same again. Nine of the players who played in that final double header had played for the team during our first ever season nearly a decade before. The best of times, the worst of times.

Chapter Fifteen

It was the season of darkness

I T WAS fortunate that the Wizards folded just before the 2010 World Cup as the release of the Panini World Cup Album™ gave me something to focus on while I waited for my appointment to see the orthopaedic specialist who could determine the extent of the damage to my knee. As Mel and I had only started going out a couple of months after the final of the previous World Cup, she had not experienced the frenzied madness of a World Cup sticker collection before. There aren't too many things that you can categorically say are better about being an adult than a child, but having enough disposable income to walk into a newsagent's and buy a box of Panini stickers outright, rather than waiting for your pocket money each week or nagging your dad to buy you a couple of covert packs, is definitely one of them. As I sat gloriously surrounded by the detritus of 100 packs I felt a bit like one of those city traders from the 1980s, rolling around the floor of a stunning penthouse apartment covered in bank notes. The only difference was I was in my bedroom, still living in the parental home, convincing my girlfriend that a good way to spend a Saturday would be putting 500 stickers in numerical order while watching repeats of *Dr Quinn Medicine Woman*. It says a great deal about the magnificence of Panini's product that Mel actually quite enjoyed this task and has subsequently helped with other World Cup albums. Panini categorically state that they print an equal number of each sticker, and so I can only conclude that it was pure coincidence that while I had a score of Kolo Toures I couldn't get a Dirk Kuyt anywhere. The downside of collecting World Cup stickers as an adult is that you haven't got a playground of friends to swap with, or to share your dismay at the fact that the England team stickers always spoil the whole album. This is because the FA have done a separate deal with another company, meaning Panini have to superimpose the England players' heads onto randomly selected bodies, judging by the difference in said players' build and ethnicity, and make the shiny sticker into a rubbish flag of St George rather than the proper three lions. There are lots of reasons to have gripes with modern football and the FA but this is the biggest for me. When the time comes, my plan is to be buried with all my World Cup albums and my Wizards medals, a bit like an Egyptian pharaoh taking with him his most important treasures to the afterlife. Hopefully the FA's commercial contracts aren't binding in that dimension and the England pages will magically correct themselves.

While I take Panini World Cup™ stickers pretty seriously, it is worth noting that a friend of mine who had to go on a business trip to Colombia ahead of the 2014 World Cup in Brazil found that in Bogotá there are pop-up street stalls that sell the stickers to crowds formed exclusively of adults. After a heist in Brazil saw 300,000 of Panini's precious cargo stolen, the prospect of a shortage of stickers in South America led to scaremongering and panic. Panini moved swiftly to see off the threat of rioting by assuring the public that the supply of stickers would keep on coming.

Although the World Cup in South Africa wasn't a particularly special one, at least on the field, I always find the day after the World Cup Final is like the worst of hangovers. Four long years to wait until it comes around again! The knowledge that nothing in the intervening period will come anywhere close! A South African friend had bought me a vuvuzela adorned in the vibrant colours of the new South African flag. One of the highlights of finally getting on the London property ladder that autumn was blowing on the vuvuzela at close proximity to unsuspecting visitors who came over to see our new flat. This fun proved to be short-lived once we realised the sound travelled through the wall and wasn't endearing us to our neighbours who had a newly born baby.

My letter to see the specialist about my knee came through, and following an inspection where no specific diagnosis was given I was referred to a lower limbs physiotherapy group at Chase Farm Hospital, Enfield. Chase Farm had seen better days. There had been a long-standing debate over the future of the hospital and particularly whether the Accident and Emergency department I'd got to know so well over the years should be closed. Though some parts of the hospital had been updated with new buildings, a lot of departments, including physiotherapy, were in what looked like wooden huts kept in use far, far beyond what was originally intended. But while the tired paintwork and waiting room furniture told a story of neglect, the physiotherapy team and the equipment available for rehab were very good. I was put on a programme of exercises that after a few weeks meant I could start to bend my knee again; and after a few months of attending every Friday I eventually got back to running.

That autumn, as well as concentrating on my knee rehab, I had the honour of being best man for my oldest friend and Wizards stalwart, Matthew Berou. Matt grew up in a warm Greek Cypriot family, and I've known him, his parents and two older sisters since he and I were in nursery school together. Although he comes over as a quiet, unassuming person, Matt's passion for the Wizards was right up there with my own and his efforts on and off the pitch were integral to the team's record of success.

He was always one of the brighter boys at school and worked hard at university,[36] but this never stopped him having lots of girlfriends. It was during his time as a Wizard that he met his future wife, Sangeeta. He and I were out together in central London on the night of an England World Cup qualifier and while Matt was trying to be a good friend and talk to me, his at that time very single friend, about the state of goalkeeping in England and our opponents for our Wizards game that week, he was also attempting to cultivate a conversation with a stranger who had caught his eye. Finally, after about the tenth time of interrupting with inane football chat, it dawned on me what was happening and I left Matt and Sangeeta to talk. Happily they have been together ever since.

I would imagine anyone who has ever had to be best man feels under pressure, but I think the combination of Greek Cypriot and Indian wedding, with huge numbers of people and cultural customs to be followed on both sides, made this one a particularly daunting task. Having known Matt for such a long time, I was fortunate to have a wealth of material for the speech. Nevertheless I agonised over it for weeks in the time between a very civilised stag do in Valencia, where we mostly played football on the beach and took in a Valencia home game at the Mestalla, and the wedding, which was to be held in a vast hotel that specialises in Indian weddings a stone's throw away from Heathrow airport.

The day before the wedding I had collected a projector screen I had rented for the occasion to put up some photos of Matt charting the three decades we had been friends. I had enlisted the help of my sister to put the finishing touches on the photo slideshow and so was en route to her house, just behind Wood Green tube station. Wood Green is a permanently busy stretch

---

36 Matt now works for the Bank of England.

of Green Lanes where you can get a full English breakfast, a kebab, any amount of fried chicken or all three 24 hours a day while listening to a pavement sermon from the religion of your choice. It can at times be a little bit wild. I once came out of the cinema by the station with Mel and my sister and brother-in-law to see a group of ten or so young men battering two others with some sort of telescopic club.

Around this time Wood Green tube station had started to pipe classical music into the ticket foyer. It was a policy based on the idea that the best way to prevent young people hanging around and causing trouble is to play music they hate so much that they'd rather be anywhere else; also it has a calming effect on passengers and staff, thereby reducing the incidence of abuse. As I exited the station and started the short walk to my sister's house, humming along with the string section, I became aware of a very pale man in a hooded jumper walking towards me, his eyes fixed on the projector screen that I was carrying in its long, thin, rectangular case. The man had the look of someone who was using a lot of drugs. He was rakishly thin, with vacant eyes aged well beyond his actual years, but there wasn't anything overtly threatening about him and I slowed down as our paths met. It was clear he wanted to say something, but I had no idea what it would be.

'Come on mate, give us a tune on your oboe.'

Clearly the tube station's classical music was having an influence on at least one of Wood Green's residents. I explained that what I was carrying was actually a projector screen, which I was going to use for a best man's speech the next day. He considered this for a moment, then said, 'Best man's speech? Wicked!' flicking his index finger to make that clicking sound of approval, which is something I have always enjoyed ever since realising years earlier that I was one of the lucky few in the playground who could do it.

'I'll give you the best, best man's joke, do you want to hear it?' How could I say no?

'First you get all the meat together and lock the doors, no actually that's wrong; first you get all the kids and you cover their faces in red paint and this is the best part coz the coppers can't do nothing, then, then you get all the meat, yeah all the meat, and remember the coppers can't do nothing.'

Then suddenly his face contorted, and he groaned and said solemnly, 'Oh no, it's not gonna work coz you'll need fireworks.' And with that he was off, leaving me the gift of being able to retell this encounter at the wedding the next day. Perhaps that was his intention all along.

When the London riots sparked into life in August 2011, following the shooting by police of Mark Duggan in neighbouring Tottenham, it came as no surprise that Wood Green's shopping centre was one of the places affected. Mostly the looting seemed to be young kids making off with Nikes from Foot Locker rather than anything political, but it's worth noting that the Borough of Haringey where Wood Green and Tottenham are located was facing big cuts to public and youth services as part of austerity measures imposed by the coalition government. As shops burned and the Greek and Turkish shopkeepers further north along Green Lanes boarded up their windows and prepared to defend their properties, my sister Rosanne and her husband Johnny went off to Los Angeles, to study and work for two years. Our family house had also been sold and my mum was moving away. It seemed that week as if things in my corner of north London were unravelling.

I had a lot of stuff in the old house, which now had to be sorted through. With great maturity I had resolved to put all my Tottenham Hotspur goals of the season VHS tapes and DVDs that spanned every (mostly dismal) season from 1988/89 through to 2011 on eBay.[37] But far more troubling than waving goodbye to these memories was the decision over what to do with the Wizards kit bag, which had been sitting in my mum's loft

---

37 Needless to say, the cost of postage was considerably higher than the winning bid.

since the team folded. It was with a genuinely heavy heart that I took it to the local authority recycling centre and left the bag full of 15 orange shirts, goalkeeper shirt, shorts and socks in the big shed marked 'shoes and clothes'. I don't think I realised just how traumatic this had been for me until later that day, while back at the dump with some more items for 'household waste' I somehow managed to throw my car keys into the skip with them. I was in such a mournful daze over the sorry send-off I had given the Wizards kit that I hadn't even noticed I had done this until one of the recycle centre staff, who must have been watching me and have climbed in to retrieve them, brought them over to me at the exact moment I was patting down my jeans and thinking 'Where are my keys?' It was a reminder amid the chaos that plenty of people in London are still happy to help a stranger.

Maybe needing something different to focus on, I fixated on the prospect of Spurs' first game of the season (against Everton) being postponed, which eventually it was because buildings along Tottenham High Road had been set alight, and the police had other things to do than marshal football fans. It was grim watching parts of the area a mile from where I'd grown up, and minutes from where both my sister and I had bought our first homes, temporarily tearing itself apart. The news footage of those four or five days' anarchy even reached western Canada, where Mel's parents became understandably alarmed. It didn't feel like the north London I knew and loved anymore. But I reasoned that at least one positive thing might come out of the mess. Surely the authorities would now have to ensure that Tottenham Hotspur would remain in Tottenham and act as the catalyst for regeneration of the whole area, one of the most depressed in the entire country.

Impossible as it seems, it was just 12 months later that the London 2012 Olympics got underway. A completely opposite feeling of goodwill and optimism swept through the city, indeed the whole country, a warm glow of brotherly love and London pride. It gripped hold from the start of the brilliant opening ceremony and lasted right the way through to the close of the Paralympics in September.

Following years of rhetoric and plans about a new stadium in Tottenham, the Spurs board had announced that it was entering the bidding process to take over the Olympic Stadium in Stratford once the Games were over. I think this is the most passionate I have ever felt about any issue in football. How could a team from north London called Tottenham Hotspur play in Stratford, east London? It seemed that the club that had been such a huge part of my life from the age of five was willing to throw away its identity purely to exploit a commercial deal, even if this meant isolating or destroying a large swathe of its fan base. Even worse, some Spurs fans declared they were fine with this and were actually championing the proposal. For me the location of the club, its history, identity and fans are the only things left that make it justifiable to spend so much time and effort caring about its fortunes. Once you strip away those things all that's left is just another multi-million-pound company.

Had Spurs 'won' the Olympic Stadium I think that would have been it for me, I would have had to walk away and effectively consign 25 years of support for the club to the past. Some people thought there was a bit of manoeuvring going on. The Olympic Stadium had been awarded to West Ham six months before the riots, prompting Spurs to request a judicial review. When this was refused, Spurs started an appeal. There was still real uncertainty about where the future of Tottenham Hotspur lay when the rioting broke out and the sorry, deprived state of Tottenham became national news.

The idea that Tottenham Hotspur could leave its own locality just at the time this community needed something to drag it out of the doldrums was anathema to me. Now it seemed politically that this was something the local authority, the mayor's office and central government could not be seen to allow. Before too long, the first announcement of government money for a major 'sport-led regeneration of the Tottenham area' was made public, with a new Spurs stadium right next to White Hart Lane at its centre.

During this time of uncertainty, Alex and I had gone along to a demonstration on Tottenham High Road before one of the games, but we were depressed to find just a handful of people holding some balloons with less than catchy and hazily printed messages on them, 'Keep Tottenham in Tottenham'. It was hard not to feel disappointment if this was all we could muster, when the very future of the club was at stake. I was however given a jolt by my dad who reminded me that protest, however small, does have its place, even if it is not successful or, in this case, always particularly coherent.

One Friday afternoon in summer 2012 I got a phone call at work. My dad had been arrested and was in Charing Cross Police Station.

I should explain that while I missed out on having my dad on the sideline when I was a boy, and I sometimes held this against him, he had his own reasons. In addition to being a journalist he was a passionate campaigner for social justice. He had made two documentaries for ITV about the 1984 disaster in Bhopal, India, where a factory explosion led to toxic gas being released into the air killing thousands of people, and he'd carried on battling away against Union Carbide to get adequate compensation for the bereaved families and the thousands of people left disabled by chronic diseases.[38] As a youngster, I had often heard my dad speaking about Bhopal, but as India wasn't really a footballing country I had never paid much attention. This changed with that phone call.

When you arrive at the police station, an officer at the front desk directs you to a funny yellow telephone, which I don't remember being a part of the Lego police station play-set, and you have to dial down to the custody officers in the detention

---

38 The explosion in the chemical plant at Bhopal is probably the world's worst ever industrial accident. Union Carbide is an American company; it retreated out of India, and was subsequently taken over by Dow Chemicals.

area who supposedly can give you more information about anyone they are holding. No information was forthcoming, so I waited in reception for a very long time wondering what my dad had done. Eventually, after a third go at speaking to the mystery voice at the other end of the yellow phone line, another person waiting overheard me saying my dad's name, Laurie Flynn. He told me that my dad had been arrested on a protest in Trafalgar Square, he even had footage on his iPad of my old man being put in the police van, which he was more than happy to show me. It turned out that the protest was aimed at Dow Chemicals, one of the official sponsors of the London Olympics. Dow had bought Union Carbide after the Bhopal disaster and was stonewalling appeals for fairer compensation for the victims. The protestors were engaged in some sort of physical theatre that involved pouring green custard on each other in a fake Olympic medal ceremony. Don't ask, I have no idea either! Security was high in central London throughout the Olympic summer and a busy Trafalgar Square warden, who clearly missed his calling as a Sunday League referee, had taken offence at the display; he'd called in the police to report an act of criminal damage. My dad tells me that by the time the 25 police officers arrived, the custard had already been cleaned up. He explained to them that he was fully willing to co-operate by demonstrating that the custard was edible if necessary. Notwithstanding, he was arrested as part of the 'Custard Seven'.

By the time he was finally released, he had been in custody for nearly nine hours and I had been waiting for four of them. The farcical nature of the events was only heightened by the fact that, in his rush to leave the cells once the fine men and women of the Metropolitan Police let him go, he had forgotten to refasten his belt, which they had taken off him; and so as he stood in the police station reception area and relayed the story of what had happened, exchanging words of encouragement with the other protesters who had just been released, his trousers fell down, but being the man that he is, he snatched them up with one hand

and continued talking without missing a beat. In the end he received a police caution and a banning order from attending any Olympic venues during the course of the games.

As the new season came round, I had decided to make a comeback to 11-a-side football. After over a year of weekly physio my knee felt OK and Alexandra Park FC was situated just up the road. I was going to be that weird, awkward fella who turns up at pre-season training not knowing a single person at the club. Anonymity gave me the chance to style myself as a ball-playing centre-midfielder and philosopher, the missing link to the Brazil World Cup team of 1982 discovered anew in north London, rather than the big clogger of a centre-half that I had been for the Wizards. The freedom of not playing with people I went to school with, and the obligatory piss-taking among mates when anyone does anything a bit out of the ordinary, had also emboldened me to grow my hair long and cultivate a bit of a beard. At Alexandra Park when I was in possession of the ball and a team-mate called me, what I'd hear would be, 'Give and go Jesus!'

As a new player you had to play a pre-season friendly for the Alexandra Park 8s against the 7s and work your way up from there, a bit like the way all policemen have to start off walking the beat. This was an analogy I came up with when I was talking to Steve, the builder working on our flat. He'd seen my muddy football boots and asked who I was playing for and I felt at pains to explain my current team was no reflection of my footballing ability – I just needed to work my way up. Steve, it turned out, had played for the Crouch End Vampires, Alexandra Park's fiercest rivals, for years and years to 'a very good standard' but he had to pack it in. He cited two age-old reasons that have sounded the death knell for so many amateur footballers' careers: the missus and work.

It was liberating playing for Ally Park, as they are known. It was just football as pure fun. While I gave it my best and like to think significantly improved the team, even though we lost every game that I played in at the start of that season, I played without any sense of pressure for the first time in a long time and really, really enjoyed myself. The fact that the team also played in the famous orange shirts and black shorts as worn by the Wizards was just a happy coincidence.

My standout memory from the handful of games I played was being refereed by a man who cannot have been any less than 80 years old. It was quite remarkable to see this old boy with such a love for football that he was still out there refereeing a parks game at his age. Judging by the size of the collar on his referee's shirt he'd been doing the same since Bobby Moore got stitched up for shoplifting in Colombia and yellow and red cards were introduced into the game for the first time. Equally amazing was the fact that some players on both teams couldn't resist the urge to give him shocking dogs' abuse for not keeping up with the play, or for getting a decision wrong; but thankfully it seemed he didn't wear his hearing aid to referee and so was happily oblivious.

After about five games the rock hard pitches of late summer gave way to the sticky mud of autumn; I landed heavily after a header and my knee went again. It was following a chat with Mickey Pearce, who had battled on through so many injuries to keep playing, that I decided to go back to the doctor and ask for an MRI scan.

I received an appointment letter to go to a clinic near Manor House. When I informed the reception I was there for a scan on my knee they said I should go round to the car park, which all seemed a bit backstreet for what was a pretty standard examination of a fairly routine body part. In the car park was a huge articulated lorry, which instantly reminded me of Optimus Prime from Transformers, with steps up the back; it led inside to a small reception room with a screen and computer monitors where a nurse instructed me to change into a hospital gown. The scan itself involved lying flat on a bench which slid into a big cylinder that periodically made loud clicking noises while taking images of the inside of my knee. After about 15 minutes the clicking sounds stopped and the nurse informed me that the results would be sent to my GP in a few weeks. But when the time came the doctor at my surgery was unsure of what he was looking at, so I was referred back to the orthopaedics team at Chase Farm where a physio, without needing to refer to the CD ROM of the scan, pulled and pushed my leg around and said he was 99% sure that I had torn my anterior cruciate ligament (ACL) as well as damaging the cartilage. He was a friendly Irish guy who said I had a lot of good years of football left in me and that surgery would enable me to play on to a good standard. Honestly, at that time there was no choice to be made. If it meant the chance to play football again, then it had to be done; that and the fact that the childish part of me felt weirdly proud at having one of the more serious injuries a footballer could have.

After meeting with the surgeon who would perform the operation, Mr Saksena, with whom I bonded instantly as he complimented me on the vintage Adidas France 1982 tracksuit top which I wore to the appointment, it was then a case of waiting a few months for the date of the surgery to come through. Previously when I had been under the surgeon's knife it had been following accidents, meaning the repairs were done immediately, and so waiting to move up the hospital orthopaedics list was a new experience for me. I was aware that people live out their life quite happily without a functioning anterior cruciate ligament, so long as they don't want to play football. But I was electing to have this operation done, which might mean I was a long way down the Chase Farm list. I remember one day turning on the radio in my kitchen at exactly the point BBC Radio 5 Live trailed that it would shortly be speaking to a man who had gone into hospital for a standard knee operation but due to an infection that had gotten into his spine had lost the use of his legs. Now while the internet is perhaps the standout invention of the 20th century, when you are waiting to have surgery done it does have its downside. Of course you could Google statistics for successful

ACL surgeries, but let's face it, who is going to do that when there are so many stories of freak mishaps to torment yourself with? Seven months passed before my letter came through, and by that time I had worried myself into a frenzy about the 'Things That Could Go Wrong'.

Before an elective procedure like this you have to go into the hospital a few weeks in advance to meet the anaesthetist, who makes sure you are medically fit to undergo the operation. You are also required to stick a cotton swab up your nose and between the join of leg and ball bag, the female nurse gave me a particularly vivid air-swab demonstration, which is used to test for MRSA. Having successfully swabbed my own groin in the toilets, I sat patiently in the waiting area, observing the misery of a receptionist trying to relay information to some people who didn't speak English as a first language. Her technique involved aggressively repeating the exact same phrase she had used the first time increasingly loudly to the point where she was shouting at them. Before I could see the conclusion of this exchange I became distracted by the middle-aged woman sitting next to me who seemed to be writing a novel via the medium of text message, and had declined to turn off the keypad noises on her phone, meaning each press was accompanied by a beep. I resolved at that point, providing I survived the operation, to start a campaign to force mobile phone manufacturers to make all keypads silent as standard.[39] This hyper-acute sensitivity to the relatively innocuous actions of other patients in hospital was to prove a regular theme over the next couple of months.

The anaesthetist takes you through a series of lifestyle questions which, being a pretty clean-living character, I smugly answered, wondering about the answers she must get from other people. The way she raised a sceptical eyebrow made me think that she was suspicious of my answer to the question about how many units of alcohol I consume a week, which is often none.

---

39 Having thought about this a lot since, I can't see any reason to have beeping buttons on a mobile phone other than to piss off random strangers.

Having told her that I had injured myself playing football and was a big football fan, I guessed she was struggling to reconcile what for her were two contradictory ideas: 'Likes football but doesn't drink.'

Providing my groin swabs came back clear, I was all set to have the operation in a couple of weeks' time at the end of November. I made plans to go with my sister, now back from the US, and our other halves to Edinburgh to see my dad. I was joking that I should make sure I see all the family before the surgery, just in case, but this wasn't that well received as it wasn't funny and also I wasn't joking. Just before we were due to get the train, the hospital called and said that they'd had a cancellation and could now fit me in early on Friday of the following week. This was good news to me as Mel and I had booked flights to Canada to visit her family for Christmas, and although it was always going to be tight I thought it would give me enough time to recover. My dad, who can be relied upon to provide exactly the information you don't want to hear, helpfully told me on the phone that Fridays were absolutely the worst day to have any kind of surgical procedure as by the end of the week doctors are so tired that the probability of mistakes increases exponentially. Nice one dad. Thanks.

Heading north, I was reading David Peace's *Red or Dead*, an amazing factual and fictional account of Bill Shankly's management of Liverpool. Entire pages of the book are just repetitions of the same text, and on the five-hour train journey I was delighting in reading out loud examples of where the team line-up for a certain game Liverpool played in the 1970s is written out in full and then repeated verbatim over and over like a chant. I wasn't making much headway with the girls, who had absolutely no idea who Emlyn Hughes even was.

Having eventually bored them into submission, I then attempted to convince Rosanne, who works in television and film, that *Red or Dead* would make an excellent TV series and she should check if anyone had bought the rights to it. She dismissed my idea saying there wouldn't be a big enough audience for it, at which point with almost perfect timing a couple in their sixties from Huddersfield sat down opposite us. The man, having noticed the book on the table in front of me and not being from London and therefore uninhibited by the capital's most important rule of avoiding conversations with strangers on public transport at all costs, told me he was reading the book too and loving it and would definitely like to see it adapted for TV. While I felt pretty good about getting one over on my sister for only the third time in 32 years, it should be noted that the man's wife was less enthused by the idea.

Following the weekend trip to Edinburgh, each night's sleep counting down to the Friday got progressively worse. I began to give serious thought as to whether I should buy some sort of weatherproof wrapping for my sticker albums so that they didn't decompose along with my corpse if the worst happened. On the day before the operation I seriously considered adding the caveat 'If I survive' to my out-of-office message about when I would next respond to emails. That night, reading the pre-op letter supplied by the hospital, I was horrified to see that I should bring an overnight bag with me. I'd somehow assumed I'd be in and out in a day. The next morning as I took the short train ride from Alexandra Palace to Gordon Hill and entered the Surgi Centre of Chase Farm Hospital, 'Hotel California' by the Eagles reverberated in my head. I wondered if I'd be checking out anytime I liked but maybe never leave. Mr Saksena's registrar, Mr Ahmed, took me through the disclaimer form where you sign that you understand all the possible complications that can arise from surgery, including serious surgical infections and blood clots.

As a result, my anxiety levels were already sky high by the time I faced the decision as to whether to answer the attractive nurse's question honestly when she asked if I needed a medium or large size in the mesh paper pants they make you wear under the surgical gown.

Just like when I felt nervous before a big Sunday morning game, I tried to pull myself together. I looked around the ward at the other people waiting stoically in their surgical gowns and told myself, 'Don't be a bottle job.' The familiar face of Mr Saksena appeared and he put my mind at rest by saying I would be first up and more than likely I'd be able to go home that evening. He also made a point this time of complimenting me on my Adidas Star Wars tracksuit top and the fetish we obviously shared for German sportswear meant I felt like I was in safe hands. I walked down to theatre in my surgical hat, gown, paper pants, one surgical sock and pristine Nike Air Max 90s reflecting that as the surgical sock, worn to guard against blood clots, came slightly above my knee, to the casual observer (of whom there were none) it would appear as an homage to Thierry Henry or worse still John Terry who always wore their socks like that.

I lay on the bed in the anaesthetic room where they knock you out before wheeling you through to theatre and actually felt relatively calm. It was reassuring to see that the arrow drawn with marker pen to indicate which knee was to be operated on had been drawn on the right knee. That's to say, on the Right Knee. The anaesthetist told me to count to ten as he put me under. I decided to try and see how many of the Spurs '95/'96 squad's shirt numbers I could recite before going to sleep, a game that helped pass the time in many a GCSE chemistry lesson back in the day.

1 Ian Walker, 2 Dean Austin, 3 Justin Edin...

The procedure for an ACL reconstruction, I know from watching a video on YouTube, involves the surgeon harvesting a strip of your hamstring via keyhole surgery, shaving off the old torn cruciate ligament and then using the piece of hamstring to make a new ligament, which with a bit of drilling and a screw is anchored to the femur and tibia bones; at the same time the surgeon repairs the damaged cartilage which usually accompanies ACL injuries. The whole process can take a few hours but my next memory, after Justin Edinburgh, was coming round and being absolutely sure that the answer to the question that someone, somewhere, was asking was 'Shania Twain'. I actually shouted it out loud. Even now I have no idea whether I was hallucinating that I regained semi-consciousness in a room where someone was doing a crossword, or if they had actually asked the question out loud, but I do know that Shania was definitely the answer. It would be nice to think it was the one answer this fella was missing and in that brief moment before I dipped back out of consciousness, I gave it to him. It was a cracker of an answer.

The passage of time when you are coming round from a general aesthetic is impossible to chart. There's a moment when you open your eyes and realise this time they are staying open. Now I was given a few sips of water and had to try to control the extreme shivering that suddenly overcomes me whenever I have come round from an operation. I was then pushed back into the ward feeling as if only five minutes had passed, even though the darkness which I could see closing in through the windows showed it had been hours.

All that was left was for two of the physiotherapy team to show me how to get up and navigate a few stairs using crutches. I confidently assured them that I was ready to do this and was not feeling the least bit nauseous before almost immediately being sick all down my front, the ward floor and my bed, in full view of the other patients, but I pushed through this and demonstrated I was OK to go home. One of the physios called Reese, who had a shock of curly hair that he managed with an Alice band, imparted to me some real wisdom that was to prove vital over the coming weeks. 'Don't leave it too long to get up to go to the toilet.' Following ACL surgery the muscles in the operated leg waste very quickly, and initially the thigh and hamstring muscles don't fire, making it extremely difficult and slow to get up. Moreover, when you do finally make it to your feet, the rush of blood through the holes that have been drilled in the bones is absolutely excruciating and immediately makes you want to lie back down. Therefore every cup of tea is followed by a very real decision: would it be easier to just wet the bed than attempt to stand up and shuffle a few feet to the toilet? Aside from facing this challenge, my spirits were high and my overwhelming emotion was gratitude to the surgeon, anaesthetist and nurses who'd looked after me.

When I returned to the hospital for a check-up two weeks later, I took a box of the ambassadors' finest hazelnut-based chocolates into the ward as an offering of thanks; also, the amount of chocolate I received from kindly well-wishers at this time was incredible and re-gifting was a strategy to mitigate exceeding my optimal game weight, seriously. I had been working hard on the basic post-surgery rehab and was walking semi-normally without crutches, all of which Mr Ahmed said he was pleased with. I mentally pencilled in my glorious Sunday League comeback for the opening game of the next season.

Then on a Sunday afternoon three weeks after the operation, as I watched a film about another zombie apocalypse, one of the scars from the surgeon's incisions began to swell into the shape of a triangle. It looked like a piece of the Toblerone bar that I had stolen from my sister and then denied eating one Christmas 20 years ago had come back for revenge and was trying to burst out of my upper shin.

By Monday morning this had turned into a big pus-filled blister and I thought it best to ask Mel to come with me to the hospital where I had a scheduled physio appointment for that afternoon anyway. The physio team seemed not to be particularly concerned by it, but advised I go over to Accident and Emergency to have it lanced. I envisaged this would involve a quick pin prick and I'd be back home in time for the start of *Monday Night Football*, however as the orthopaedic doctor asked me when I had last eaten and began explaining that infections that have entered the knee can destroy the whole joint, my mind returned to the disabled man I had heard on the radio. It became clear that dinner with Gary Neville was off the menu.

Mel went off to fetch the things you need when you are going to be admitted to hospital, and at that moment, sitting alone, I started to panic. What was wrong with me that having had so many great years playing football I couldn't just accept that it was time to hang up my boots? Why had I gone chasing a knee operation that might now result in who knew what? I remember getting up off the triage bed and walking up and down the room in a defiant attempt to show the doctor that there must be a mistake as I could walk almost normally.

The doctor on duty, following some input from another colleague, decided to drain the fluid from the wound and I can only compliment his professionalism as I was absolutely disgusted by the colour and volume of what came out. As I had succumbed to the delights of a vending machine while waiting to be seen in A&E, Ribena and a Milky Way, the doctor explained it would not be possible to operate that evening. The plan would be to go back into the knee tomorrow and wash it out with saline solution. In the meantime I was to be admitted to a ward and put on intravenous antibiotics.

The ward was relatively quiet; I was in the furthest bed from the door and was lucky to have a window. There were elderly men in the two beds furthest from me, one of whom, Mr Bose, looked in a terrible state and didn't ever appear to be conscious the entire time I was on the ward. Next to me was a man around my age who was pretty fed up having been on the ward for a week, but it seemed he would be going home the next day; this is what I was hoping for as I struggled to sleep that first night. On Tuesday morning I awoke to find a 'nil by mouth' sign on my table so I knew breakfast was out. Mr Saksena came by, the first time I had seen him since the operation, and remarked that the doctors I had seen on A&E should have drained the wound the night before. I didn't want to tell him that they actually had, and that it had just filled up again overnight, as this would have meant admitting to myself that things weren't heading in the right direction.

It was around 4pm that the porter came by to take me down to theatre. He was annoyed that I hadn't managed to get into my paper pants in the eight lonely, hungry hours I'd been waiting for news of when they would come for me. He had a flag of St George tattooed on his arm which I optimistically decided to take as a sign he liked football rather than the English Defence League, and we had a chat as he wheeled me through the labyrinth of corridors before handing me over to the anaesthetist, wishing me good luck.

3 Justin Edinburgh, 4 David Howells, 5 Colin Calderwood...

When I came round, Mel and my mum were already waiting for me back on the ward. I was at last able to sample the NHS macaroni cheese I had selected from the menu on the advice of my ward neighbour when the catering staff had come to take orders in the morning. As getting up to go to the toilet independently during the night was not going to be possible, I was presented with the hospital alternative, a phallic-shaped cardboard container which with some difficulty you can manoeuvre your manhood into and release all from the comfort of your own bed, lying down even. The only problem is that you can never be entirely sure the capacity of the container is sufficient for the contents of your bladder; suffice to say on my first attempt it was not, and henceforth I always politely requested the nurse to leave two containers.

It was a unique time to be at Chase Farm Hospital. The Accident and Emergency department was to be permanently closed at the end of the week along with some in-patient wards. While the kindness shown towards me that week is something I will not forget, there was a dispirited air about the place.[40] No doubt the staff were worried about their futures. But one nurse, a man called Alan, from the Philippines, was a constant source of positivity; his smile made me almost feel guilty for feeling sorry for myself. The prognosis was that I would need

---

40 This sense was added to by the news coming through that Nelson Mandela had died.

a further operation to wash the knee joint out for a second time, and so I resigned myself to the fact that I would be in the hospital for a few more days. It is incredible how quickly you become institutionalised by the routines on the ward, and also how quickly inhibition and shyness give way to necessity. I had never envisaged that my mum would be flannel-washing me at the age of 32, or having to pretend that she hadn't noticed the skid marks on the flannel as she wrung it out in the cardboard washbasin. Who knew that hospitals were such huge benefactors of the cardboard industry?

Two new men came into the ward. The first was a man called Stewart, who could not have weighed more than eight stone and said he hadn't eaten solid food in three months. He was a quiet but friendly man, exactly what you want. Stewart spent all day in his pyjamas, only moving to put on a huge sleeping-bag-style Adidas Ukrainian manager's jacket in order to go out for a smoke. I could see that it took my mum a lot of self-control not to point out the cigarettes were probably not improving his condition. Opposite me, the bed became occupied by a man aged around 50 who had been admitted with an extremely sore throat but spent the whole time on his mobile phone loudly calling every one of the contacts in his phonebook to tell them how much his throat hurt when he spoke. On the basis of his gold-hooped earring, meticulously gelled hair that was thinning at the back, matching tracksuit top and bottoms and the most pristine white trainers this side of centre court at Wimbledon, I reckoned on him being a fellow Spurs fan, and so it proved. During our first day together, once we had exhausted all Spurs talk, we got on to the subject of Sunday League. It turned out he had played in the Edmonton and District Sunday Football League before a knee injury had put him out to pasture. But things turned sour that night. On falling asleep he began to snore as loud as a pneumatic drill. It was going to be a long night.

At about 2am an elderly man was admitted who had fallen and struck his head. This poor old gent was suffering from dementia and seemed to think that one of the other elderly men on the ward was his best friend from the war; he kept calling out to him to check that he was OK. He would then try to get up and walk over to what he thought was his comrade, risking another fall each time. All I could do was press the button to call the nurse to put him back on the bed, to start the cycle all over again. There was something hugely endearing about this but also massively depressing, an insight into what old age might look like for my parents and one day for me, which sent a shiver down my spine and still does right now thinking about it.

Eventually Alan, the nurse, put up the sides of this man's bed to stop him getting out and the night settled into a rhythm of his calls and the other man's snores. There was nowhere to go and so I took the only path I could see open to me; I put Enya's 'Orinoco Flow' on repeat on my iPod in a futile attempt to sail away, but not before texting Mel and my sister to bring me earplugs and a sleeping mask when they visited the next day.

I recently saw the snoring Spurs fan. He was ahead of me as we left White Hart Lane following a poor home defeat. It always amazes me how you can recognise some people just as quickly from the back of their head as from seeing their face. He was talking loudly on his phone, of course, so I overtook and walked on to the bus stop where I took a seat and waited for the W3 to take me home. After a minute or so he came walking past and for a second our eyes met but nothing was said. I guess some experiences that people share bond them forever and others most certainly do not.

On day three my leg was still bandaged and very painful. Belatedly one of the nurses remembered that the bars at the end of the bed could be removed, meaning I could actually lie down flat for the first time with my legs from the calf downwards hanging off the end of the mattress. But the doctor came to deliver the news that my blood tests had come back from microbiology and they hadn't been able to identify specifically what the infection was. They would therefore need to continue treating it with intravenous antibiotics and have another go at washing the knee out under general anaesthetic. So down to theatre I was wheeled to be knocked out again.

6 Gary Mabbutt, 7 Ruel Fox, 8 Ilie Dumitrescu...

I was finally allowed out at the end of the week. Mr Saksena said my white blood cell count showed that the infection was heading in the right direction and that I could go home with one week's course of oral antibiotics. I left Chase Farm on the day Accident and Emergency closed. A TV crew was filming a small pocket of determined protestors who knew their battle to save that part of the hospital and the service it provided to their community was lost, but who wanted admirably to be there to show defiance.

Mr Saksena had instructed me that should there be any further issues I would now need to go to Barnet Hospital, which is a considerably longer journey from where I live. I spent a nervous week at home with my leg propped up making sure that I took my antibiotics bang on time. I knew that there was now no chance of making the trip to Canada for Christmas as planned, and realised that all those years of tempting fate by insisting on playing Sunday League right before travelling had finally caught up with me.

At the end of the week the wound promptly started to leak again, and so in low spirits Mel and I set off by taxi to Barnet Hospital first thing on the morning of Sunday 15 December. Having learned the lesson of experience, we packed everything that I might need for a lengthy stay, including the earplugs and a much-read copy of Bret the Hitman Hart's autobiography.[41] Yet again waiting in hospital reception on a Sunday morning, I wondered at the sheer volume of young men hobbling into A&E dressed in muddy football kit having clearly been driven from the park by one of the unused subs. It took a long time to be processed that Sunday as things were so busy, and Barnet was

---

41 Bret Hart is the five-time World Wrestling Federation champion and one of Canada's most famous sons.

now taking in all the patients who would previously have gone to Chase Farm. This time I was careful not to eat anything so as to ensure I didn't hold up my opportunity to recall more Spurs players' shirt numbers from bygone days. It was clear I would need another operation and so by 7pm when I had finally done all the necessary blood tests and X-rays it came as a real kick in the bollocks when I was told they could not fit me in for surgery until the next day. Modern-day Spurs were at the same time getting hammered 5-0 by Liverpool in what was yet another Spurs manager's last game in charge. At least I would have the speculation of who the next man in charge would be to keep me busy during my stay.

That first night at Barnet Hospital I was put on a ward that seemed to be exclusively for elderly women, and so I reasoned that opportunities for football chat of any sort, let alone Sunday League, were slim. I was also at this stage feeling very sorry for myself as I lay flat out on the bed, my phone buzzing with messages about the state of Tottenham Hotspur. Usually the first to reply to our Spurs group text chats, my silence prompted one of the boys to text, 'Where's Flynny, is he dead?' For the first time in my life I didn't care about the Spurs result or the manager. All I could think about was the yellow liquid leaking from my knee onto the crisp, white hospital bed sheets. When I spoke to my sister on the phone I was struggling to hold back tears of self-pity but not doing a very good job of it, bottom lip quivering and voice cracking.

In similar style I tried to hold it together when I said goodbye to Mel. We had decided she should not miss her trip home to Canada for two weeks, which only added to my sense that fate was conspiring against me.

It ended up being a ten-day stay in Barnet Hospital, where from the second day I was given my own room rather than being on a shared ward. I underwent three further operations, with a general anaesthetic each time, and tried to settle into what I began to think of as my new pre-match routine:

9 Darren Anderton, 10 Teddy Sheringham, 11 Chris Armstrong...

However, I stopped playing this game after the fifth trip down to theatre. On this occasion the porter came to collect me a bit early and so I arrived in the anaesthetic room ahead of schedule. Consequently there was a few minutes' wait before they could put me under. As I lay on my back trying to jump the gun in recalling who wore number 12 for Spurs in 1995/96 (Jason Dozzell, obviously) suddenly the loudest series of screams I have ever heard started to emanate from beyond the double doors leading to the operating theatre.

'Arrrrrrrrr! Fuck! Fuck! Fuck! Arrrrrr!' The screams seemed to go on for an eternity.

The anaesthetist matter-of-factly turned to me and said, 'Try not to let that worry you, Mr Flynn.' Worry me? How could it possibly? 'There are some procedures we have to do where it is not possible for the patient to be anaesthetised, which can lead to some discomfort for them during surgery.' And with that the screaming abruptly stopped. I hoped it was due to the surgery being successfully completed rather than the other alternative, at which point I was instantly told to 'think of something nice'. Rather than number 13, Erik Thorstvedt, I racked my brain for my best Wizards goal of all time as the room around me began to blur.

Soon after I came round, my sister rang me to say she and my brother-in-law were on their way to the hospital, and they were going to smuggle in a KFC. She'd remarked that I had a bit of a Bobby Sands look about me the last time she'd visited, and I'd have to admit it was true. The hospital does a great job of making sure the meals are served on time, so there is never any danger of you going hungry, but when you are lying in the same room day after day doing nothing more than reading football managers' cliché-riddled autobiographies, you don't build up much of an appetite. I felt pretty nauseous at this mention of fried chicken and told my sister I didn't think I'd be able to hold down a date with the Colonel, but she said that they were getting some for themselves and would bring some extra for me just in case I changed my mind. This was a patent lie. My sister is a very healthy eater and wouldn't go near KFC on her own behalf. I, on the other hand could eat it all the time, though fortunately my sense of self-preservation means I have reined in my consumption to twice a year.

It speaks volumes for the secret recipe that as soon as Rosanne and Johnny arrived and the smell of fried chicken started to escape from the bucket, any thoughts of sickness dissipated and I ate what must have been the equivalent of three chickens' worth. Afterwards I reflected on how lucky I was to have a sister who loved me so much that she would eat KFC with me, wiping my greasy hands on my hospital gown. Dignity had long gone out the window.

As the doctors were unable to determine exactly what the nature of the infection was, it was necessary for them to test my blood for HIV and other diseases. The intravenous antibiotics and repeated surgery didn't seem to be having the desired effect. As a person who has a strong belief in science and who doesn't have any religious beliefs, it was alarming to hear the doctors say they weren't sure what the cause of the infection was and that the treatment was not yet getting on top of it. I have to confess I did even make a little vow to whoever might be up there that if I could just get better and come out of this able to walk normally, I wouldn't even mind not being able to play football again.

Under the new arrangements the orthopaedic team I had seen at Chase Farm were now also working at Barnet, so Mr Saksena and Mr Ahmed were both regularly popping by to check up on me. I was genuinely frightened when Mr Ahmed said to me that along with the treatment they were administering we had to pray for God to help. When a doctor, someone I imagined was the very personification of a man of a science, invokes a 'higher power', you have to think all is not well. It was a good lesson for me not to be so dismissive of other people's religious beliefs.

Following my sixth operation in the space of six weeks, I geared myself up for the fact I would be spending Christmas in hospital. On the morning of Christmas Eve, former Wizards Mickey, Alex and Neil, three of my oldest school friends, came by to see me. Alex even brought me a copy of *Match of the Day Magazine*, which came with 'posters, stickers and a lolly'. It is very difficult to quantify how much of a difference visits like that from my friends and family made. I saw there were patients who had no visitors at all and felt absolutely awful for them. Even when one of the boys stuck an Arsenal sticker above the toilet door in my room that they knew I wouldn't be able to reach to take down, I felt nothing but love towards them.

Later on Christmas Eve, microbiology prescribed a new stronger antibiotic, so strong it is the same thing they give to people with leprosy; because it can harm your liver, it can only be given under strict supervision and injected very slowly. But it was decided at 8pm that I would be allowed to go home for Christmas, and that I could come into the hospital each morning for the next couple of days to have this drug injected. I felt overcome with emotion to be going home. The elderly lady two rooms down would also be going home that day and I was intrigued to see the nurses so excited at this prospect that they formed a guard of honour and kissed and hugged her like an old friend as she made her way along the corridor. It turned out she had been there for almost two years. I suddenly felt embarrassed at how sorry for myself I'd been feeling. As I sat in the back of the car on the journey through north London, the Christmas lights and people spilling out of busy pubs seemed to belong to a world I was no longer part of. It was totally disorienting. I wondered how people cope after a long stretch in prison.

On Christmas morning, as we drove back into the hospital, it was hard not to feel sad for the patient in slippers and pink dressing gown I saw out the front in the freezing cold, having a smoke. She was there every morning at the same time on each of the subsequent days I came into the hospital for my injection, and

I couldn't help but forecast a bleak outcome for her. After a few days I was fitted out with a pic line. This is a tube fed into your arm towards your heart using ultrasound as a guide. From then on I could have the district nurse come to visit me daily at home to administer the antibiotics through the pic line. I also had to go to the doctor's surgery for regular blood tests to check my liver function. After a few weeks of this, my blood tests showed that the infection was gone.

I began attending physiotherapy at Chase Farm Hospital every Thursday and worked really hard at the gym to try and get my right leg muscles built up.

I was the star student of the lower limbs physio group. When I say star student it should be noted that one of the other patients in the group was an overweight middle-aged woman who turned up for her first physio session in a long floral dress and knee high, brown leather boots. She proceeded to use the treadmill by standing with one foot on and one foot off doing a skateboard-motion without the machine switched on. After a minute of this she made some pretty unconvincing noises of exhaustion and then spent the rest of the time outside the rehab gym on the phone to her husband. The following week she complained that her condition wasn't improving. She didn't come back again after that. I then took great satisfaction in how much more weight or repetitions I could do on the leg press machine compared to the people alongside me recovering from hip and knee replacements. Happily I progressed, until in springtime one of the physios took me out to the car park with a football to dribble round some cones. He also had me jump for some headers. Having been away from playing football for so long, I was buoyed by his interest in just how far I can head a football; he even pulled his colleague out of the gym to witness my gift.

This was a short-lived display as my very next header sent the department's one and only ball onto the roof of one of the outbuildings and would require the caretaker and his ladder to retrieve it.

At my gym in Wood Green, however, I was embarrassed by how feeble I actually was compared to the regular clientele, many of whom wouldn't have looked out of place in a 1980s action film that required them to have a homoerotic arm wrestle with Stallone or Schwarzenegger they were so ripped. I made sure to stop halfway through my set to very conspicuously rub my knee and draw attention to my scars to anyone who might be watching or judging my severe lack of muscle.

* * * * *

It was the final day of the Premier League season in May 2014. Spurs were playing Aston Villa, it was Tim Sherwood's last game as manager, and I had decided to watch at home where the legroom compares very favourably to that between the rows of seats at White Hart Lane. Spurs were 3-0 up by the interval, which meant the second half was a formality played out in the north London spring sunshine. With little happening in the game I took my eyes off the TV. When I looked back at the screen a familiar face was looking back at me, from the seat usually occupied by the manager. There seemed to be some amusement in the crowd and disbelief among the commentators. Danny Grimsdell, our Danny, wearing Tim Sherwood's Spurs gilet, was in the manager's seat next to Les Ferdinand! From behind, Brad Friedel was leaning over saying something to him.

For the best part of 20 years Danny and his brother Aaron have had their season tickets at Spurs close to the tunnel, well within earshot of the home and away dugouts and members of the press. Over the years many a Spurs manager, and many a player too, have received honest feedback from Danny about the level of their performance. In a game earlier in the season, multi-million-pound signing and Brazil international Paulinho, not for the first time, had pulled out of a tackle. This had prompted Danny, always particularly interested in how those occupying the central midfield berths in any Spurs team perform, to shout out, 'You're a disgrace Paulinho, you're a disgrace! This is Tottenham

Hotspur you are playing for!' Danny's words about Paulinho, which Sherwood heard from his position in the technical area, seemed to resonate with him, as he turned round to face the crowd and nodded to Danny.

On this last day of the season, Danny was calling out for youngster Alex Pritchard to be brought on as sub, the opportunity of a run-out in the first team that Danny had never been given in his own professional career. Sherwood relented and brought Pritchard on. Then to everyone's amazement, Sherwood turned to Danny and called him out of the crowd, installed him in the manager's seat and handed him his own gilet! The television cameras picked this up instantly and so it was broadcast live.

White Hart Lane is notorious among Spurs fans for its patchy mobile phone reception. However, on this occasion Danny's phone started 'going mental' as word of what had happened spread among his friends and family. His dad Mick, who wasn't watching the game, recalls receiving a text from someone he worked with saying, 'I think Danny has taken the Spurs manager's job.' Such was the pace with which the news spread that Danny even received a message from Wizards team-mate Marc Johnson who was away in West Africa.

At full time Danny realised that the story was going to be far bigger than he could have possibly imagined. Print and television journalists swarmed round him, pointing cameras and mics in his direction as he tried to make his way to the gangway to leave the stadium. Suddenly a group of stewards arrived on the scene telling the journalists to step aside and announcing that Danny was to be detained 'until the police arrive'. This was on the instructions of the stadium security team who monitor everything happening inside the ground from a tower located in the roof of the south-west corner. Danny was still wearing the gilet given to him by Tim Sherwood at this stage and stood back as a row between the journalists and security team ensued. Andy Burton of Sky Sports News leapt to his defence, asking why Danny was being held. The stewards confessed they didn't know, they were just following orders. Burton, obviously seeing that a good story was in danger of being sabotaged by overzealous security, again went in to bat for Danny. 'He hasn't done anything wrong, Tim Sherwood invited him down.'

There was a stand-off until a PR man for Spurs emerged. Burton then said decisively, 'This goes one of two ways: it's a great story, a great PR story for Spurs, we make it the story it should be. Or we turn it into how you have killed it.' At this, the Spurs PR man quickly called off the stewards and cancelled the police.

Ironically, in a post-match press conference, Tim Sherwood jokes, 'We've got the police looking for him 'cause he's nicked the gilet.' A journalist asks Sherwood if this is genuine, and Sherwood laughs and says, 'No, he can have it. Of course not, he's all right, it was fine. I invited him down and I would have been more annoyed if they wouldn't have let him come.'

The press now had Danny's phone number and he was contacted by BBC Radio 5 Live during their post-match phone-in show and was interviewed on air. The fixer who lines up the calls and runs the 5 Live Twitter feed asked Danny for his Twitter handle and tweeted it out. Danny recalls the soundtrack to his evening from that point on was the buzz, buzz, buzz of his phone as people in increasing numbers started to follow him on social media. By the end of the night he had 2,000 followers on Twitter. The next day his cameo appearance was covered in all the national newspapers' match reports. He was contacted by Talksport while at work and gave his second radio interview standing outside the van while Ed sat inside listening to it on the radio, trying not to catch his eye through the windscreen and make him laugh. He then graduated from radio to television. As the two drove back to Danny's house to pick up some gear, they found a huge Sky broadcast van, complete with a satellite dish on the roof, waiting outside. Danny still isn't sure how Sky had got hold of his address, but distinctly remembers the woman who introduced herself apologising for being early for their live television interview. This was news to him, as he had no idea they were coming and he had a day's work to do. But Ed said Danny should not pass up the opportunity and went off to cover the jobs, while Danny recounted his time in the White Hart Lane hot seat live on air. Before the cameras started to roll the interviewer asked, 'Have you still got the gilet?' which of course they wanted him to wear.

Looking back, the only slight regret Danny has is that when he was asked to come on Sky's *Soccer AM* the following weekend, he didn't get a chance at the end of the show to have a go at kicking the ball through the hole with all the other guests – something anyone who has ever watched *Soccer AM* over the last 20 years would want to do. What he'd really like is one day to bump into Tim Sherwood. 'It would be nice just to say, "Thanks mate."'

* * * * *

After nine months of physio and gym rehab and a few trips to the park where Mel went in goal and I shot mostly wide or over, I felt ready to give playing football a go. I sent out a message to the old Wizards email group and suggested we have a reunion game on a Tuesday night which maybe we could make a regular thing. Deep down I realise that as much as being about playing football, it was about seeing the boys regularly again. The fact is I missed them.

The response was overwhelmingly positive; it looked like we might even have enough for 11-a-side. Ahead of the game, of course, drop-outs started coming through thick and fast, and we were left desperately asking the boys if they had any brothers or mates who fancied playing. On the night when we arrived the pitch had been double booked, but thankfully I had printed out the confirmation so we weren't the ones to miss out. Twenty minutes past kick-off time and with only five of us there, my phone rang. In the time-honoured Sunday League tradition, half of the boys had gone to the wrong pitch despite the full address and postcode being in the email I had sent them in bold and underlined. Once the rest finally arrived we played out a 7-7 draw and it was just like old times, even if a few of the hairlines had receded and waistlines expanded in the four and a half years since we had last shared a pitch together. At the end of the game Robbo said to me, 'You know what, Flynny, it's only a couple more years and we'll be eligible to set up the Wizards veterans' team.' I'm polishing my boots already.

Postscript

IN spring 2015, I contacted Ken Martin from the Edmonton Sunday League hoping to tap into his vast knowledge of the League's history, and his wider reflections on Sunday football. I wasn't sure whether Ken would remember me but happily he did and he was as I remembered him, polite and friendly. As I explained the reason for my call, Ken said that he was busy preparing for the end of season cup finals and financial accounts, so could I call him back once the season had ended. I called again in June.

This time Ken seemed very down, cryptically saying that he didn't really want to talk as 'A man's views on amateur football are his own.' He also seemed sceptical as to why I or anyone would be interested in the history of Sunday football, which given the amount of his life he has dedicated to it took me aback.

I realised perhaps the timing of my phone call had been ill-judged. It was a few days before the League's annual general meeting, which involved a lot of work for Ken at the end of a long, hard season. I decided to lay my cards on the table and told him how grateful I was to him and his colleagues for how they ran the League. This seemed to strike a chord with Ken; despite his initial reluctance he began to talk. It occurred to me that the men who run amateur Sunday football leagues year after year, long after their playing days are over, probably don't receive much gratitude.

As Ken began to reflect on all his years involved in the Edmonton League, I realised there was more to his initial downbeat mood than it just being end of season fatigue. Ken explained that the season marked the Edmonton League's 90th anniversary and it has been his long-held ambition to see the League make it to a centennial season in 2025. However, he explained he now felt this was unlikely and that the League would die out in the next five years or so. Ten teams had withdrawn in the last 12 months and it looked likely the Edmonton and District Sunday Football League would be reduced to just three divisions for the new season. This phenomenon was not exclusive to Edmonton as figures announced by the FA in 2011, a year after the Wizards folded, showed that 1,600 teams had disappeared across the country in the previous three years alone. This decline continued unabated to the point that in 2014 Sport England reduced funding to the FA for amateur football by £1.6 million. In Ken's opinion there has been a generational shift. 'If it hasn't got a touch screen young men aren't interested nowadays.' Expanding on this bleak assessment of the outlook for amateur football, Ken explained that young men's idea of Sunday football these days was getting up at midday to go down the pub and watch the Premier League on big-screen TVs. 'Pubs are open all day, commercialism is killing the amateur game.' He also reflects how the emergence of five-a-side football centres like Powerleague, where a group of mates can pay a few quid each for a game at any hour of the day, was chipping away at organised amateur football.

Ken went on to talk about some of the men who had first set up the Edmonton League and ran it without the assistance of computers and mobile phones, plotting out the fixtures in pen and ink, only pausing to go off and fight in the Second World War. He told me about H.W. (Bert) Skeggs, a remarkable man who had been at the Normandy landings and who from the early

1950s to his retirement in 1978 acted as both general and fixtures secretary and ran the League with military precision, while at the same time insisting on one of the League's more peculiar traditions: apparently goal nets were not used in Edmonton until the 1970/71 season. Ken recounted how initially Mr Skeggs, who retired to Suffolk, had intended to commute down to north London twice a week in order to continue his service to the League, but Mrs Skeggs vetoed this idea. And then abruptly Ken ended our conversation, said goodbye and hung up the phone.

I decided to write to him by hand to thank him for his time on the phone, and for his work in running the League for all those years, enabling the Wizards and so many other teams to have footballing memories to look back on for the rest of our lives.

About the Author

We Are Sunday League is Ewan Flynn's first book and was written in Haringey, north London. Ewan captained the Wizards FC for nearly a decade, leading them to the Edmonton and District Sunday Football League First Division title.